D0624990

*The Emperor Nicholas II is one of the most pathetic figures in history. ...Had he lived in classic times, the story of his life and death would have been made the subject of some great tragedy by the poets of ancient Greece. They would have represented him as a predestined victim pursued, on each successive act, by some relentless fate, till the curtain fell on that heart-rending scene in the basement of the house at Ekaterinburg...*

SIR GEORGE BUCHANAN,
*My Mission to Russia*

# The Sunset of the Romanov Dynasty

*By Mikhail Iroshnikov,*
*Liudmila Protsai and Yuri Shelayev*

«ТЕРРА» «TERRA»

MOSCOW
1992

63,3(2)5
H 63

*Editor: Juri Pamfilov*

*Designer: Yevgeny Bolshakov*

*Translated from the Russian by Paul Williams and Juri Pamfilov*
*(captions to illustrations)*

*Editor of the Russian text: Mikhail Iroshnikov*

«TERRA» Publishing Centre
Produced by a/o Alliance and the private enterprise Julia
Type-setting and production of films by Aurora-Design, St Petersburg,
with the participation of the Autopan-Service, Moscow
Printed and bound in Russia:
Pervaya Obraztsovaya Printing House, Moscow

ISBN 5-85255-223-2

© «TERRA» Publishing Centre, 1992
© M. Iroshnikov, L. Protsai, Yu. Shelayev,
a/o Alliance, text and illustrations, 1992
© P. Williams, translation, 1992
© Y. Bolshakov, design and layout, 1992

H $\dfrac{5002000000-109}{A\ 30(03)-92}$ Без объявл.

# CONTENTS

CONCORDIA UNIVERSITY LIBRARY
PORTLAND, OR. 97211

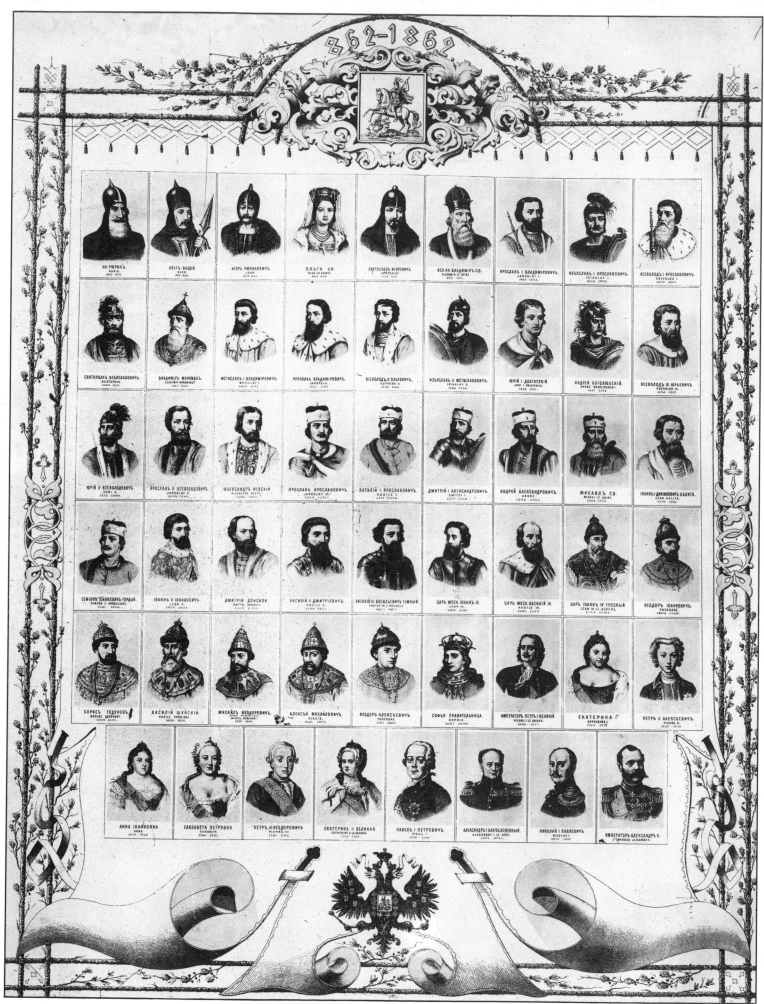

*Collage with portraits of grand princes, tsars and emperors who ruled Russia from 862 to 1862*

# PROLOGUE

---

At the turn of the twentieth century photographers were only just beginning to experiment with symbolist and avantgarde approaches to their art, and could hardly have suspected that what must have seemed to them ordinary landscape or genre shots or pieces of photo-journalism would almost a century later take on a profound, at times truly symbolic, significance.

At one time paintings and photographs of the Emperor, his family and other members of the ruling dynasty adorned not only the halls of state institutions, but also studies and drawing rooms in people's homes, as a regular part of their everyday lives. If you look carefully among the photographs on this desk belonging to Count A.D. Sheremetev, a close friend of the royal family, you can easily make out some of those used in the present book.

*Writing-desk in the study of Count A.D. Sheremetev.*
*Ligovo Station. St Petersburg Province. 1908*

I N Soviet times history became faceless. Individuals, especially political figures, were practically divorced from their context and, for whole generations raised in the conviction that the creators of history were some abstract "popular masses", the past was made to seem an incessant fight, sometimes quiet, sometimes intense, waged by the autocrats and ruling circles against their own savagely-oppressed people.

Pre-revolutionary historians saw these matters differently. In their descriptions history appears as a succession of characters who were probably far better known to any senior schoolboy of that time than to many of our social scientists now. In Russia's thousandth anniversary year Karl Bulla, the photographer of the Ministry of the Imperial Court, produced a collage containing a whole gallery of the country's rulers from the legendary Rurik to Alexander II — men and women whose desires and actions undoubtedly counted for far more than millions of the subjects of the great state. Each of them was linked to a distinct period in history and each contributed his brick to the masonry of the state — some greater, some smaller — and these formed the look and the traditions of the gigantic edifice that was the Russian Empire. And, above all, it was the concept of autocracy which bound it all together.

Historically no other people has produced anything which could fully match Russian absolutism. From the seventeenth or eighteenth century there was no longer any Western monarch who possessed the degree of power wielded by the Russian tsar. They could not disregard the unwritten rules of society, which since ancient times had come to be expressed in the formula describing the monarch as "first among equals". The traditional "God-given" power of the Russian tsar left its mark on each and every aspect of life: from the fundamental questions to the way the person of the tsar was perceived by a people, which, from the bottom to the top, historically took its bearings from the tsar, to borrow the words of the Soviet writer Nathan Eidelman.

As an example of this, the outstanding Russian historian Sergei Solovyov cited a typical instance of the rules governing behavior at the court of Tsar Mikhail Feodorovich, Peter the Great's grandfather: "At last the doors open; the great ruler enters and, on catching sight of him, everyone bows down to the ground. The Tsar sits in a large armchair in the foremost corner of the chamber and summons those who are to be dealt with to him; if the Tsar calls a boyar and he is not present then the tardy noble is sent for straight away and can expect a threatening reproof over the cause of his lateness. The reckoning with those who committed a mistake, failed to carry out, or to carry out properly, an order from the Tsar is brief: the ruler gives immediate orders for them to be sent far from the palace or put into prison..."

In the following century the famous Prince Feodor Yuryevich Romodanovsky, a comrade-in-arms of Peter the Great and one of those who educated him, was left as vice-regent with unlimited authority and power in Moscow when the Tsar was on his travels or campaigns, yet in his letters he never addressed Peter in any other way than the following: "Your base-born bondsman, Fed'ka Romodanovsky, beats his brow before Your Majesty..."

And, right up to the end of the empire, the Russian autocrat was a towering figure at the pinnacle of the pyramid of state, exercising total power in the country. His was the last word in the issuing of laws, the imposition of taxes and the appointment of ministers and senior officials; the entire business of government was under his command, including questions of war and peace; and he had practically unrestrained access to the Treasury. With far greater justification than Louis XIV, the Russian tsar, even as the twentieth century dawned, could proclaim: "L'etat c'est moi!"

In contrast to the course of events in Europe, the absolute rule of the tsars met, in the last resort, with no opposition from society (if we discount spontaneous popular revolts, whose leaders were not averse to assuming the throne themselves if the opportunity arose), neither in the form of a parliament, nor from municipal councils or self-governing religious bodies, while the third estate — the bourgeoisie which the Frenchman de Boulard called the "soul of a society" ("Any state which lacks the third estate is incomplete, however powerful it may be") — had only begun to gather strength here.

The sources of Russian autocracy were, according to its ideologists who propagated the formula "Moscow is the third Rome", to be sought in Byzantium, itself heir to the might of Rome. It was far more than chance that the double-headed eagle of Byzantium was adopted as the coat-of-arms of the Muscovite tsars and later of the Russian Empire, and that it endured over the centuries. The imperious bird of pray turning its crowned heads to East and West was a symbol more fitting than any other for the dual nature of a great state which extended for many thousands of miles across the land-mass of Europe and Asia. This state with its unusually multifarious mosaic of a population accommodated the traditions and ways of life of many different peoples. It was Asiatic in the eyes of the Europeans and too European for the Asians. Adopting over the course of many centuries elements of such diverse cultures, it was ever vulnerable to being torn apart by their very incompatibility.

While the best of those at the head of the state leant towards European culture, enlightenment and democracy, the Russian monarchy retained features of Eastern despotism and remained practically right to its very end "a country of slaves, a country of masters". The Russian peasants were fully and completely enserfed by the articles of the new legal code of Tsar Alexei Mikhailovich, father of Peter the Great, in 1649, the very year in which the English overthrew their king. They were granted freedom only in 1861, when the Civil War broke out between the Northern and Southern States of America and the last generation of Europeans who could remember from their childhood a similar despotism in their own countries — albeit in far milder form — were going to their graves. While by the middle of the nineteenth century parliamentary democracies or constitutional monarchies had been established throughout almost all of Europe, the Russian peasant was still an article which could be bought, sold, exchanged or presented as a gift of friendship like a Borzoi puppy or a thoroughbred stallion from the landowner's stable.

"The entire process of historical development in early Russia," the renowned historian and theologian G.P. Fedotov wrote, "took the opposite course to that of Western Europe; it was a development from freedom towards slavery. A slavery dictated not by the whims of rulers, but by a new national goal: the creation of an empire on the basis of a meagre economy. Only extreme all-embracing tension, iron discipline and terrible sacrifices could maintain this beggarly, barbarian, continuously expanding state. There are grounds for believing that the people of the sixteenth and seventeenth centuries had a better understanding of the needs and the general state of the country than those of the eighteenth and nineteenth centuries. Consciously or unconsciously, they made the choice between power as a nation and freedom..."

The submissiveness, patience and muteness of the slave, inherent first and foremost in the serf population, ate away in a crippling manner at the moral foundations of their owners, the holders of the land, who grew accustomed to exercising unrestrained arbitrary rule over the unfree peasant "souls" (as they were officially known), which was terrible even in its most benevolent guises. (This accounts for the taking up as a popular saying of the words from Griboyedov's comedy *Woe from Wit*: "Deliver us from those worst of all ills, a master's anger and a master's love".) On the other hand they themselves were wholly dependent on the whims and benevolence of the powerful in this world, not to mention the monarch. Russian history can provide thousands of instances to confirm the fact that even for those close to the tsar with all their honours and riches life was like a walk on the rim of a volcano. Yet even the Russian autocrat himself was a hostage to the system that had formed in the state over the centuries. He was no less dependent on the support of the great landowners, and later of the influential middle class, and had to take their interests into account. The memory of the "universal remedy" for all kinds of political disputes and clashes — a death from the strangler's cord — was very much alive in the opulent halls of the imperial palaces. It caused even the most august pupil of the European Enlightenment, Catherine the Great's grandson, Alexander I, to postpone the liberal reforms he had in mind when he ascended the throne at the beginning of the nineteenth century, until better times — beyond the end of his own life. He too feared to meet with the same fate as his father, murdered by conspirators — officers of the guard and noblemen — in what seemed to be the most secure palace in St Petersburg, his own Michael's Castle.

"The joint operation of despotism and freedom, enlightenment and slavery" seemed to Vasily Kliuchevsky to be a squaring of the political circle and a puzzle which remained unsolved in Russia even into the twentieth century. The influence of Europe on its eastern neighbour, which became particularly strong at the time of Peter the Great, had a character entirely of its own.

*Monument to the Millennium of Russia in the square in front
of St Sophia's Cathedral, Novgorod. By Mikhail Mikeshin.
Early 1910s*

"... In adopting European technology," the historian wrote of Peter, "he remained rather indifferent towards the life and peoples of Western Europe. That Europe was for him a model factory and workshop, while he considered the concepts, feelings, social and political attitudes of the people on whose work this factory relied to be something alien to Russia. Although he visited the industrial sights of England many times, he only once looked in on the parliament..." "We have need of Europe for a few decades yet, and then we will already be able to turn our back on it," Kliuchevsky wrote in an obviously toned-down version of the words tradition attributes to the first Russian tsar to style himself "Emperor".

Crafts and science, as we know, really took off in Russia, and even within a short time the country could compete with her Western neighbours in matters maritime and in the art of building fortifications. A great surge took place in many branches of technical learning; manufacturing industries sprang up and were improved; trade expanded.

Yet anything to do with making the life of society more humane and democratic remained as before truly neglected and it was difficult for any ideas on these spheres to reach the hearts and minds of the Russians. The first really serious attempts at reform in this area were made by Catherine the Great — the spiritual heir of the reformer-tsar — who dreamt of going down in history as an "enlightened ruler" and a friend of the French Encyclopedists. Something then happened, however, which would subsequently occur with an inexorable logic of its own, to stay the hand of more than one Russian emperor with ideas of bringing about a "revolution from above". The mass revolt led by the Cossack Yemelyan Pugachev put an end to a process that had not even started, and so a state built on the rule of law did not even begin to form in Russia. Seemingly all that needs to be said about the political history of the second half of the eighteenth century can be found in a single sentence from the Empress's personal conversation with her private secretary Khrapovitsky about the role of the monarchy: "One motion from me — and Catherine made a gesture to show this royal motion — gives directions, what is to move and where..."

In her native German lands others, such as Emperor Joseph II in Austria or Frederick the Great in Prussia, also flirted with the ideas of the Age of Reason and the "spirit of the law", and there too everything came full circle. But, nevertheless, changes did somehow take place, because neither of these rulers had unlimited autocratic powers.

Many senior officials recognized the necessity of making changes in the social organization of the Russian state. In 1801 Count A.P. Vorontsov reported to Alexander I that under autocratic rule it was hardly possible to assure the "quiet and personal security" of the citizens, and advised the restoration of the rights of the Senate, on which "depends both the future structure of Russia and, perhaps, the very trust that the administration should command". The young Emperor did not, however, place much hope in the existing power structures. Even in his youth he had decided on "his government" consisting of long-time friends — Stroganov, Novoseltsev, Chartoryiski and Kochubei and he preferred to prepare serious reforms aimed at establishing due order, legality, a transformation of the social structure and a spread of education (which would in turn create the conditions for a rise in industry and culture) not in the halls of influential official institutions, but in an intimate private committee. The basic rule adopted in all this work was that all the intended transformations should be instigated by the Emperor personally. In this way the planners reckoned to safeguard their own creative freedom and also the independence of the monarch from the pressure of those around him, from premature rumours and opposition, from excessively high expectations or dissatisfaction. In Stroganov's opinion, "absolute secrecy" was also necessary so as to "be perfectly aware of the true state of minds and to adapt the reform in such a way that its introduction might give rise to the least degree of discontent".

However, the work of reforming, which they were only just on the point of beginning, as the noted historian Alexander Presniakov observed, "was immediately hampered by the danger of somehow evoking too strong a discord between the government and the society being reformed... The memory of 11th March [Paul I's murder] was still too fresh. And at the same time there was another aspect to things which was as strong if not stronger: Alexander's group of advisers, whom he jokingly called the 'Committee for Public Safety' but angry critics branded as 'jacobins', belonged to the same stratum of powerful aristocrats and was only prepared to concede the minimum of reforms necessary and that only with haste and without the least 'upheavals', acknowledging that otherwise it was better to do nothing. Their theoretical understanding of the defects of autocracy and serfdom lost its strength and importance when it came to drawing up measures for reform because they wanted to carry it through without any very noticeable break with the social structure which they condemned in principle."

Alexander I had been raised on a mixture of enlightened absolutism and military despotism, and dreamt of the role of "benevolent dictator", while in reality he was obliged only to temper his plans to the interests of the great landowners and the nobility. As a result, the "great reforms" were restricted to a mere transformation of the highest organs of administration with the aim of strengthening the central power.

Again, as in the first years of Catherine's reign, the hands of the Russian clock seemed to be moving to catch up with Europe, and once again they then slowed down. The staggering contrast between Europe and the everyday life of Russia came home with full force to the members of the Russian army who pursued Napoleon across Europe. It caused the most advanced people in Russia to feel a profound sense of shame and pain for their homeland and to recognize the burning need for reform at the earliest possible opportunity. So it was that the members of what were known as the Northern and Southern Societies sought to put into practice Alexander's timid ideas about the liberation of the peasants. They counted on seizing power by means of a military coup on the day the oath of allegiance to Alexander's brother and successor, Nicholas I, was to be taken.

The selfless act of these noblemen revolutionaries on 14th December 1825, when they formed up their mutinous regiments on Senate Square in St Petersburg in the hope of forcing Nicholas to renounce the throne, marked the opening stage of the Russian liberation movement. The first initiatives towards the introduction of decisive changes came, not from some "philanthropic" monarch, but from members of what was then the most influential and powerful class in society. Future generations of revolutionaries in Russia saw the Decembrists' stand as the fountain-head of their movement and considered them national heroes, yet the reaction of their own contemporaries (with very few exceptions) proved wholly negative. The Decembrists were condemned not only by the law, but also by the court of public opinion, and even by many of their own close friends and relatives.

The imperial manifesto, published at the time the Decembrists were coming to trial, contained hints of future plans to "move with the times" at a modest gradual pace. The Decembrist Rebellion was defined as something imported, alien, an "infection" from the West, "neither the character nor the morals of Russians could harbour such a design". Nicholas I called on all the estates to unite in trust in the government and reminded the nobility of its importance as "the wall around the throne" with access to all types of military or civil service, and also of the necessity of supporting "the steadfast order, the security and the property of its custodian" and of spreading education that is native, natural and not alien to our land". The need for change should take as its starting point "not daring dreams which are always destructive", but the path of a gradual improvement of the existing order.

All strata of society were thus to bow down to the God-given power of the monarch and, as far as they were able, to assist in the realization of his conservative national programme. The main points of this programme had, incidentally, already clearly formed in the last years of Alexander's reign. Nicholas's rule was thus practically the implementation of a course of action drawn up in the last years of his brother's life.

Count Sergei Uvarov, a former liberal who had once associated with the Decembrists but later became Nicholas's minister for education, tried to advance education and the spiritual life of society as a whole towards an "imperceptible concord" with a Russia based on serfdom. He developed an entire theory of spiritual principles which was summarized in the celebrated formula: "Orthodoxy, Autocracy, *Narodnost.*" This theory incorporated everything: the innate religiosity of the Russian people who allegedly had no need of Western rationalism and the people's special relationship with the "little father tsar" caring like a true parent every hour of the day and night for his children and answering for them directly to God; an idyllic patriarchal relationship between the childlike simple-hearted peasants incapable of thinking for themselves and the landowners who care for them like fathers; the alienness to the Russian soul of

Western ideas of social progress, a social contract, democracy and the reconstruction of life on non-traditional principles; the vanity of fruitless "philosophizing" and the pre-eminence of faith over frail human reason; and the necessity of absolute supreme autocratic power based on "the law of God" with an all-embracing system of spiritual and civil supervision. This is the sort of "direction of thoughts and spiritual inclinations" that would henceforward be regarded as "truly Russian" and patriotic, and the Russian state, borne up by the trinity of "Orthodoxy, Autocracy and *Narodnost*", was held to be the sacred Motherland.

Who made up this immense edifice that was Holy Russia? Data from the census taken in the 1830s informs us that out of a population of 52—53 million, 25 million were peasant serfs, another 18 million or so were peasants tied to state or royal lands, and if we exclude all the members of the armed forces from the remaining 9 million, then it is relatively easy to gain an idea of the number of "freemen". At the one pole 272,000 land- and serf-holders, at the other 25 million serf "souls". The same Count Uvarov asserted that "the question of serfdom is tightly bound up with the question of autocracy and the monarchy: these are two parallel forces which developed together; they have, both the one and the other, the same historical origin and their legality is the same." Thus in speaking of serfdom he had sufficient ground for concluding: "This tree has spread its roots wide — it supports both the church and the throne, and to uproot it is impossible."

Be that as it may, the task certainly proved beyond Nicholas I, although he did foster the idea of making the ownership of land itself, rather than serfs, the basis for the privileged position of the nobility. All aspects of the social life of the state were so inalienably bound up with the fundamental principles of serf-holding that, until a solution to the basic issue was found it fatally inhibited the resolution of many other, more specific problems. This became clear once and for all in the mid-nineteenth century — during the Crimean War of 1853—56 — when against the rifles of the English and French Russian soldiers took the field still armed with antediluvian smooth-bore muskets. The decline in Russia's international prestige, industrial stagnation, mediaeval agriculture with its almost thirty million effective slaves, extreme social and national tensions across the immense territory of a country which by now extended from Poland to Alaska, prompted Nicholas I to tell his son shortly before his death: "I am handing you a command not in complete order."

Alexander II tried to be more decisive and the circumstances on his accession were completely different too. Now it was a matter of saving an already sinking ship and the Reformer Tsar, as history recorded him, needed a mere five years to convince himself of the inevitability of major changes in the structure of both society and the state and to plan their course. The manifesto he then published in the belief that "it is better to liberate the peasants from above than to wait for them to liberate themselves from below" freed the peasants, but left them effectively without land. The minimal allotment of land which the former noble serf-owners were obliged to provide to their peasants so that they could feed themselves had to be redeemed by whole decades of hard labour. To do more was beyond the power of even the Tsar, who had himself constantly to look over his shoulder at the mood on the noble estates.

The explosion was averted for the moment, but the potential for a tremendous historical cataclysm remained deeply rooted in what was still a mighty empire. Industrial development, which at last began to take off in Russia, coexisted with agricultural conditions no less wretched than before; a combination which was socially more explosive still. The "inbuilt tension" at the very core of Russia burst out in the peasant revolts that continued to flare up, as well as in a growing wave of strikes among industrial workers. It was reflected too in the activities of revolutionary parties which operated illegally, since, right up to 1905, any political party, even if it supported the monarchy, was illegal in Russia.

Alexander II also did away with scourgings and almost all corporal punishment, brandings with red-hot irons, running the gauntlet and beatings in the forces; replaced twenty-year military service with general conscription; introduced an adversarial legal system and grandly proclaimed the principle of presumption of innocence and the independence and security of tenure of the judiciary. This period saw the state budget made public for the first time, and it was now too that the word *"glasnost"* — openness — first came into general use.

The will of this far-sighted emperor gave rise to one more projected reform — an epoch-making advance for Russia — the constitution which the country had never had before and which was supposed finally to lay the basis for the first national parliament, a voice for the population in its own administration and perhaps at least the beginning of some degree of accountability to the long-suffering people on the part of their ruler, God-given or fate-ordained. More specifically, it meant an abandonment of the mediaeval doctrine of autocracy, the demise of the Russian tsar as an absolute ruler answerable only to God and his own conscience...

But it was already late: the time for reforms had expired and processes that began far earlier would not submit to the will of the new tsar — they had their own historical inevitability. On 1st March (13th March by the Western calendar) 1881, Alexander, who had already survived several attempts on his life, was murdered on the embankment of the Catherine Canal in St Petersburg by members of the revolutionary "People's Will" group who were firmly convinced they were acting in the name and best interests of the Russian people. They paid for their courage and their convictions with their lives and the spirit of reaction triumphantly turned back the clock wherever possible: dreams of a parliament were abandoned as pernicious Western liberalism which had brought the Reformer-Tsar to his tragic end...

In the mid-nineteenth century many states found themselves brought face to face with fundamental questions which would decide the fate of whole peoples. It is a curious fact that matters came to a head in two of the world's great powers at practically the same moment in time. Exactly a year separated the abolition of serfdom in Russia and passing of the Homestead Act in the United States in 1862. This act granted each American citizen the right to acquire, for a small, more or less symbolic, payment, a piece of land which would in the course of time become his own property. This marked the victory on a national scale of the farmer's or the American approach to agriculture, which in the long run laid the basis for America's subsequent prosperity.

Russia, in very different circumstances, did not manage to come to terms with its problems so successfully, and later the country paid the price for this. Alexander Golovnin, once Minister for Education under Alexander II, said something in this respect which proved to be truly prophetic: "In the past forty years the government has taken much from the people and given them little. And since every injustice comes home to roost, I am convinced that the punishment for this will not be wanting. It will be due when the peasant children who are now still feeding at the breast come of age and fully grasp what I have just said. This may happen during the reign of the grandson of our present monarch."

And indeed, a half-century later, these peasants and their own grown-up children took part in the street demonstrations and armed skirmishes in Petrograd in February and March 1917 which proved to be the straw that broke the back of autocracy. In the October of the same year, they would storm the Winter Palace and arrest the ministers of the Provisional Government. The "grandson of our present monarch" was Nicholas II, the last Russian emperor.

In contrast to his distinguished grandfather, Nicholas II felt no inner drive to reform the realities of Russia, quite the contrary, he seemed to avoid anything of the kind, preserving the semi-feudal, patriarchal structure of life in his empire — it is no coincidence that the predecessor he chose as his ideal, the object of his veneration and the one he sought to imitate, was not one of the reformers but Peter the Great's father Alexei Mikhailovich, who has gone down in history as the "quiet tsar". Superficially Russia attained its greatest degree of freedom during Nicholas's reign with the creation of the State Duma, a parliament of kinds, and the proclamation of freedom of speech, of the press and of assembly, and so on, but all of these were literally extorted from the Tsar, and at the first possible opportunity he withdrew them again.

The situation which gave rise to the famous manifesto of 17th October 1905 can easily be pictured from a few lines left us by Count Sergei Witte, one of those responsible for drafting the document: "To assess the mood around the tsar in those days in October, it is only necessary to cite the following fact. When we took the steamer to Peterhof (the railway was on strike all through this period), the Head Chamberlain of the Court, Adjutant-General Benkendorf (brother of our ambassador in London) travelled with us, an educated man, far from stupid, devoted to the tsar and one of the cultured nobles who surrounded the throne. He, among other things, let Vuich who was accompanying me know of his sense of sympathy, that in the present situation it was a pity that their majesties had five children, the four grand duchesses and the poor, dearest (as they used to say) boy — the heir to the throne, Alexis; that if it became necessary to leave Peterhof by the sea to seek a refuge abroad, the children would present a great hindrance..."

Tension was running so high in the country that, on the evidence of Prince Nikolai Obolensky, one of those closest to the emperor, there were realistically only two ways out of the crisis. One way was to "invest some trusted person with dictatorial powers so as to energetically and irrevocably suppress at the very roots all semblances of opposition to the government — albeit at the cost of massive blood-letting." The second was to recognize the inevitability of "a shift of ground to making concessions to public opinion and to give a future cabinet orders to move along a constitutional path."

In the opinion of many high-ranking figures Grand Duke Nikolai Nikolayevich might have become the "trusted person" of the first route. However, Count Fredericks, the Minister of the Imperial Court, related that when he put the idea to the Grand Duke that a dictatorship was necessary and that he should assume dictatorial powers, the Grand Duke drew a revolver from his pocket and said: "See this revolver. I'll go now to the tsar and beg him to sign Count Witte's manifesto and programme; either he signs or I let him have a bullet in the forehead from this revolver." And having said that he quickly left Fredericks.

The Grand Duke did not have to pull the trigger. Despite long and agonizing vascillations the Emperor eventually agreed to sign the paper that was put before him. "Soon after five in the evening," Prince Obolensky recalled about a year later, "the work was complete. Count Witte who had already arrived from St Petersburg made the journey to Alexandria [the name given to the summer residence of Empress Alexandra at Peterhof — *The authors*] and in his presence the Emperor signed the manifesto and affirmed the programme. Thus, although not without some struggles, hesitations and doubts, the monarch

found fit, in the light of various internal and external circumstances, to put Russia back on the path of reform it had left and to bring to fruition the great cause of his most august grandfather."

On the evening of the same day the witnesses to this event so important for the fate of the country returned by steamer from Peterhof to the capital. To those around him Grand Duke Nikolai Nikolayevich had an extremely satisfied and gratified air. In talking to Count Witte he compared what had happened with the dramatic episode in October 1888, when luck had spared the whole of Alexander III's family injury during the derailment of the royal train. "It's the 17th October today," he said, "the seventeenth anniversary of the day when the dynasty was saved at Borki. It seems to me that this time too the dynasty has saved itself from a danger no less great by the signing today of that historic document."

The Grand Duke was mistaken. The Romanov dynasty was not fated to survive, although back then it still had a chance to survive, to stay on as a symbol of Russian statehood, as occurred in a number of European states in the twentieth century, where the fact that they retained the monarchy did not in any way impede social advance or stand in the way of a parliamentary system and democracy.

On that same day — glorious for some, joyless for others — Nicholas himself made a laconic, yet frank entry in his diary: "*17th October. Monday. Anniversary of the accident... Signed the manifesto at 5 o'clock. After such a day my head has grown heavy and my thoughts confused. O Lord, help us, pacify Russia."

That last sentence of Nicholas's is a sufficiently eloquent reflection of what truly worried and disturbed him. Yet despite this he did not take the course of far-reaching reforms which the country and the times were waiting for. Not having ventured to make a lesser sacrifice, Nicholas ended by losing everything. Only a few years were to remain before the fall of the Romanovs, the dispersal of members of the imperial house around the world, and the death of the tsar himself and those closest to him, while Russia would be plunged into an endless sea of troubles...

# THE
# CORONATION

---

*Absit omen* — let this not be a bad omen.

THE LORD GOD HAS ENTRUSTED US WITH ROYAL POWER OVER
OUR people and We shall answer before His throne for the
fate of the Russian state..," ran the manifesto published on
the accession to the throne of the new emperor Nicholas II,
signed by him while still Tsesarevich, two hours before the
death of Alexander III on 20th October 1894. "...We command that all Our subjects swear fealty to Us and to Our
successor the Grand Duke Georgi Alexandrovich who is to
be known as Tsesarevich and heir until such time as it shall
please God to bless with the birth of a son Our forthcoming
marriage to Princess Alice of Hesse-Darmstadt."

THE PREMATURE DEATH OF EMPEROR ALEXander III at the age of forty-nine literally shook the entire country. Despite the fact that in recent years this ruler, whom nature had endowed with great physical strength — he was able to bend horseshoes and break coins — had suffered a considerable decline in his health, what happened was completely unexpected. It is hard to say what the true cause of the Emperor's death was, perhaps his immoderate indulgence in food and strong drink, perhaps the railway accident which he had been in a few years previously, since which time his appearance, always "very sickly" according to Count Witte's memoirs, grew noticeably worse, "but the tsar himself did not acknowledge his illness". "In general," this former minister stressed, "the royal family has a strange half custom, half sense of not acknowledging one's own illness and of avoiding treatment as far as possible, and this habit was particularly strongly developed in Emperor Alexander III."

The ruler's growing indisposition in recent years had changed little in the royal family's accustomed way of life. In accordance with established custom Alexander took part in the celebrations of the marriage of his daughter Xenia to Grand Duke Alexander Mikhailovich (known in the family as Sandro), visited the traditional annual military camps and manoeuvres. Against the advice of the noted physician, Professor Zakharyin, who had been summoned from Moscow, the Emperor did not travel to the Crimea but, again in keeping with the family custom, went to hunt at Bialowieza and Spala in Poland. Even another noted medical man, Professor Leyden of Berlin, who confirmed a diagnosis of acute nephritis, could not persuade him against this. Years later the German doctor spoke warmly of the Emperor while calling him one "of the most disobedient patients I have ever had to deal with".

When Alexander finally did arrive in the Crimea his condition was practically hopeless. His close relatives spent the whole of September and October under the shadow cast by the sharp decline in the health of the family's head. This is fully reflected in Nicholas's diaries, in which barely a single day's entry does not contain notes and observations on his father's condition: "*4th October. Tuesday.* Unhappy day! Dear Papa felt so weak that he himself wanted to go to bed... *6th October. Thursday.* ...Papa was up this morning, but lay down after breakfast, he was overcome with drowsiness... *8th October. Saturday.* ...Darling Papa felt a little better and ate more! Read reports and papers. *9th October. Sunday.* Dear Papa felt weak, although he slept a little more; the doctors were satisfied with his condition. He suffered several nosebleeds. *10th October. Monday.* ...Papa was weaker today and Alix's arrival besides seeing Father John fatigued him... *14th October. Friday.* Dear Papa passed the night quite well, but after breakfast he again felt weaker... *15th October. Saturday.* Papa felt a little better!... *16th October. Sunday.* ...Papa felt better, but vomited during the doctors' visit... *17th October. Monday.* In the morning Papa received the Sacrament from Father John. He felt weak from the agitation, and besides, slept badly at night..."

Nicholas's diary entries for the last three days of his father's life contain virtually nothing else. "*18th October. Tuesday.* A sad and painful day! Dear Papa did not sleep at all and felt so bad in the morning that they woke us and called us upstairs. What an ordeal it is. Then Papa became a little easier and dozed interruptedly through the day. I did not dare be out of the house for long... About 11 o'clock the doctors held a conference in Uncle Vladimir's rooms — it's terrible! ...*19th October. Wednesday.* ...In the morning dear Papa slept continuously for four hours and sat in an armchair in the afternoon. Our worries began again towards evening when Papa moved into the bedroom and went to bed: again his weakness has become terrible! Everybody wandered about the garden separately... *20th October. Thursday.* My God, My God, what a day. The Lord has summoned our adored, dear, deeply beloved Papa to Him. My head is spinning, I don't want to believe it — the awful reality seems so unjust. We spent the whole morning upstairs by him! He had difficulty breathing and they kept having to give him oxygen to inhale. About half past 2 he received the Holy Sacrament; soon he began to have slight convulsions ... and the end came quickly! Father John stood by the bed for more than an hour holding his head. It was the death of a saint! O Lord, help us in these difficult days! Poor dear Mama! The requiem was held at 9.30 — in the same bedroom! I felt devastated..."

*Icon commemorating the accession of Emperor Nicholas Alexandrovich to the throne, made in 1895 by the Russian Theatrical Society for the Elderly Actors' Home. St Petersburg. Early 1900s*

*Members of the Imperial family in front of the palace in Livadia: standing Alexander III (third from right), Grand Duke Nicholas Alexandrovich (fourth from left), Grand Duchess Xenia Alexandrovna (fifth), Grand Duke Georgi Alexandrovich (sixth); seated (right to left) Grand Duke Mikhail Alexandrovich, Maria Feodorovna, Grand Duchess Olga Alexandrovna. Livadia. 1894*

That day — 20th October 1894 — was the actual beginning of the new reign, that of the nineteenth tsar of the Romanov dynasty. The period of mourning, however, meant that coronation celebrations were put off until a later date. They were destined to be held only a year and a half afterwards, in the spring of 1896. There was nothing unusual in this. As a rule the accession to the throne in Russia did not coincide with the coronation ceremony and its accompanying festivities. The actual length of time between the two events varied and depended directly on the will of the new monarch. In was customary to hold the celebrations in spring or summer since they were traditionally accompanied by popular outdoor festivities. Thus, Alexander I, for example, was crowned a mere month after the tragic death of Emperor Paul I, on 15th April 1801 (Paul's murder took place on 12 March that year), while his brother Nicholas I — displaying a greater sense of decorum and also, apparently, having waited for the end of the investigations into the Decembrist Rebellion which marred his actual accession in December 1825 — appointed 22nd August 1826 as the day of the ceremony. Alexander III had felt it possible to hold the coronation celebrations only in May 1883, more than two years after the dramatic explosion which killed his father on 1st March 1881.

Nicholas took the decision about his own coronation on 8th March 1895. Once this had been done, a special coronation commission was set up under the Emperor's uncle, Grand Duke Sergei Alexandrovich and including Hilarion Vorontsov-Dashkov, the Minister of the Imperial Court and Domains, Vladimir Fredericks, his deputy and the Chief Master-of-Ceremonies Konstantin von der Palen. This commission drew up an extremely detailed programme for the coronation celebrations. Three main documents laid down the way in which they were to be conducted: *The Coronation Ceremony, The Regulations for the Issuance of Allowances to Officers Travelling on Orders to Moscow on the Occasion of Their Majesties' Coronation Service* and *The Timetable from the 6th to 26th May 1896*. To finance these events considerable sums of money were allocated from the treasury, totalling, it was found later, some 110 million roubles. It was proposed that the main ceremonies be held in Moscow in keeping with tradition. Ever since the coronation of Prince Dmitry Donskoi in the mid-fourteenth century, these ceremonies had always been held in the Assumption Cathedral inside the Moscow Kremlin — a tradition unaffected by the transfer of the capital to St Petersburg. Other towns and cities also organized celebrations, though, depending on the local possibilities.

It would be no exaggeration to say that for those weeks in May the eyes not just of Russia, but of the whole world were focused on events in Moscow. Moscow played host to the most noble of guests: kings and crown princes, ruling dukes and the representatives, official and otherwise, of many countries. Those heads of state who were for various reasons prevented from coming to Russia's ancient capital did their best, nevertheless, to express their respect for the Russian tsar in every way possible. The President of France, Felix Faure, personally met the Dowager Empress Maria Feodorovna as she was returning from Villafranca to Moscow, in order to express his best wishes to her son the tsar and the Russian people. The French who saw the coronation service as a symbol of three things — power, concord and peace — were generally highly enthusiastic about the forthcoming Russian festivities and the days were celebrated in great style, not just in the land of Joan of Arc itself, but everywhere that French people had settled. In the German capital Berlin the Kaiser attended a magnificent military parade which was accompanied by the sounds of the Russian anthem. There was also a banquet breakfast at which Wilhelm, noted for his gift as an orator, made a

*Archpriest John of Kronstadt. Late 19th century*

Alexander III died literally in the arms of the "great griever of the Russian land" Father John of Kronstadt (1829—1908) who was specially summoned to Livadia to "ease the sufferings" of the Tsar. By that time this archpriest who worked in the naval town of Kronstadt on an island out in the Gulf of Finland from St Petersburg was already very well known, not just for his prayers and church services, but also for his charitable deeds: in 1874 he established a Parish Board for the Assistance of the Poor at Kronstadt Cathedral; in 1882 the first House of Diligence in Russia, where up to 25,000 people worked, and a night shelter; and another decade later a hospice. In the words of Chekhov "the eyes of the entire poeple were turned [on him] with hope". He kept up his activities throughout the rest of his life. He established four religious houses and found his last resting place in the cloistered community which he himself had built on the embankment of the Karpovka River in St Petersburg and which bore the name of his patron saint, John of Rylsk. He was canonized by the Russian Church in Exile in 1964 and exactly a quarter of a century later he was recognized as a saint in his homeland too.

highly emotional speech. At a banquet in Sofia, capital of the fraternal kingdom of Bulgaria, friendly greetings and toasts rang out in honour of Russia and her young Emperor.

*Reproduction of Zichy's drawing* Alexander III Ascending to Heaven. *1894*

The number of representatives from Eastern nations was greater than at the previous coronation. For the first time the festival of the coronation and anointment of a Russian monarch was to be attended by plenipotentiaries extraordinary of the Ecumenical Patriarch in Constantinople and of the Patriarchs of Antioch, Jerusalem and Alexandria. For the first time too, the Vatican and the Anglican Church had sent representatives to the celebrations.

Every day masses of trains brought thousands of men and women from all corners of Russia to the stations of its old capital. These guests, who included large delegations from the peoples of Central Asia, the Caucasus, the Russian Far East, the various groups of Cossacks and so on, completely changed Moscow's usual appearance. The overwhelming majority, however, were citizens of Russia's northern capital — as the newspapermen joked "all those, whom we are accustomed to call 'the whole of St Petersburg', have now gathered here."

A special international group was formed by the arrival not only from all parts of the empire, but literally from all over the world, of newspaper reporters, journalists, photographers and even artists — all those who were destined to create a chronicle of the events with the help of a pen, brush or lens and set it down in print for posterity.

The Academy of Arts commissioned works for its forthcoming *Coronation Album* (published in 1898) from such venerable artists as Victor Vasnetsov, Vladimir Makovsky, Valentin Serov, Ilya

Repin and Andrei Riabushkin. A no less responsible task fell on the shoulders of the imperial photographers who were to create a photochronicle of the coronation for later publication in several albums. The photographs which accompany this chapter are reproduced from some of those very albums — authentic souvenirs of the celebrations which are almost "too heavy to lift". Each of them is a real work of art from its beautifully finished leather binding with colour tooling to the immaculate quality of the wonderful photographic reproductions.

It was not only professional men, however, who were called upon to make great efforts for the May festivities. Navvies and carpenters, house-painters and plasterers, electricians, engineers, cooks, tailors, firemen and janitors, policemen and gendarmes also worked like Trojans. The restaurants and theatres of Moscow were full to overflowing for the duration. On the days leading up to the festivities Tverskoi Boulevard, one of the horseshoe of streets around the centre of Moscow, was so jammed with traffic that, tn the words of eye-witnesses, "you had to wait hours in end to cross from one side to the other. Hundreds of splendid carriages, coaches and landaus and other conveyances stretched the length of the boulevards." The main thoroughfare of old Moscow — Tverskaya Street — was transformed in anticipation of the passage along it of the magnificent royal procession. It was adorned with all manner of decorative fixtures. The whole route was lined with masts, arches, obelisks, columns and pavilions. Flags were hoisted everywhere, the houses hung with carpets and beautiful fabrics, decked with garlands of flowers and greenery which hid thousands upon thousands of electric light bulbs. A stand was built for those who were to watch on Red Square.

Work was in full swing everywhere, including Khodynka Field out to the north-west of the city which was to be the venue for popular festivities

*Group of distinguished nobles during the coronation festivities:* seated (right to left) *Princess Trubetskaya, Countess Stroganova and Countess Vorontsova-Dashkova;* standing (right to left) *Counts Stroganov, Palen and Vorontsov-Dashkov. Moscow. 1896*

*Members of the British delegation:* standing (left to right) *Count Ribopier, Colonel Edgerton, Admiral Fullerton, Colonel Welby, General Grenfell, Captain Lord Bingham, Cavalry-Captain Prince Kochubei, Colonel Water and Sotnik Orlov;* seated (left to right) *S.D. Edgerton, General Prince Golitsyn, the Duchess and Duke of Connaught. Moscow. 1896*

*The Imperial Petrovsky Palace: here the Romanov family stayed for three days before their ceremonial entry into Moscow. May 1896. Photograph by L.L. Konoshevich*

and the distribution of commemorative royal gifts and refreshments on 18th May. Apart from stands for the guests of honour and an imperial pavilion in old Russian style, there rapidly sprang from the ground here 20 plank huts, each filled to the roof with barrels of spirits; 150 buffets, the majority of which stretched in a line from the St Petersburg Highway south-west towards Vagankovo Cemetery; stages for theatrical performances and church services; and smooth pillars set into the ground on which it was intended to hang various prizes for the agile, ranging from well-made boots to samovars produced in the famous metalworks at Tula.

The 9th May saw the tsar's grand entry into the Kremlin. Nicholas, his wife, and their retinue had already left St Petersburg on 5th May and following old-established tradition they spent the three days before the entry into Moscow at the Petrovsky Palace in the park of the same name, close to Khodynka. It was from here, past the Triumphal Arch, the Convent of the Passion and so on,

---

*Triumphal Arch decorated for the coronation of Nicholas II. Moscow. 1896. Photograph by I.N. Alexandrov*

*The Imperial palace in Neskuchny Garden where the Romanov family lived during the coronation festivities. Moscow. May 1896. Photograph by L.L. Konoshevich*

and down the whole length of Tverskaya Street, that the royal procession was to make its way to the Kremlin. The few kilometres of this route were full of people from six in the morning. Indeed many people did not go to bed at all on the night of the 8th May and, judging by the newspaper accounts, it must have been something like the Orthodox celebration of Easter.

One reporter, working for the *Vsemirnaya Illustratsiya* (Universal Illustrated), wrote that in a very short period of time the Petrovsky Park took on "the appearance of a bivouac or immense camp. Under each tree groups of people who had come from all ends of the city settled down for the night and amongst the huge trees and on the small lawns lit by the soft light of the moon; they presented a picturesque spectacle... Tverskaya Street in all its splendid finery, dressed up like a bride in her wedding day, looked especially striking. Along the street and the adjoining boulevards there was a ceaseless stream of carriages carrying the participants of the procession: generals, foreign princes, ambassadors extraordinary and so on, speeding to the Petrovsky Palace where according to the ceremonial they were to assemble just after ten.

*Building of the Bolshoi Theatre where a gala performance was held on 18th May to mark the coronation. Moscow. May 1896*

"The gleaming uniforms, the glittering helmets, the plumed tricorn hats and the magnificent robes of the representatives of Asia all looked most splendid in the bright light. The people watched and hailed this great multitude of foreign guests driving past with visible satisfaction and an expression of serious dignity on their faces, taking a pride in such a display of respect for us from the whole world... By twelve all the side streets leading onto Tverskaya Street were roped off and filled with a mass of people. Troops lined the road on each side."

Having taken up a position opposite the house of the Governor-General of Moscow, Grand Duke Sergei Alexandrovich, who had put his apartments at the disposal of guests of honour not participating in the procession, the journalist had an opportunity to observe a truly captivating spectacle. "There was a mass of spectators looking out of every window: here were the gleaming uniforms of British admirals, and Spaniards, and Japanese and Chinese, and beautiful French cavalry officers in gleaming, gilded helmets in the Ancient Greek style with horsetails streaming out behind. The whole of the long balcony was taken up by a great number of extremely elegant society ladies in magnificent white costumes and hats."

The artist Mikhail Nesterov had found a convenient place near the stands on Red Square a few hours before the start of the ceremony and was later able to give a detailed and eloquent account of watching the final stage of the procession: "At 12 o'clock nine cannon salvoes announced the start of preparations. Grand Duke Vladimir Alexandrovich rode out of the Kremlin with his retinue to meet the Tsar. At half past two the bells of all the churches in Moscow and a cannonade announced the fact that the ceremonial entry had begun and it was only at five o'clock that the advance guard of field gendarmes appeared and behind them His Majesty's party and the others.

"They drove the senators past in golden carriages. The old men were so tired that on the drive up to the Kremlin they were already sleeping like babies...

"The senators were followed by 'people of different ranks'. There were footmen, moors, a troop of horse-guards. The rulers of the Asian peoples pranced past — the Emir of Bukhara, the Khan of Khiva — all in robes embroidered with goldon wonderful race horses.

"More horse-guards and only then could a re-sounding hurrah be heard in the distance. It came quickly closer, became louder, bigger, and finally thundered somewhere close to us with startling force.

"The soldiers presented arms, the music struck up and the young Tsar appeared on a white Arab horse. He rode slowly bowing to the people in greeting. He was excited, with a pale, pinched face...

"The Tsar proceeded through the Saviour Gate into the Kremlin. People began to disperse...

"At ten in the evening the illuminations were turned on. A magical fairytale began, a waking dream. People walked as if spellbound among glowing precious stones, the million lights of the city and the Kremlin, admiring the exotic sight. The trees in the Alexander Garden were hung with illuminated flowers and fruit. Everything was aglow, iridescent, sparkling with gold, diamonds and rubies against the dark background of the evening twilight and then the quiet of the May night..."

The next day, after all the highest dignitaries and invited princes had driven to the Petrovsky Palace, breakfast was served for one hundred and eighty people. In the evening Their Imperial Majesties, Empress Maria Feodorovna, Grand Duke Mikhail and Grand Duchess Olga moved to the Alexander Palace to the south-west of the city. On the 11th the ambassadors extraordinary from France, Spain, Japan and Korea were presented to the Emperor and Empress in the Great Kremlin Palace. That same morning on Senate Square in the Kremlin, where representatives of the embassies and other guests had assembled by eight in the morning, heralds officially announced the day of the Coronation Service. At this ceremony batons were raised, a fanfare was blown and then one of the secretaries, who did not dismount from their horses, read the text of the proclamation. The people listened to this ritual in complete silence and without moving. It finished with the anthem, a thunderous hurrah from those present and the distribution by the heralds of copies of the proclamation cleverly printed in festive shades of red and gold. Further copies were handed out by servants of the imperial household from specially equipped carriages.

On the day of the Coronation, the 14th May, from earliest morning all the central streets of Moscow were filled with a moving mass of people. "Before nine in the morning," one eyewitness reported, "by the Kremlin the entire area between the Alexander Garden and the History Museum was — without exaggeration — an uninterrupted sea of heads, and only a small space right by the History Museum opposite the gate leading into the Kremlin was left for vehicles to pass."

Official figures who were to participate in the ceremonial procession to the Assumption Cathedral began arriving in the Kremlin Palace from seven in the morning onwards. By about nine o'clock the Dowager Empress Maria Feodorovna had arrived in the Kremlin. Some time later two masters-of-ceremony descended from the Red Porch followed by a whole "golden" stream of Russian and foreign nobles in uniforms which shone in the sun to mark her emergence. The empress appeared to the sound of the anthem and deafening hurrahs, wearing purple with a great eagle on the back of her robes and a dazzling crown of diamonds and walked beneath a golden baldachin to the Assumption Cathedral.

The grandest moment of the Imperial Procession took place about half an hour later and was described many times down to the last detail in the newspapers and magazines of the capital and the provinces. "A platoon of dashing horse-guards descended from the porch, trumpets and kettle-drums struck up on the terraces of the palace," one reporter wrote, "another brilliant mass of courtiers, representatives of the rural districts, towns and district councils, the nobility, the merchant class, the professors of Moscow University,

*Heralds announcing the day of Nicholas II's coronation inside the Kremlin. Moscow. 11th May 1896. Photograph by L.L. Konoshevich*

behind them the Chief Procurators of the Senate, Senators, Secretaries of State, Ministers and members of the Council of State. Finally, after deafening ecstatic hurrahs and the sounds of *God Save the Tsar* played by the court orchestra, the Emperor and Empress appeared on the Red Porch. They too processed to the cathedral under a golden baldachin, the Emperor in front, the Empress following.

"Suddenly, in an instant everything falls silent — the music, the bells and the cries of the people — and in this reverent silence Sergii, Metropolitan of Moscow, greets Their Majesties at the south door of the cathedral with a speech. Preceded by three metropolitans, bishops and other clergy and to the singing of a sublime psalm Their Majesties enter the cathedral where at about 10 o'clock there begins the solemn ceremony of the coronation and anointment of the monarch which the Orthodox Church invests with such deep significance and which is filled with such great importance for every Russian who understands his own history."

The tradition of coronation already stretched back four hundred years to old Russia. On 3rd February 1493 Dmitry Ivanovich, grandson of Grand Prince Ivan III, became the first to receive the crown of the principality "of Vladimir, Moscow and Novgorod". At that time, due to a great influx of Greeks to Moscow (the Grand Prince was married to Sophia Paleologus, niece of the last Byzantine emperor), the court was particularly keen to observe the customs of the court of Constantinople. However, the crowning of a tsar in the full modern sense did not take place until a century later on 31st May 1584, when the new tsar was Ivan the Terrible's son and heir Feodor. It was then for the first time that a description of the coronation ceremonies mentions the sacrament of anointment with chrism (holy oil) as an inseparable part of the whole ritual. This chrismation, which, according to Church teaching, goes back to the time of the kings of Israel, was carried out by the Eastern and Western Churches and the established Church of England according to the same rite and accompanied by prayers with roughly the same content. In contrast to certain Catholic countries with amended rites, such as Poland, where during the prayers preceding the anointment the monarch lay down with his arms out like a cross on a carpet spread on the floor while the officiating clergy knelt beside him, the Russian rulers like the

Holy Roman Emperors in Germany and the kings of France and Hungary said prayers while kneeling.

Special items of church plate played an important role in the conduct of these ceremonies. At the coronation of the Russian monarch it was required to have for exaltation "a cross containing a fragment of the Life-Giving Cross that had been sent to Vladimir Monomakh (the early twelfth-century Grand Prince of Kiev) and the *krabitsa,* or jasper vessel, which was also sent to him and had at one time belonged to Caesar Augustus, possessor of the 'whole universe'," the nineteenth-century historian Yevgeny Karnovich wrote in his article *The Coronation of Monarchs.* "This bowl was first used at banquets. It was made of jasper, decorated with precious stones and on its lid there is a snake twisted into a ring in a standing position. At the coronation of the French kings the chrism was poured from a piece of broken crockery set with gold and precious stones, which according to legend was brought by a dove that flew into the church during the baptism of Clovis, King of the Franks. One of the holy relics present at the coronation of the Holy Roman Emperors was some eartht soaked with the blood of the first Christian martyr, St Stephen. The shrine which contains it is kept nowadays in Vienna. Formerly only the emperor, and he only once in his life, on the day of his coronation, could open the casket and look at what it contained."

In its main details the coronation ceremonial of Nicholas II followed already established tradition, although every emperor had the right to introduce some changes into the ritual. Thus, for example, his grandfather Alexander II, and that emperor's two predecessors, Nicholas I and Alexander I, did not dress in the dalmatic — the ancient robe of the Byzantine emperors, similar to a garment now worn by Catholic deacons — for the ceremony. During his own coronation Nicholas II presented himself to the congregation not in a colonel's uniform, but in a magnificent ermine cloak. The young emperor demonstrated his liking for the past from the very beginning of his reign. This expressed itself in a renewal of old Muscovite customs. (Thus, after a break of more than half a century, the imperial couple celebrated Easter solemnly and with great ceremony in Moscow; in St Petersburg and abroad churches in Muscovite style increased in number; in 1903 a great costume ball was arranged with dress as in the time of Tsar Alexei Mikhailo-

*Reproduction of the painting* The Coronation of Nicholas II.
*St Petersburg. 1896*

vich, Peter the Great's father; in a desire to please
the Emperor even his Minister of the Interior
Dmitry Sipiagin took to wearing clothes cut in a
seventeenth-century fashion and had his ministerial offices reconstructed in the style of the
Chamber of Facets, the oldest building in the
Kremlin; and so on.)

The Ceremony of Coronation took place at
10.30. The service was conducted by Pallady,
Metropolitan of St Petersburg, and the Metropolitans of Kiev and Moscow also participated.
Many bishops were present at the ceremony, as
were representatives of the senior Greek clergy.
In a loud, distinct voice the Emperor recited the
Creed after which he placed the large crown on
his own head and a smaller one on Empress Alexandra Feodorovna, then his full imperial title was
read out and the artillery salute and numerous
congratulations began. While kneeling and saying the appropriate prayer the Emperor was
anointed with chrism and received communion.

Throughout all this, the people outside the
walls of the Assumption Cathedral responded in
an highly sensitive manner to every action that
took place within. "Everything that occurred in
the Assumption Cathedral," the chronicle recorded, "just like a jostling in the heart, passed
out through the entire vast crowd and like a pulse
beat made itself felt even in its most distant ranks.
Now the Emperor is down on his knees praying,
saying the holy and great words of the appointed
prayer that are full of such profound meaning.
Everyone in the cathedral is standing, the Emperor alone kneels. And the crowd on the squares
also stands, but how they all fell quiet at once, the
reverent silence all around, the pious expression
on their faces! And now the Emperor has risen.
The Metropolitan now kneels, followed by all the
clergy, all the church and, after the church, all the
people covering the squares of the Kremlin and
even those standing outside the Kremlin. Now
even the wanderers with their knapsacks have
got down and everybody is on their knees. The
Tsar alone stands before His throne in all the
majesty of His high office amid the people who
pray fervently for Him."

And finally with ecstatic hurrahs the people
greeted Their Majesties who processed in all the
royal regalia into the Kremlin Palace, bowing to

the assembled crowd from the Red Porch. The day's celebrations were completed by a traditional banquet in the Chamber of Facets. The walls of this ancient hall had been repainted before the coronation of Alexander III, giving it the appearance it had had when the tsars ruled from Moscow.

And yet three days after such a splendid beginning to the festivities a real public tragedy took place. The programme of the forthcoming popular celebrations included the distribution of royal presents to everyone who waited from 10 in the morning. (400,000 packages were made up, each consisting of half a pound of hard sausage, bread rolls, sweets, nuts, gingerbread and an enamel mug gilded and decorated with the tsar's monogram, all wrapped up in a coloured kerchief.) Between 11 and 12, musical and theatrical performances were due to start and at 2 in the afternoon a "royal appearance" was expected on the balcony of the Emperor's pavilion.

The gifts on offer — and, by the way, even today, a hundred years later, such a collection would bring people in droves — together with the promise of spectacles unseen before (an improvised stage was to be used to present extracts from *Ruslan and Ludmila*, *The Humpbacked Horse* and *Yermak Timofeyevich* and a circus programme featuring Durov's performing animals), a desire to see with their own eyes the Emperor "in the flesh" and, perhaps, the wish at least once in their lives to be a part of such an event — a combination of all these factors brought huge masses of people to Khodynka Field. Explaining his motives for being there that day Vasily Krasnov, a workman, reflected in many ways the general mood of the people: "To wait until morning so as to come for ten o'clock, the time appointed for the distribution of gifts and commemorative mugs, seemed plain stupid to me. With so many people there'd be nothing left when I arrived in the morning. And am I going to live to see another coronation?.. To be left without a reminder of such a celebration seemed to me — as a Muscovite through and through — a disgrace: was I to be like some corner of a field they'd forgot to sow? They said the mugs were very pretty and would 'last forever'... Back then enamel cups and things were a real marvel..."

A strangely negligent attitude on the part of the authorities had resulted in an extremely unfortunate choice of venue for the popular festivities. At that time deep ditches, gullies and trenches were dotted all over Khodynka Field; full of pits, mounds and abandoned wells, it was good for nothing apart from military purposes and indeed it was used as a training ground for the troops of the Moscow garrison. And even on the eve of the festivities, when it became obvious that huge numbers of people were gathering here, no strong emergency measures were taken which might have averted the catastrophe.

Those who survived the events of "Bloody Saturday" recalled it as the worst shock of their lives. "Wonderful weather had set in then," P. Shostakovsky wrote later, "and the prudent people of Moscow ... decided to spend the night on Khodynka Field, in the open air, so as to be on the spot right at the start of the festivities... That night, as ill luck would have it, there was no moon and Khodynka Field filled up in complete darkness. The people kept arriving and, unable to see the way in front of them, they stumbled and fell into the gullies... The immense crowd became ever more tightly packed. More and more people kept arriving. No less than half a million were jammed together by morning between the city boundary and a wall made up of the 100 buffets. The handful of police and cossacks sent to 'maintain order' on Khodynka Field sensed that the situation was becoming threatening and that they were out of their depth... The morning turned out still, without a breath of wind. There was no flow of fresh air over the packed crowd. It became harder and harder to breathe. Sweat poured down pale bluish faces and they seemed to be in tears..."

The famous reporter Vladimir Giliarovsky, a correspondent for the newspaper *Russkiye Vedomosti* (*Russian Gazette*), was the only one among the two hundred Russian and foreign journalists covering the coronation celebrations who happened to spend the night on Khodynka Field. He recalled: "Steam began to rise over the million-strong crowd, looking like the mist over a swamp... The crush was terrible. Many felt faint, some lost consciousness, having no chance to get out or even to fall: lacking sensation, with eyes closed, caught as in a vice, they jostled along together with the mass of people... A tall, handsome old man, standing near me, next to my neighbour had long since stopped breathing: he suffocated in silence, died without a sound and his corpse had grown cold as it jostled along with us. Someone alongside me vomited. He could not even lower his head..."

Leo Tolstoy, who in his time collected information about this disaster, was staggered by evidence that the merchant Morozov promised to pay 18,000 roubles to anybody who saved him. Markuyev, one of the characters in Gorky's novel *The Life of Klim Samgin*, recounts: "I arrived there at midnight... and I was sucked in... By morning some had gone mad, I think. They were shouting. It was very eerie. Someone like that was standing by me and wanted to bite everything. People were butting each other, forehead against the back of the head, back of the head against the forehead... And one... man... dug his nails into the back of the head of a fat man by me and tore off a piece... the bone was exposed."

Fearing to be swept away by this avalanche, the men whose job it was to hand out the ill-fated gifts decided to begin the distribution of the presents without waiting for the appointed hour. "And a mass of people half-a-million strong, pressed together as tightly as possible," Shostakovsky wrote, "staggered with all its unimaginable weight in the direction of the buffets. People by the thousand fell into a ditch and ended standing literally on their heads at the bottom. Others fell straight after them, and more, and more, until the ditch was filled to the brim with bodies. And people walked on them. They could not help walking on them, they were unable to stop..."

According to the official statistics, 2,690 people suffered, 1,389 of whom died, in this "deplorable incident" which cast a shadow over the "brilliant course of the coronation celebrations", as Khodynka was described in the terse official account published that evening. The true number of those affected — crippled, injured physically, or left with some psychological trauma — could scarcely be calculated. In any case, records show that for a long time afterwards, the bodies of those who had fled from the scene were being found around Moscow.

Even in the morning all the fire-brigade units in Moscow were occupied in removing the horrific consequences. String after string of carts were driven away with the bodies of the dead and injured. The soldiers, doctors and firemen had already seen some sights, nevertheless their hearts stood still at the spectacle that opened before them. Here were scalped heads, bones sticking out through the skin, seemingly well-built men with their rib-cages crushed and premature babies rolling in the dust...

Pierre d'Algeim, the correspondent of one of the Paris newspapers, set off for Khodynka Field in the morning and met one such string of carts, carrying away the dead. "On the way to Khodynka there are a lot of carriages and landaus. The harness of the horses, the lacquered carriages, helmets and weapons shine in the bright sunlight... And on the left in two lines gloomy crowds of people drag themselves in single file away from Khodynka. They all have gloomy, downcast looks... Suddenly the carriages have stopped. They wait. The coachmen try to see what is happening. The military men lift themselves out of their seats. They are irritated, nervous: this could easily make them late for the royal appearance! Suddenly policemen rush up, shout something, give orders, take the horses by the bridles and make a passage for vehicles to come through. And right away, along this passage a cart comes, slowly, slowly — and I do not understand," the journalist wrote, "what it is carrying. The load has been hastily covered with some kind of hopsack and sackcloth. Some ladies in a landau let out a cry; the men look at the carts in astonishment. Now it is passing me by. And I see, sticking out from under the sacking and shaking with the jolting motion, hands, legs and blue swollen heads. And the coaches and carriages start off again..."

The official figures who travelled out to Khodynka Field included Count Witte who was literally on the point of boarding his carriage when he heard of the tragedy that had occurred. "I was in such a frame of mind setting off..." he recalled, "and this was of course the mood in which all the other figures, who were meant to be present at these festivities, arrived. The question that troubled me above all was: how would they deal with all the people who had been maimed; how would they deal with all the bodies of people who had been killed; would they manage to take all those who had not yet died to the different hospitals and to take the corpses away to some place where they would not be in view of all rest of the celebrating people, the Emperor, all his foreign guests and all the thousand-strong retinue. And then the question struck me: will there not be an order from the Emperor in the light of the disaster that has occurred to turn these happy celebrations into a solemn expression of grief and to hold a solemn religious service in place of the performance of songs and concerts?"

*Ceremonial procession in the Kremlin. Moscow. 9th May 1896. Photograph by Möbius*

Nicholas probably found himself faced with the same questions that day. However, neither the reminiscences of others, nor his own writings, shed complete light on what was going on in his heart. "The crowd which had spent the night on Khodynka Field awaiting the start of the distribution of meals and mugs," he wrote in his diary, "pressed towards the stands, and a crush took place there, in which, terrible to add, about a thousand three hundred people were trampled to death. I learnt about this at half past ten... This news has left an abominable impression."

Faced with the choice whether to carry on with the programme of festivities as originally planned or to introduce changes to it in response to the situation that had arisen, Nicholas found himself in an extremely difficult position. It is hardly credible that he did not feel natural human distress and sadness at what had occurred. At the same time he could not help but be concerned by the fact that the great mass of people who had travelled to Moscow from all over the world had come expressly for the celebrations, and that, moreover, no small amount of money had been spent. Nevertheless, neither his moral feeling, nor his religious sentiments, which were a matter of common knowledge, prompted him to take the only proper decision.

By the time Witte reached the spot there were no visible signs of what had occurred, "nothing that struck one's eye... everything was concealed and smoothed over." But what more than anything stunned him and with him many guests and inhabitants of Moscow was the fact that "the festivities were not cancelled, but continued in accordance with the programme: so, a concert was performed by a mass of musicians under the direction of Safonov, the famous conductor; in general, everything took place as if there had never been any disaster." The festival on top of the corpses, to use Giliarovsky's expression, ran its course...

At 2.05 p.m. the court chroniclers noted the appearance of Their Imperial Majesties on the balcony of the royal pavilion. The Emperor's standard was raised over the roof of this specially constructed building, an artillery salute rang out, and the many thousands of people in the crowd bared their heads. Infantry and cavalry regiments marched past in formation below the balcony. Later the Emperor and Empress returned to the Petrovsky Palace and, after having received deputations from the peasantry and the nobility of Warsaw in front of the building, they attended a banquet for the nobility of Moscow and the heads of the rural districts inside. A mere one and a half or two versts from Khodynka Nicholas declared to the assembled company in high-sounding words that concerns about the well-being of the people were as close to his heart as they had been to his grandfather and his dear, unforgotten parent.

In the evening, having changed into the dress uniform of the Life-Guards Uhlan Regiment with the sash of the Legion of Honour, the Emperor set off with his wife to the ball planned as part of the ceremonial at the residence of the French ambassador Count (later Marquis) Montebello. Under the circumstances many also suspected that, even if the ball itself was not cancelled, then at least it would take place without the Emperor, the more so since, in the words of Grand Duke Sergei Alexandrovich, His Majesty had been advised not to come here. However, Nicholas did not agree, expressing the opinion that, although the catastrophe had been a very great misfortune, it should not be allowed to cast a shadow on the coronation festival. And he danced the first country-dance with Countess Montebello, while Alexandra Feodorovna was partnered by the count. They left, incidentally, soon afterwards. This same evening the guests who had not been invited to the ambassador's had the opportunity to admire a brilliant gala performance at the Bolshoi Theatre.

The next day another ball, no less grand and opulent, was given by the young Emperor's own uncle Grand Duke Sergei Alexandrovich, then Governor-General of Moscow, and his wife Elizabeth Feodorovna, who was also the Empress's elder sister. The festivities in Moscow continued unabated until they were concluded on 26th May with the publication of Nicholas II's Royal Manifesto, which contained an assertion of the unbroken link between the monarch and the Russian people and his readiness to serve the good of his beloved country.

Nevertheless the impression left by the Moscow festivities on public opinion, not just in Russia, but also abroad, remained quite negative. One of the emigre pamphlets published in Geneva the same year accused the Emperor of being incapable of observing even the outward forms of decency. This applied in full measure to his closest relatives as well. Nicholas's uncle, Grand Duke Vladimir Alexandrovich, for example, on the day the victims of Khodynka were buried at Vagankovo Cemetery, organized a competition to shoot "pigeons in flight" for high guests at his nearby range.

And although royal donations amounting to 90,000 roubles were made to benefit those who had suffered and a thousand bottles of port and madeira were sent to various hospitals for the injured, while the Emperor himself visited the wards and attended the requiem service, his reputation was shaken and it was not only considerable sections of the populace who turned away from him, but also many people close to the throne who had pinned their hopes for change in Russia on the young Tsar. From this time on Sergei Alexandrovich was popularly given the offensive title "Prince of Khodynka" and Nicholas II came to be known as "the Bloody".

All that which happened during the days of the coronation festivities was to have a truly symbolical significance in the years to come and not only because this was the starting-point of the chain of consequences which pushed the country inevitably towards a catastrophe. One can even say that this tragic episode represented a projection in concentrated form of Nicholas II's entire reign. It was precisely at this point that the inability of the Emperor, not in general a stupid person, to react precisely and sensitively to changes in the situation and to make suitable adjustments through his own intervention, became patently obvious. In all probability he simply had not been endowed with the proper capacity to respond to the living, changing course of public life. But, if this is of little significance in the fate of a private individual, for the head of such an authoritarian state as the Russian Empire, it was a shortcoming fraught with the most serious consequences.

The coronation festivities, which started so well and finished so tragically, extended symbolically for the whole two decades and more of Nicholas's reign. He ascended the throne in a time of relative peace and was met with hope and sympathy by fairly large sections of the country's population; he ended with a state to all intents and purposes brought to its knees, rejected himself by a patient and submissive people who only the day before had loved their tsar.

*The Romanov family during the coronation festivities:* standing (left to right) *Grand Duke Cyril Vladimirovich. Nicholas II and Grand Duke Sergei Alexandrovich;* seated (left to right in the second row) *Empress Alexandra Feodorovna with Grand Duchess Olga* (third), *Grand Duchess Elizaveta Mavrikiyevna (wife of Grand Duke Konstantin Konstantinovich) with her son Igor* (fourth), *Grand Duchess Elizabeth Feodorovna* (fifth); *(in the first row) Grand Duchess Maria, daughter of Grand Duke Pavel Alexandrovich,* (first) *and Grand Duke Pavel Alexandrovich* (third)

*Members of the Vatican delegation:* standing (left to right) *Count
Marino Salluzzo, Duke de Corigliano, and Count Mario Carpegna;*
seated (left to right) *Genarro Granito de Belmonte, Aliardi, Nuncio
Extraordinary Ferdinand de 'Cron and Francesco Tarnassi. Moscow. 1896*

*Members of the Turkish delegation:* standing *General Faik' Pasha,
Maikov;* seated (left to right) *Member of the State Council*
← *Karatheodori' Effendi, Colonel Butakov, Ambassador Extraordinary
Ziya' Pasha and Secretary Faik' Bey. Moscow. 1896*

*Members of the Danish royal family with their retinue:* standing (left to
right) *Lieutenant Prince Bariatinsky, Colonel Bull and Captain
← de Kefed-Hansen;* seated (left to right) *General Engelbrecht,
the Crown Prince of Denmark and Adjutant-General Kremer.
Moscow. 1896*

37

When the regalia of royal power are described it is usual to mention the crown first. One of the most ancient Russian crowns is what is known as the Cap of Monomachus, which, according to legend, was sent by the Byzantine emperors Basil II and Constantine IX to Grand Prince Vladimir (the Saint) in 988 on the occasion of his baptism and marriage to their sister Princess Anna. It was made up of eight plates of gold each of which was adorned with filigree work and decorated with precious stones and a number of pearls. On top of the cap was a bulb bearing four stones: a ruby, a pearl, a sapphire and a yellow corundum. The bulb is surmounted by a cross whose tips are decorated with pearls. Originally the lower part of the crown was fringed with pearls, but later it was lined with sable.

The first European-type crown in Russia was created for the coronation of Catherine I, Peter the Great's wife and successor, in 1724. The same crown was used by Peter II, but on his orders it was decorated with the immense ruby that had been bought from China at the command of the seventeenth-century Tsar Alexei Mikhailovich, while a cross of diamonds was placed on its top. The same type of crown, only more opulent (adorned with 2,605 stones, including the ruby from Peter II's crown) was prepared for the coronation of Empress Anna. The same crown, somewhat reworked, was worn by Elizabeth Petrovna at the start of her reign. For the coronation of Catherine II, however, a new crown was commissioned, which was finished with 58 very large and 4,878 smaller diamonds, the great ruby and 75 pearls. It weighed some two kilogrammes. For Paul I in 1796 it was expanded a little and the pearls were replaced, and this crown was used for the coronation of all the subsequent emperors.

Empresses had so-called lesser, or processional, crowns which were their own private property. Each was broken up after the death of its owner and the stones distributed in accordance with her will. The lesser crowns of the later empresses were modelled on the large emperor's crown.

Another very ancient symbol of power was the sceptre. The first time a Russian tsar was solemnly invested with the sceptre was at the late sixteenth-century coronation of Feodor Ivanovich. At the coronation and on other formal occasions the tsar held the sceptre in his right hand; during grand public appearances it was carried in front of the tsar by special officials. From the reign of Paul I, Russian emperors used a sceptre in the form of a gold rod strewn with diamonds and other precious stones. It was surmounted by the *Orlov* diamond.

Symbol of the tsars' sovereignty over the earth was the orb — a spherical object topped with a cross. This arrived in Russia from Poland and was first used at the coronation of the imposter known as False Dmitry. Since Paul I Russian tsars had an orb of sapphire, strewn with diamonds.

The royal regalia also included the sword of state, the shield of state (carried only at an emperor's funeral) and the seal of state, all of which (as well as the state banner) were first used by Empress Elizabeth in the mideighteenth century. These items too would be carried as part of various formal processions.

*The Tsar's throne. Moscow. May 1896. Photograph by K.Fischer*

At 3 p.m. on 3rd April 1896, in accordance with the pre-established order of ceremonies which had been announced to the capital's inhabitants, the imperial regalia were formally sent off to Moscow. They comprised two chains of the order of St Andrew the First Called, which the Tsar and Tsarina were to put on in the Assumption Cathedral, two imperial crowns — the Greater and the Lesser, the orb and sceptre. They were destined to remain in the Kremlin Armoury until the day of the coronation service.

The Assumption Cathedral which the fifteenth-century Bolognese architect Aristotle Fioravanti built on the site of an earlier church exceeded in both size and astonishing simplicity all other buildings in the Kremlin. "That church is wonderous in its majesty and height and brightness and space; the like has never been before in Russia, except the churches of Vladimir" — was how one chronicler expressed his delight in this radiant, resounding, harmonious edifice. With its capacity and location in the centre of the Kremlin as if just made for large-scale formal ceremonies, the cathedral was from the outset a place where the most important acts of state were played out: here fealty was sworn to the Muscovite tsars, patriarchs and metropolitans were installed, blessings were given before military campaigns and services of thanksgiving held, the chief festivals were celebrated here and here too the rulers of Moscow were crowned as tsars.

Immediately before Nicholas II's coronation, in 1894—95, the cathedral was thoroughly restored and brought back to something like its original appearance. Its domes were covered in pure gold. The outside walls were cleaned of plaster and weathered stones replaced, while the plinth around it was partly restored to its original form. As for the interior, in the nineteenth century the abundance of silver, gold and precious stones on the icon frames and service books created a magnificent effect. Inspiring too were the great many glowing lamps, the splendid painting on the walls and the bright, sumptuous robes and vestments, prompting anyone who entered to think of the expression "in church as in Heaven". For the coronation ceremonies the cathedral took on an even more superb appearance.

*Interior of the Assumption Cathedral, the coronation place of Russian emperors. Moscow. May 1896. Photograph by L.L. Konoshevich*

*The royal regalia (crown, mantle, staff, sceptre) prepared for the coronation festivities. Moscow. May 1896. Photograph by K.E. von Gan*

41

"As the Tsar and Tsarina came out of the cathedral a large baldachin was waiting for them, carried by the senior generals of the retinue wearing white lambskin caps. The royal trains were carried by senior civilian officials, and, walking behind them, we had nothing to stop us looking around. In the front and rear the procession was closed off by splendid detachments of horseguards in their palace dress uniforms — white jackets and red cloth breast-plates or tabards with a large St Andrew's cross on front and back. They were followed by countless clergymen. In the air the keals of the Moscow church bells blended with the sound of military bands playing the anthem. Everything fell silent, when, after paying respects to the Muscovite tsars buried in the Archangel Cathedral, we followed the royal couple onto the Red Porch of the Pleasance Palace. From there, in accordance with the tradition of the Muscovite tsars, Nicholas II was supposed to bow to the ground before the people. I knew about this beforehand and regarded it as a piece of symbolism, but the people was just what was missing, since the small area in front of the porch was completely packed with military men, officials and ladies in hats."

*From the memoirs of*
*General A.A. Ignatyev*

*Nicholas II, in the royal mantle with crown, sceptre and staff, processing beneath the baldachin in the Kremlin. Moscow. May 1896*

*Emperor Nicholas II drinking a glass of vodka on Khodynka Field.
Moscow. May 1896. Photograph by K.E. von Gan*

*The royal pavilion on Khodynka Field. Moscow. May 1896.
Photograph by L.L. Konoshevich*

*Popular festivities on Red Square. Moscow. May 1896.*
*Photograph by Bychkov and Zhdanov*

*Gostiny Dvor (trading arcade) decorated for the coronation of Nicholas II.*
*St Petersburg. 1896*

# THE MOST AUGUST FAMILY

WHEN THE FUTURE EMPEROR NICHOLAS II, THEN ONLY THE EL-dest son of the Tsesarevich and heir to the throne Grand Duke Alexander, was coming up to his thirteenth birthday, tragedy struck at the very heart of the royal family. On 1st March 1881, having had sentence passed on him by the Executive Committee of the "People's Will" organization, Nicholas's grandfather — the Russian Emperor Alexander II — was killed in the prime of life.

*Tsesarevich Grand Duke Alexander Nikolayevich. St Petersburg.*
*Before 1855*

IT WAS THE TSAR'S CUSTOM TO REVIEW HIS troops in the Mikhailovsky Riding School on Sundays. These parades were famous and even the heads of foreign missions often attended them. The ceremonies were a festive occasion for the young horse guards officers from among whom the Emperor chose his orderlies. It was a very rare occurrence for Alexander not to take part. On that fateful day, after the end of the parade, the Emperor was driving along the Catherine Canal at about two o'clock, when the terrorist Nikolai Rysakov threw a bomb under his carriage. The explosion killed or injured several of the Emperor's Cossack escort and other people who happened to be passing by. The Emperor got out of his carriage and turned on the assassin, who had been held by grenadiers, with the words: "What have you done, you madman?"

The story goes that Alexander was asked by one of those who came up, "Your Imperial Majesty has not been injured?" and replied, "No, thank God." Rysakov smiled and said "What? Thank God? Look again, aren't you mistaken?" and at that very moment another young man, Ignaty Grinevitsky, threw his own bomb at the Emperor's feet.

These events and their consequences were fully described in the many eyewitness accounts in the *Diary of Events from 1st March to 1st September 1881* which was published in St Petersburg the following year. After the column of smoke and snow raised by the explosion had settled a shocking sight met their eyes: "Twenty people, seriously injured to a greater or lesser degree, lay on the pavement and the road, some of them managed to raise themselves up, some, crawled while others were doing their utmost to free themselves from under those who had been thrown on top of them by the blast. Amongst the snow, debris and blood you could see the torn remains of clothing, epaulets, sabres and bleeding lumps of human flesh."

The glass of a street lamp had been shattered and its metalwork bent. The carriage in which the Emperor never managed to retake his seat was mangled by the explosion, while he himself, deathly pale and covered in blood, his military hat lost and his greatcoat in tatters (only the collar and no more than fifteen inches of the upper part remained — the rest had been shredded), was half lying on the ground, leant over backwards supporting himself on his arms. His shattered legs were exposed; the blood flowed in rivulets; one of his feet had been torn off completely.

The half-fainting monarch was laid in a sledge and in accordance with his wishes brought to the Winter Palace. Although losing consciousness, the Emperor still struggled for life. Fearing for his son, Alexander asked "Is my heir alive?" and when he was answered in the affirmative, he even tried to make the sign of the cross. He was still able to understand the words spoken by his brother Grand Duke Mikhail who had rushed to the scene of the catastrophe and he asked to be taken "home quickly". He was shivering violently and kept repeating that he was cold. Kuryshev, the Quarter-Master of the 3rd Naval Corps, reported that the Tsar said: "Cover me with the shawl," and when he was told that it was dirty, he repeated his request. Kuzmenko, one of the Cossack escort, heard him ask Cavalry Captain Kulebiakin who had also been caught by the explosion, but who supported the legs and lower part of the dying Emperor's body during that final journey: "Have you been wounded too?". But Alexander had only a few hours left to live. When the sledge stopped at the entrance to the palace, there was so much blood inside that it literally had to be poured out.

Overcome with distress, those accompanying him failed even to open the door straight away. The lift was small, so they carried the Tsar in their arms up to his study where a bed was already made up. "It was here," the 1912 Stuttgart publication *The Truth About the Death of Alexander II. From the Notes of an Eyewitness* reported, "that he was given medical attention — but it was all in vain.

"Grand Duke Mikhail informed the Tsesarevich and all the members of the family of what had happened.

"In the study the first person at the monarch's bedside was that unhappiest of women Princess Yuryevskaya, pleading and sobbing for her husband to return to life and consciousness...

"The Heir and Tsesarevich soon arrived with his Most August Consort. The horror showed in their faces and they sobbed like little children...

"The study filled with the Most August members of the Royal Family and senior officials. An undescribable horror showed on each of their faces, — what had happened and how was somehow forgotten and they saw only the terribly mutilated Tsar... In the meantime there was a real hullabaloo going on in front of the palace. People gathered in their thousands waiting for news from the palace. The reports grew more and more dismal... The Royal Standard was lowered above the palace. At half past three Almighty God was pleased to put an end to the sufferings of the Tsar Liberator. The people, in tears, fell on their knees crossing themselves incessantly and bowing down to the ground!..."

News of this grievous event spread quickly throughout the country, causing agitation not only in the twin capitals, but also in the distant provinces. Few in Russia were left indifferent when they learnt the painful details of what had taken place. But in the highest echelons this tragedy came as a real shock. "Such a terrible villainy has been committed that I am still not myself," Alexandra, the wife of General Yevgeny Bogdanovich, wrote in her diary on the evening of that same day. "We had many people here. Some had still not left when Skalon ran in with a terrible cry: 'There's just been an attempt on the Tsar's life. He's badly wounded, two of the escort were killed and 8 more people have been cut or worse.' Ye.V. [her husband — *The authors*] ran up to him, not believing the news. Skalon was here a few minutes after two. Ye.V. immediately set off for the palace. There was a mass of people there, troops, the royal retinue, ministers crowding around the palace. Nobody was allowed inside except members of the Imperial Family... It happened at 1/4 to 2 and by 3.35 the Tsar was no more. It is hard to bear such a disgrace. People have been coming and going here all day — everyone is indignant about this terrible business. Ye.V. was at the Metropolitan's and at Loris's. The sorrow is great. God grant that no further disgraceful blot appear on the pages of Russian history..."

Many of those who gathered in the Winter Palace at that distressing moment had been in the Mikhailovsky Riding School but a few hours before and seen the Emperor in all his glory enter on a magnificent black horse to a resounding hurrah from the troops under the command of the Tsesarevich. Watched by some fifty generals and adjutant-generals Alexander II bowed to all sides, greeted the troops and received the customary reply "Good health to Your Imperial Majesty!". Nobody had known that this would be the last time the troops' greeting would ring out for him. On that day the Emperor had seemed a little paler than usual, but nevertheless fully

*View of the Church of the Resurrection (Our Saviour on the Spilt Blood). St Petersburg. Before 1914*

The Church of the Resurrection of Christ on the Site of the Fatal Wounding of the Late Emperor Alexander II, or in popular parlance the Saviour on the Spilt Blood, was constructed on the embankment of the Catherine Canal at the spot where on 1st March 1881 the bomb thrown by the People's Will terrorist Grinevitsky put an end to Alexander II's reign. The church was some 24 years in the building. It was opened in August 1907. The consecration service was attended by Emperor Nicholas II, the murdered man's grandson, and members of the imperial family. The church was designed by A.A. Parland in the style of seventeenth-century Moscow and Yaroslavl architecture and is particularly interesting for the mosaic decoration of the façades and the interior, created in the workshop of the Frolov brothers from sketches by such noted Russian artists as Victor Vasnetsov, Mikhail Nesterov and Andrei Riabushkin. Much use was made of valuable types of stone in decorating the inside of the church.

*Canopy in the Church of the Resurrection constructed on the spot where on 1st March 1881 Alexander II was fatally wounded by I.I. Grinevitsky, a member of the People's Will organization. St Petersburg. 3rd June 1909*

justified the opinion of many contemporaries who, not without some reason, regarded him as "one of the most impressive and magnificent personalities ever to sit on the throne".

Such comments had accompanied Alexander since his youth. The famous biographer of Nicholas I, Nikolai Schilder, conveys the impression he created in the following manner: "The heir to the throne, Grand Duke Alexander Nikolayevich, on reaching the age of sixteen combined within himself all that one could wish in a young tsarevich, destined for such high things. Fine stature and a charming face, which displayed kind-heartedness and thoughtfulness, and an attractive noble bearing with an innate politeness. He was equally capable of carrying on a conversation himself and of profitably listening to others. He was always adroit in his movements; he rode splendidly and excelled in all forms of gymnastic exercise; he was diligent in his lessons, always displayed a great thirst for knowledge and made rapid progress in all his studies; he was full of tender respect towards his parents, loving them with all the ardour of his years, was caring towards his sisters and his younger brothers and genuinely fond of those who shared his lessons and games, the young Count Wielgorski and Patkul. All in all he left nothing to be desired, neither by his parents, nor by the public, who every day grew more and more attached to him."

These words the court historian wrote about Alexander II were, like as not, no great exaggeration. His father, the future Emperor Nicholas I, had been unable to devote time to his son himself, but nevertheless managed, and here he must be given his due, to make a splendid selection of teachers and mentors for him. When Alexander turned six, his father decided the time had come to pass his education over into male hands. As a tutor for the young Grand Duke, Nicholas chose Life-Guards Captain Karl Karlovich Merder of the Izmailovsky Regiment, whom he personally knew as an excellent regimental commander in the school for junior guards ensigns which he himself had founded.

Merder took up his post straight away, devoting himself totally to his charge, who became attached to him and loved him with all his heart. It would be difficult to imagine a more flattering testimonial for any teacher and educator than the one given Merder by another of Alexander's teachers and mentors, the well-known Russian poet Vasily Zhukovsky. "There was no artifice," he wrote, "in the education he gave; the whole secret was in the quiet but constant beneficent effect of that splendid heart of his... His charge... heard only the voice of truth, saw only unselfishness... he could not have failed to develop an affection for goodness in his heart, to acquire that respect for humanity that is so necessary in any life, particularly one spent close to and on the throne."

In 1826 Zhukovsky, who had accepted his royal commission with great enthusiasm, presented to the new Emperor Nicholas I the detailed *Plan of Studies* he had carefully worked out for the heir to the throne. This plan included a programme for the moral and intellectual development of his royal charge. The full course was divided into three periods: "preparatory" from eight to thirteen; "detailed studies" from thirteen to eighteen; and "applied studies" from eighteen to twenty. The programme for the education of the future emperor envisaged him mastering several foreign languages: French, German, English and Polish; Russian literature and grammar; history; physics; chemistry; geography; botany and zoology; mineralogy and geology; logic and psychology; the fundamentals of law and statistics; various military and, of course, religious studies. Besides this, the natural talents of the Grand Duke were fostered quite well by lessons in drawing, music, gymnastics, fencing, horse-riding, handiwork and so on.

It was not only Alexander's teachers and mentors who strictly supervised his studies; his illustrious parents also took a serious interest. The boy was obliged to take an examination each month in the presence of his mother, and twice a year in the presence of his father the Emperor.

On coming of age Grand Duke Alexander went on a journey around Russia accompanied by Zhukovsky and other tutors — Aide-de-Camp Yuryevich and General Kavelin — and he also became the first member of the royal family to visit Siberia. As a consequence of this journey the conditions of convicts and political exiles were significantly alleviated. We note too that Alexander's accession brought an amnesty for the exiled Decembrists still alive, the members of Petrashevsky's revolutionary circle and the participants in the Polish uprising of 1831.

The results of an enlightened and humanitarian upbringing could be seen in Alexander even at a young age. When he began to play his part in the affairs of state he was already — in terms of both spiritual attitude and sense of responsibility — a fully formed personality, possessed also of an enviable degree of bravery. During his journey through the Caucasus, on the way from the Vozdvizhenskaya Fortress to the settlement of Achkhai he was involved in a skirmish with some Chechen raiders which earned him the Order of St George 4th Class. Galloping with the advance-guard as was his habit, Alexander noticed an enemy skirmish line and dashed up to it, carrying all his retinue, the generals of the detachment and the Cossack escort with him. The encounter ended with the leader of the Chechen party, the Sword-Bearer of Naib Sambdula dead, his body and weapon captured by the Cossacks. The Governor-General of the Caucasus, Prince Vorontsov, who himself witnessed this episode, wrote to the Emperor with satisfaction that "not only all the troops comprising the detachment and almost all the generals of the army in the Caucasus, but also a huge number of militia from various tribes... personally witnessed the true martial spirit and, I may even say, noble daring born in the illustrious breast of the Heir to the Russian throne."

These excellent qualities — bravery and coolness at moments of danger — did not desert Alexander in later years and once, in 1879, they quite simply saved his life. Alexander did not lose his self-composure under the bullets (five revolver shots) fired at his back by the would-be assassin Alexander Solovyov and was quick-witted enough to cover the distance to the nearest doorway not straight, as a natural instinct for self-preservation would have prompted him to do, but in zigzag fashion, throwing himself from side to side and not giving his assailant the chance to take aim.

It was, however, in the last resort these same qualities that brought about the Emperor's death, when on that 1st May 1881 he left his carriage and walked towards the wounded and towards his murderer.

Being the heir apparent of the Russian Emperor, Alexander prepared himself very seriously for such a responsible calling. For almost twenty whole years, from the day he came of age to the day he ascended the throne, he was very actively engaged in the running of the state. Not only did he hold responsible military posts, but his father also introduced him into the Senate and Synod, the committee of ministers and even the State Council. He frequently deputized for Nicholas in the Tsar's absence. In 1848 he carried out a great variety of diplomatic tasks at the courts of Vienna, Berlin and other European capitals. Thus he passed through a sort of higher course of the sciences of state — military, diplomatic and legal. It should be noted that, all in all, Alexander spent a significant portion of his life away from home — in foreign travel or journeys about his own country.

His accession to the throne on 19th February 1855 came at a very difficult time for Russia. It would be no exaggeration to describe the situation on both the foreign and the domestic fronts as extremely grave. The failures of the Russian army in the Crimea were so obvious and so dispiriting that they even provided grounds for talk about Nicholas having deliberately taken his own life (there is a fully-argued theory that the Emperor did in fact commit suicide). Therefore, the main task, politically and militarily, facing the new ruler was to end the Crimean campaign as quickly as possible on terms which were more or less acceptable, and this did indeed soon take place.

On taking the throne Alexander adhered to tradition in promising his subjects in his manifesto that he would follow in the footsteps of his predecessors — Peter the Great, Catherine II, Alexander the Blessed and his own father. But his real intentions remained for the moment unclear.

Filled with hope, Alexander Herzen addressed him in an open letter. "Your Majesty, your reign begins under a strikingly happy constellation," the publisher of *Kolokol* (*The Bell*) wrote from exile in London. "You have no blood stains on you, your conscience is untroubled. You did not learn of your father's death from his murderers. You did not have to walk across a square running with Russian blood to take your place on the throne. You did not need to announce your accession to the people with executions. There is scarcely a single example in the chronicle of your house of such a clean beginning. To be sure, my pennant is not yours: I am an incorrigible socialist, you an autocratic emperor; yet our banners might have one thing in common, namely... — a love of the people... And in the name of that I am willing to make a great sacrifice. What long years of persecution, prison, exile, tedious wanderings from country to

ИМПЕРАТОРЪ АЛЕКСАНДРЪ II и ЕГО СПОДВИЖНИКИ

*Bust of Emperor Alexander II by N.A. Lavretsky set up at the Alexander Hospital (132, Fontanka Embankment) in memory of 19th February 1861. St Petersburg. Early 1900s*

country could not achieve, I am willing to do for love of the people. I am prepared to wait, to efface myself, to talk of something else, if only I have alive within me the hope that You will do something for Russia.

"Sire, grant liberty to the Russian word. Our mind is cramped, thought is poisoning our breast for lack of space, it groans in the pillory of censorship... Give us freedom of speech... We have things to tell the world and our own people.

"Give the land to the peasants — it belongs to them anyway."

On 19th February 1861 the Imperial Order on the Emancipation of the Peasants from Serfdom

*Emperor Alexander II with his associates (photomontage created for the 50th anniversary of the Emancipation Reform of 19th February 1861): top left D.N. Bludov, (on his right) P.P. Gagarin, (then clockwise) Grand Duke Konstantin Konstantinovich, D.A. Miliutin, F.F. Berg, N.A. Miliutin, V.A. Tatarinov, Ya.I. Rostovtsev, A.M. Gorchakov and A.I. Bariatinsky*

was decreed; on 1st January 1864 it was followed by the publication of regulations about the *zemstva*, which granted all classes of the population in the provinces and districts the opportunity to elect these bodies which would decide practically all questions concerning the administration of the local economy. Six years later, in 1870, the municipal reform was introduced, which also granted the right of internal self-administration to all classes of the population in towns and cities.

On 20th November 1864 the Judicial Statutes were enacted, laying the basis for profound reforms in the administration of justice. The courts were completely separated from other departments of state and became open and independent with the participation of juries drawn from the local population. Justices of the peace were now to be elected by the population. The adversarial trial system was introduced for the first time, as was an independent bar and the right to counsel.

In 1874 shortly before another in the series of wars with Turkey, a military statute was adopted which imposed compulsory military service on all the male population for a period of between six months and six years depending on education. Major changes were begun too in the field of female education: many courses for women appeared providing an education which followed university curricula. A statute of 1863 had given the universities themselves elected boards of professors and rectors and thus self-administration. General primary education got off the ground.

Russia also achieved major undoubted successes in foreign policy at this time. Thanks to the skill of her diplomats, first and foremost Prince Alexander Gorchakov, in the autumn of 1870 Russia was able with impugnity to cease observing the extremely unfavourable conditions of the Treaty of Paris limiting her naval strength in the Black Sea. In the period between 1865 and 1880 the Russian Empire made a series of strategically important acquisitions in Central Asia — Turkestan, the Khanates of Khiva and Bukhara and other territories. 1859 saw the final annexation of the Eastern Caucasus, followed in 1864 by the Western Caucasus. In the 1858 Treaty of Aigun, China conceded the Amur region to Russia, while the Treaty of Peking in 1860 gave her the Ussuri region as well. The campaign for the liberation of the Balkans in 1877—78 ended victoriously almost at the very walls of Constantinople and not only liberated the Bulgarians from the Turkish yoke they had endured for many centuries, but also greatly enhanced Russian influence throughout the Balkans.

This is probably a good place to stop, although it would be possible to continue enumerating Russian achievements and successes under Alexander for much longer. Sadly an equally long list could be produced of those things the Emperor failed to accomplish. In the letter quoted above Herzen said he was willing to wait, to efface himself, to talk of something else, only in return for the hope that the Tsar would do something for Russia. Very quickly, however, the public came to regard this "something" ambiva-

lently at the very least. Far from everybody saw Alexander as a great reformer and a wise statesman, who had managed by dint of his own personal authority to influence even the numerous conservative elements in society and to "move the country from the spot"; many looked on him as merely a more refined version of the reactionary than his "papa" — the swindler tsar, who had left the peasants to complete ruination without land.

The abolition of serfdom really did not improve the position of the largest section of the country's population — the peasantry, who, burdened now with payments for the redemption of their small plots of land, were just as poor as before.

The peasant commune remained as strong as it had been in the villages. "It played an immense role in the life of the peasants," V. Diakin, one of the leading Soviet historians, considers. "Together, as a community, it was easier to find protection from natural calamities, from the master and the overseer. It was advantageous for the village to have common pasture and woodland, a common place for watering the cattle. The commune looked after orphans and childless old people. But it was the commune, and not the individual peasant or peasant family, that had control of the arable lands. The lands under the plough were divided up periodically according to the number of "souls", working males. The striving after a just distribution degenerated into petty levelling. A peasant household would be given a whole number of strips in different places, low-lying and on the hill, on sandy soil and on clay, close to the village and further away. This number sometimes amounted to dozens, while the width of the strips was measured with a yardstick or even the traditional peasant's bast shoe. On such strips only a common rotation of crops was possible: sow the same as everyone else, and at the same time as everyone else, harvest along with everyone else. Otherwise the animals let onto the field will trample your strip. It makes no sense to fertilize or improve the soil — at redistribution somebody else might be given it. The commune stands in the way of agricultural progress. It prevents people dying from hunger, but it leaves no room for the more enterprising and resourceful to get ahead."

Despite having embarked on the road of "great reforms", the country remained in essence as before an autocratic monarchy with no place

*Chapel on the site of Dmitry Karakozov's attempt to assassinate Alexander II. Summer Gardens, St Petersburg. Early 1900s*

The first attempt on the life of Alexander II took place on 4th April 1866. It was carried out by Dmitry Karakozov, a member of the nobility from Saratov Province, who had been a student but was expelled from Kazan and later Moscow universities for participating in disorders. Karakozov came up to the Emperor after the customary royal stroll in the Summer Gardens and fired a pistol at him. It was only a lucky chance that spared the monarch — the peasant Osip Komissarov standing next to the terrorist (according to the official version) jolted his arm and prevented the murder. This patriotic act brought the man both personal ennoblement and a reward of money, while a school named after him even appeared in the Shchukin Dvor, one of the lively trading centres in St Petersburg. Karakozov was hanged on Smolensk Field on 3rd September at the end of the authorities' investigation into the revolutionary underground.

The incident so affected the Emperor that without stopping at the Winter Palace he went to the Kazan Cathedral to give thanks to God for his miraculous deliverance, and in the evening, this time accompanied by his entire family, he again attended a service of thanksgiving there. The general public were struck by the affair as well. For the rest of that day and the two following the Tsar received numerous delegations — from the State Council, the ministries and departments of state, the Ruling Senate, the nobility of St Petersburg and of the province, representatives of various societies and associations — who expressed their loyal sentiments and delight at the outcome of the event. The foreign envoys brought the best wishes of their governments and rulers, while telegrams came in from all corners of the country.

A chapel was erected on the site of the assassination attempt (1866—76, designed by Academician R.I. Kuzmin).

for either a constitution or a parliament. As before the landowners, the nobles and their children enjoyed many privileges as classes, while the rights (both civil and property) of other estates, particularly the peasantry, were still restricted. It is true that, after twenty years of rejecting the idea of some form of representation for Russia as a whole, the Tsar gave his consent to the adoption of a draft constitution drawn up by Mikhail Loris-Melikov, his Interior Minister, and even called a session of the Council of Ministers for 4th March to discuss the question of convoking in St Petersburg provisional preparatory commissions and a General Commission comprising representatives of the *zemstva* and the urban authorities, but this was to take place only hours before his death, which abruptly cut short the government's policy of liberal transformations.

The "People's Will" terrorists who killed Alexander II gave the grounds for their action in an appeal to "honest laymen, Orthodox peasants and all the people of Russia" published on the day after the Tsar's death. In it they gave their view of the Emperor's 'merits': "For many years now the people of Russia have been suffering from lack of land, famines, heavy taxes, unfair courts and all manner of injustice. The late tsar Alexander II did not concern himself with his people, burdening them with intolerable taxes, depriving the peasants of land, delivering the worker up to the ravages of all manner of robbers and extortioners, and not heeding the tearful complaints of the common man. He protected only the rich and himself feasted and lived a life of luxury while the people were dying of hunger. He destroyed hundreds of thousands of people in a war that was ventured needlessly. He allegedly protected other peoples from the Turks, but he laid his own people open to the ravages of the officers and men of the police, who harassed and slew the peasants in a manner worse than the Turks. Ordinary people who stand up for the people and for truth, the Tsar had hanged or sent for hard labour or exile in Siberia. He did not allow messengers from the peasantry access to him and did not accept petitions from the villagers. For all of this, he was punished with a terrible death. Great is the sin weighing on the soul of a tsar when he does not concern himself with his people. Great is the sin weighing on his advisers, ministers and senators: they surrounded the Tsar and did not allow the peasants' tears to reach him..."

The first response of the most radical circles in Russian society to Alexander's rule had been heard near the Summer Gardens in St Petersburg on 4th April 1866 when Dmitry Karakozov opened fire on him. When interrogated later, the gunman declared that he had wanted to take vengeance on the Tsar for the people deceived by the semblance of emancipation. Alexander spent the next fifteen years under the constant threat of death. (It is a curious fact that a fortune-teller once told him that there would be seven attempts on his life.) A year after Karakazov a certain Berezovsky tried to kill the Tsar while he was visiting Paris. On 2nd April 1879 Alexander Solovyov managed to fire off five shots at the Tsar from close range and ... again the attempt failed.

*Reproduction of the painting* Alexander II Ascending to Heaven. *1881*

That same year, on 18th November, members of "People's Will" tried to blow up the imperial train just outside Moscow. The blast completely destroyed the bed of the railway, but the Tsar had already passed on an earlier train. Another supporter of "People's Will" Stepan Khalturin achieved the seemingly near-impossible — he got himself employed as a stoker on the Winter Palace boilers and managed, little by little, to smuggle a sufficient quantity of dynamite into the guard room which lay below the imperial dining-room. On 5th February 1880 he set off the explosives at exactly six in the evening, the very moment when the imperial family should have entered the dining-room. Again luck saved Alexander (a visiting Bulgarian prince was late), but forty soldiers of the Finnish Regiment who were unfortunate enough to be next to the bomb were either killed or injured.

On that fateful 1st March, when the last two explosions in the Emperor's life took place, Count Loris-Melikov asked him to postpone the review, because the police had evidence of the most precise kind that an assassination attempt was in preparation and had already the day before arrested one of the leaders of "People's Will", organization, Andrei Zheliabov — frequently referred to at the time as "the chief of the nihilists". The Emperor was not persuaded by this and so the Count approached Alexander's wife Princess Yuryevskaya, with whom he had lived happily in a morganatic marriage for 12 years, even while Empress Maria Alexandrovna had still been alive, and by whom he had three children. It is said that the Princess managed to persuade her husband to cancel the parade, but, it seems, there was already no escaping fate. The Tsar's sister-in-law Grand Duchess Alexandra begged him not to cancel the parade — her younger son Dmitry had been chosen as orderly and was waiting this opportunity to present himself to his uncle in his new role. A final decision was made and the Emperor's hours were now numbered, as he rode off to meet his death...

The following day, in a room from which all the furniture had been removed, Alexander's body lay on a simple iron camp bed in the uniform of the Life-Guards Preobrazhensky Regiment. The lower part of his body was covered with a thin counterpane; there were several minor wounds on his face and one large one near the left eye. But in the room next door to the deceased, a "celebration" was taking place, if that word can properly convey the exact quality of what occurred: the new Emperor was giving his first reception; the acclamation of his subjects resounded from the walls of the palace... life continued on its course...

The duties of the new emperor, Alexander III, began with participation in the painful, sad ceremony for the interment of the tsar who had died before his time. His remains were to be taken to the SS Peter and Paul Cathedral, the traditional last resting place of Russian tsars. The ritual of transferring the body of an emperor from his official residence, the Winter Palace, to the Peter and Paul Fortress, dated back to Peter the Great. Then, early in 1725, after forty days of lying in state, Peter's body was taken across the ice of the Neva on a specially-built bridge lined by an honour guard of 1,250 freezing grenadiers holding burning torches in their hands. Subsequently, although details of the ritual were changed, the final destination of all the rulers remained the same. And Alexander III, following behind his father's coffin on 6th March 1881, cannot have foreseen that he was destined to be the final link in this chain, the last of the Russian autocrats who would rest in the SS Peter and Paul Cathedral.

The procession began from the Winter Palace and moved slowly downriver along the Palace, Admiralty and English Embankments to the Nicholas Bridge (at that time the only permanent one across the main channel of the Neva), and then along the 1st Line of Vasilyevsky Island to reach the Tuchkov Bridge over the other arm of the Neva and through the Alexander Park entering the fortress by the St John Gate. "There was no small amount that was tedious in the procession, but also a great deal that was bright and attractive," Andrei, the son of the famous Russian writer Nikolai Leskov, later recalled. "The 'highlight' was what was called in the ceremonial a 'warrior', or more precisely a knight, riding on a white horse, wearing golden armour with white ostrich feathers on his golden helmet; his visor was raised and he held his sword unsheathed before him. But even more memorable, by way of contrast, was the 'foot soldier' tramping after him in black bronze armour, black plumes on his helmet, his visor half-lowered and his sword pointing down. Others behind him carried a 'black taffeta banner of mourning' and led a horse in black harness.

"These were symbols for the Emperor who had ascended to the throne and the Emperor who was going to his grave.

"Then came the city council, the ministers, the heralds and small squads of gleaming horseguards. The numerous crowns of the realms and principalities which had at one time or another become part of Russia, the orbs, the sceptre and the imperial crown were carried past. The clergy of the court followed with Bazhanov, the royal confessor. Finally the carriage bearing the coffin appeared with adjutant-generals and generals of the household standing by the cross bars and holding the tassels of the pall.

"The new wearer of the crown followed directly behind.

"It was obvious to everyone that the black knight was having difficulty walking. Soon the rumour spread through the city that the eager minor official who had agreed to depict the late emperor for a hundred roubles, had had too much faith in his own strength, overstrained himself and, having somehow made it to the fortress, collapsed and within a day or two was in the grave himself.

"The capital, like the country as a whole, was full of conjecture — what could be expected next; what would the new reign be like; would things move forward or back; which way would the rudder of the ship of state turn?"

In contrast to his Most August father, the new Russian tsar, the seventeenth to bear the title, had not reckoned on taking the throne either in his childhood or in his early youth. For almost ten years the heir apparent and Tsesarevich had been Alexander II's eldest son, who had been born on 8th September 1843 and named in honour of his grandfather Nicholas. It was only after his death in Nice on 12th April 1865 that Alexander's third child, Grand Duke Alexander Alexandrovich, was declared the heir to the throne. By that time Alexander had already turned twenty. His education had been mainly in the hands of Professor Chivilev, a famous economist from Moscow University, with Adjutant-General Perovsky, who had been appointed the Grand Duke's mentor, also participating. Besides general and military instruction, Alexander was given courses in political science and jurisprudence by invited professors of the universities of both capitals. After Alexander had been declared the heir his studies became more intensive, since he had also to begin carrying out many state duties. He held the posts of ataman of the Cossack forces, Chancellor of Helsingfors University, head of various military units, including the command of the St Petersburg military district, a member of the State Council, and more. Alexander travelled extensively throughout Russia and displayed a very keen interest in the life of the people and the history of the country. During the Russo-Turkish War of 1877–78 he was sent into active service and appointed commander of the separate Rushchuksky detachment.

Many people considered that, through becoming the heir at such a late stage, he missed out on even a minimum of the education befitting a tsesarevich. Alexander himself, incidentally, having grown up among officers, frequently jokingly called himself "a meticulous regimental commander". We know too that on a report from the Governor of Tobolsk lamenting the poor standard of literacy among the population of his province, Alexander III wrote: "And thank God for that." Perhaps this was just a piece of fun, but the jottings in the Emperor's diary also contain quite a number of demonstrations of his simplicity and ingenuousness. On the day of Karakozov's attempt on Alexander II, he recorded his impressions of the celebration in the Winter Palace in the following way: "The reception was magnificent, the loudest of hurrahs," and later: "Then they summoned the man who saved him. Papa kissed him and made him a nobleman. Again the loudest of hurrahs." (The author of these lines had already reached his twenty-first birthday.)

"We know from reliable sources," Count Witte recalled later, "that when Tsesarevich Nicholas was hopelessly ill (and he himself was aware of it), he replied to an exclamation made by one of those attending him: 'What will be, if anything happens to you? Who will rule Russia? After all, your brother Alexander is totally unprepared for it?' — he replied: 'You do not know my brother Alexander: with him heart and character completely replace and even excel all other abilities which might be inculcated in a man.' And indeed," Witte continued, "Emperor Alexander had a completely ordinary mind, you might even say, a below average mind, below average abilities and a below average education; outwardly he resembled a big Russian peasant from one of the central provinces; the costume that suited him best of all was a sheepskin jacket, a long tight-fitting coat and bast shoes; and nevertheless that exterior of his, which reflected his enormous character — a magnificent heart, kindliness, fairness combined with firmness — undoubtedly impressed and, as I said earlier, if it was not known that he was the emperor and he went into a room wearing any kind of clothing, there is no doubt, that he would attract everybody's attention... And really, the Emperor's figure was very imposing: he was not handsome, in his manner he was more like a bear than anything; he was very tall, but, for all his build, he was not particularly strong or muscular, rather somewhat fat and plump."

The simplicity, certain degree of severity and even asceticism of the Emperor were not only inherent in him, but, with his accession, they began to influence many aspects of life in the state. For example, the customary military parades, reviews and ceremonies so beloved of Alexander II declined under his son. The brilliant "changing of the guard" held in the Riding School in the presence of the Emperor became nothing more than a guardsman's memory, while the affairs of the corps were delegated to the Tsar's brother Grand Duke Vladimir Alexandrovich. Contemporaries considered this to be a consequence of the fact that Alexander III did not ride well.

As General Count Alexei Ignatyev noted in his memoirs, after the accession to the throne of the new Emperor "under the slogan 'autocracy and *narodnost'* there began a period of 'simplification' and 'russification', which in the army resulted in the wearing of short caftans, coloured sashes, lambskin hats, wide trousers and so on. At the first court reception when all the senior officers who were members of the royal household were supposed to wear the new uniform of the household, Prince Bariatinsky, the commander of the Horse-guards, appeared in his regimental uniform, and when this was remarked on by the Minister of the Court he replied that 'he did not intend to wear a peasant uniform'. As a consequence he was obliged to spend the remainder of his life in Paris."

The Emperor was the first to set the tone in the change of dress-style to the Russian. Anatoly Koni, a leading lawyer and public figure, recalled his visit to the palace at Gatchina outside St Petersburg: "I caught sight of the master of Russia's destiny. He was wearing a grey double-breasted jacket with, peeking out from beneath, a Russian shirt with a soft collar and sleeves, embroidered with a coloured Russian design. His height and powerful build seemed all the greater in that fairly low room."

On occasion the Emperor's overtly peasant-like ways bewildered those around him, who simply did not know how to react. Alexander's valet, Kotov, who was forever darning his trousers, complained many times about the Emperor's habit of wearing one frock-coat or one pair of trousers without changing: "Until all the seams come apart, he won't throw them away for anything. It is the most unpleasant thing in the world for him to be forced to wear something new. And it is just the same with boots: give him patent leather boots — and he'll throw them out of the window for you." It is typical that when living in the palace at Gatchina Alexander chose to occupy not the relatively pleasant ground floor,

nor the completely luxurious second floor with its audience, ball and concert halls, but the mezzanine-like first floor with its small rooms, and not even all of that — only half the floor.

The monument to Alexander III set up after his death on a splendid pedestal by the great Church of Christ the Redeemer in Moscow fully conveyed the personal qualities of the emperor they called "the soldier on the throne". This idea was expressed inventively and quite openly: the crown on his head, the sceptre in his hands, the tsar's robe — and sticking out from under it, a coarse soldier's boot. Still more impressive for contemporaries was the monument set up in St Petersburg, which, in contrast to the one in Moscow, was destined to survive, albeit tucked away in the backyard of a museum. The sculptor Pavel Trubetskoi succeeded not only in achieving a likeness to the Emperor but also in conveying the very spirit and manner of his rule. It was not by chance that the massive rider on his heavy, squat mount, reminiscent of an ordinary Cossack sergeant, was perceived as a symbol of a Russian autocracy which had reached its limit. Curiously enough, the sculpture raised no objections from the "highest censors" — the Dowager Empress and Nicholas II.

The characteristic features of Alexander's reign had already appeared soon after his succession when he overcame his main vacillations: to continue his father's cause and take the country along the path of reform or to impose a stable order and calm in the empire with a firm hand. There can scarcely be any doubting that the incessant succession of attempts on his father's life and particularly the events of 1st March 1881 left their mark on him. It was for this very reason that he and his family spent virtually all the years of his reign in the suburban palace of Paul I, earning him the jocular nickname "the prisoner of Gatchina".

Prince Piotr Kropotkin left us a description of this residence: "... I know that old building, designed like one of Vauban's fortresses, surrounded by moats and defensive watch-towers which have secret staircases leading to the royal study. I saw a trapdoor in the study through which you could throw an enemy into the water — onto the sharp rocks below, and then secret staircases lead down to underground dungeons and an underground passage leading to the lake. All Paul I's palaces were built to the same design. Meanwhile an underground gallery fitted with automatic electrical devices to prevent undermining by revolutionaries was dug out around the Anichkov Palace where Alexander III lived before coming to the throne."

Many suspected that fear of assassination was also not the least of the motives behind the Emperor's two-and-a-half year postponement of the coronation festivities with their many-thousand strong crowds. Even the infrequent royal departures to St Petersburg or the Crimea were accompanied by such precautionary measures that they provoked smiles not only within the country, but further afield in Europe too: extra guards were posted along the routes, passenger trains were shunted onto side lines, the railway points were wedged in position and so on.

All the same, his fears were not so amusing and unfounded. Suffice it to recall that over the 1880s many attempts were made to revive the "People's Will" organization (by Lopatin in 1884, by Yakubovich in 1883—84, by Orzhikha in 1885, by Alexander Ulyanov in 1886—87, by Ginsburg in 1888, and others besides), many of whose members regarded terror as the main method of struggle against autocracy.

The explosion on the Yekaterininsky Canal echoed horribly throughout the whole country, and its "rumblings" were heard for a long time after: memories of this event would to a significant extent determine the attitude of those in power to democratic forces in the country, while direct consequences were the increased influence on the Emperor of conservative and extreme reactionary forces, a curtailment of the reforms and the hardening of all domestic policies.

Many astrologers have calculated that precisely the 1st March 1881 was the zero point, when Russia and its people became caught up in a twelwe-year cycle of critical moments in history which can be clearly traced right up to the present day. We need do no more than recall the dates — 1893, the financial reforms introduced by Witte and Vyshnegradsky and the abrupt change of course towards capitalism; 1905 and 1917, years that rocked Russia; 1929, the "year of the breakthrough", the first in the destruction of the peasantry; then 1941 when the Second World War reached Russia; 1953 which saw the death of the Great Leader of All Times and Peoples; 1965, the end of the thaw and a return to a neo-Stalinist course; 1977, the year of the adoption of a new constitution, the very apotheosis of the society of the absurd, so-called "de-veloped socialism"; and finally 1989, the year of the beginning — of the end, or of rebirth.

Not a month had passed since the execution of Zheliabov's group, when on 29th April 1881 the Emperor published a manifesto affirming the unshakeability of autocracy and formulating basic positions in domestic and foreign policy: the preservation of order and power, the maintenance of justice and thrift, a return to true Russian principles and the guaranteeing of Russian interests everywhere.

Alexander's reign greatly favoured the spread of slavophilism, and it became almost a part of state policy. His reign saw the closing of Catholic churches in Poland, which provoked massive discontent among the population, and the bringing of the Uniates back "into the bosom of Orthodoxy". The phrase which Alexander had pronounced while still Tsesarevich as the staff of a particular army corps were being presented to him became widely known. After a whole row of officers whose names began with *von* and ended in *-heim* or *-bach*, the tenth or twelfth in line was a Major-General Kozlov, upon which the artless heir to the throne exclaimed "At last!". Besides his Russian surname, the general had done nothing to distinguish himself, but Alexander had no great liking for people of the empire's minority nationalities: Finns, Poles, Armenians, Jews and others. This was common knowledge, yet, despite this, he had no desire to use pogroms, say, as an instrument of domestic policy.

To a significant degree Alexander III's rule was a negation of the reign of his father. And this did not only apply to foreign and domestic politics. The entire mode of his domestic and family life would seem to be a counterweight to Alexander II in setting an example of the most worthy kind, not only to the numerous members of the imperial house, but to all his other subjects as well. Those around him, incidentally, noted that the tsar's attitude even to relatives and others close to him depended to a large extent on the way they fulfilled their matrimonial and family obligations. "In general any impropriety in the royal family immediately shocked the Emperor... and was always the main cause of the ruler's displeasure at one member of the royal family or another," is how Witte put it in referring to the fact that the wife of the thoughtless Grand Duke Eugene of Leuchtenberg conducted herself in a rather undignified manner and appeared everywhere mainly in the company of Grand Duke Alexei Alexandrovich. One of the causes of the Tsar's dislike for his father's brothers, Nicholas and Konstantin, was also the fact that both had taken ballerinas as mistresses. "Emperor Alexander III was a real head of the royal family," Witte recalled later when trying to compare the mores of the royal house under Nicholas II and his father. "He kept all the Grand Dukes and Grand Duchesses in their appropriate position; everyone not only honoured and respected him, but was also extremely afraid of him... The Tsar had a heart-felt understanding that the large imperial family, made up of dozens of people of different character and differing morality, should in its private, social and public life serve as an example to its subjects, since any piece of awkwardness that took place in the family of the Emperor or one of the grand dukes would undoubtedly become public knowledge and provide food for all manner of gossip, exaggeration and legend." The situation which arose in the royal family during the later years of his father's life was undoubtedly distasteful to Alexander. For a period of twelve years Emperor Alexander II, having left his royal consort Maria Alexandrovna, lived in civil matrimony with Princess Yekaterina Dolgorukaya, and had two daughters and a son, George, from this union. In doing this he failed in the eyes of many to behave with due respect towards the Empress. "There can be no doubting," Prince Kropotkin wrote of Alexander II, "that he retained an affection for the mother of his children, although at the same time he was closer to Princess Yuryevskaya-Dolgorukaya, whom he married immediately after the Empress's death. 'Don't remind me of the Empress: it's so painful for me,' he said to Loris-Melikov on more than one occasion. But at the same time he completely abandoned Maria Alexandrovna, who had loyally helped him earlier when he had been the Liberator. She died in the Winter Palace, in utter oblivion. A well-known Russian doctor, who is already dead now,

told friends that he as an outsider was disgusted at the neglect of the Empress during her illness. The ladies of the court, with the exception of two deeply devoted ladies-in-waiting, deserted her, and all the world at court, knowing that was what the Emperor himself demanded, made up to Dolgorukaya. Alexander lived in a different palace and made only a brief daily visit to his wife." Soon after the death of the Empress, in the same year, 1880, without even waiting the amount of time considered decent, Alexander arranged a religious wedding ceremony in the palace church at Tsarskoye Selo. The witnesses at the service were two people close to the tsar — the Minister of the Court Adlerberg and the Minister of the Interior Loris-Melikov (this was another cause of Alexander III's dislike for both men). After the wedding ceremony Yekaterina Dolgorukaya was given the title Most Serene Princess Yuryevskaya.

The story of Alexander III's own marriage was extremely dramatic. Dagmar, the daughter of Christian IX of Denmark, was betrothed to his brother, the eldest son of Alexander II and Maria Alexandrovna and heir apparent to the Russian throne, Tsesarevich Nicholas. Shortly before the wedding was due to take place, Nicholas, incurably ill with tuberculosis, died in Nice. And, having taken his place as next in line to the throne, the new heir decided to marry his prematurely deceased brother's fiancee. In the following year, 1866, a wedding was celebrated between Alexander and Princess Marie Sophie Frederike Dagmar, who took the name Maria Feodorovna on her conversion to Orthodoxy. It is hard to say for certain what the chief motivation behind this marriage was — love, dynastic tradition or a noble sense of duty, but, whatever it may have been, in all his almost thirty years of married life Alexander's behaviour as a husband was never anything short of exemplary. This marriage produced six children, including the next Russian emperor, Nicholas II.

# Empress Maria Alexandrovna

Maria Alexandrovna (1824—1880) — daughter of Grand Duke Ludwig II of Hesse, known before her adoption of Orthodoxy as Maximiliane Wilhelmine Auguste Sophie Marie — arrived in Russia in 1840. On 16th April 1841, the eve of Grand Duke Alexander Nikolayevich's birthday, he and she married, an event that brought no great delight to the Tsesarevich's parents. They were concerned by the rumours that the German princess was in fact the child of a lover of her mother, Wilhelmine of Baden, who led an independent style of life, and that she had only been acknowledged by Ludwig to protect the honour of the family and the throne. Convinced, however, of the firmness of their son's intentions — he was prepared to renounce the throne rather than renounce his bride — they gave their consent to the marriage and the young princess, despite the mystery surrounding her birth, was, in the words of Maurice Paléologue, "welcomed by her new family and future subjects. She was generally acknowledged to be beautiful and splendidly educated. Despite her youth, she displayed all the seriousness of her character. She gave herself heart and soul to good works and delighted the Most Holy Synod with her piety. At court she was accused only of being stern and reserved as well as of a love of etiquette. Her husband showered her with signs of attention and tenderness."

Of the eight children which came out of the marriage, only six were destined to reach adulthood. Their first daughter, Alexandra, died a few months short of her seventh birthday; the son who followed (the heir apparent who was prepared for succession to the throne) Nikolai died at the age of twenty-one, from tuberculosis.

A few years after the birth of their last child, Pavel, in 1860 and the celebrations of their silver wedding anniversary in 1866, the royal marriage ceased to exist in any real sense. Alexander's affections had cooled towards the sickly Empress who was worn out by her frequent pregnancies and badly affected by the climate in St Petersburg. Following no small number of previous love affairs, the centre of his personal life until the end was occupied by Princess Yekaterina Mikhailovna Dolgorukaya. Empress Maria Alexandrovna lived out the years left to her in complete oblivion in the Winter Palace, receiving a further insult to her feminine self-esteem in the late 1870s when, in accordance with the Emperor's wishes, her successful rival was installed in the palace.

Proud and reserved, her strength sapped by illness, she bore her heavy burden with dignity, leaving many charitable deeds by which to be remembered. Throughout her life in the country Maria Alexandrovna played a very active role in the organization of female education in Russia: she assisted in the opening of girls' grammar schools and diocesan colleges for girls. The Russian Red Cross and other charitable institutions were founded on her initiative.

*Emperor Alexander II with his family;* seated *Empress Maria Alexandrovna;* standing *Grand Duke Alexander Alexandrovich and Grand Duchess Maria Feodorovna. St Petersburg. 1866-69. Photograph by Bugrimovich*

*Emperor Alexander II with his sons:* (left to right) *Grand Dukes Alexander Alexandrovich, Alexei Alexandrovich and Vladimir Alexandrovich. St Petersburg. 1865. Photograph by Denier*

*Grand Duchess Maria Alexandrovna, daughter of Alexander II,
at the age of 12. St Petersburg. 1865. Photograph by Denier*

*Emperor Alexander II with Empress Maria Alexandrovna on their
25th wedding anniversary. 1866*

# Yekaterina Mikhailovna Dolgorukaya

Yekaterina Mikhailovna Dolgorukaya (1847—1922) was the descendant of an ancient Russian family who could count among her direct ancestors Rurik, founder of Russia's first royal dynasty, St Vladimir, the Kievan prince who had his people baptized, and the Great Martyr Prince Mikhail of Chernigov. She was one of the six children of Prince M.M. Dolgoruky who were taken "under royal guardianship" after his death. At the age of only seventeen this graduate from the Smolny Institute for the Daughters of the Nobility and exceptional beauty became emotionally tied to Alexander II and for many years she represented the strongest attachment in his life. This late love (the Emperor was thirty years older than his beloved), in the words of Maurice Paléologue, "turned into the chief impulse in his life; it suppressed the obligations of a husband and father; it had an influence on the resolution of fundamental political questions; it subjugated his conscience, indeed all of him right up to his death."

Four children were produced from this liaison — a son Georgi (1872), a girl Olga (1873), a boy Boris who lived only a few days (1876) and a second daughter Yekaterina (1878). By Alexander's decree to the Ruling Senate they were given the rights of the nobility, the title of most serene princes or princesses and the appellation "Yuryevsky", in honour of their great ancestor Yury Dolgoruky, founder of Moscow.

A month and a half after the death of the Emperor's lawful wife Maria Alexandrovna (on 22nd May/3rd June 1880) the Russian autocrat was secretly married to Dolgorukaya at the Great Palace in Tsarskoye Selo. From this point she too was known as Princess Yuryevskaya and given the additional title "Most Serene". The heir to the throne learned of this *fait accompli* only three days later after he returned from the spa town of Haapsalu in Estonia where he had been taking a cure.

As Alexander II's morganatic wife, Dolgorukaya openly took up residence in the Winter Palace where, even during the Empress's lifetime the Tsar had given her three modest rooms on the second floor, directly above his own apartments. Yet she could not take the place becoming to the wife of the Emperor among the grand dukes and duchesses and Alexander was seriously concerned to strengthen her position. He aimed to elevate Yuryevskaya to the rank of empress and, observing the necessary formalities to legalize his marriage, explored ways to make changes as painless as possible in the ceremonial and rites associated with the coronation of a tsarina. At the same time, as if sensing that his end was close, he drew up a will, leaving his wife and her children materially secure and leaving his beloved family to the care of his son Alexander in the event of his death. By Yuryevskaya's own account the Emperor supposedly intended to see her coronation through and carry out important matters of state due to arise in the near future, then to abdicate in favour of the Tsesarevich and, having become an ordinary mortal once more, to spend the rest of his days abroad. He had visions of an idyllic family happiness there, which he was fated never to realize.

Princess Yuryevskaya spent her own last years outside of Russia, living the life of a rich emigré. She devoted herself entirely to her children and never had any other romantic attachment. She lived for a long time in Nice and died there in 1922.

*Princess Yuryevskaya (a photograph from the album presented to Alexander II by Princess Yuryevskaya to mark the twelfth anniversary of their life together). 1868*

*Alexander II and Princess Yuryevskaya with their children (a photograph from the same album). 1868*

*Grand Duke Alexander Alexandrovich. Autographed portrait:*
*"Alexander 1866 11/23. Fredensborg. Denmark."*

*Grand Duchess Maria Feodorovna, wife of the heir apparent*
*Grand Duke Alexander Alexandrovich. Late 1860s — early 1870s*

*Grand Duke Alexander Alexandrovich with his family:* (left to right)
*Grand Duke Nicholas Alexandrovich, Grand Duke Alexander Alexandrovich,*
(on his lap) *Grand Duchess Xenia Alexandrovna, Grand Duchess Maria Feodorovna*
and (on her lap) *Grand Duke Georgi Alexandrovich. The photograph was taken in 1880*
*during a visit to the Pulone post (near Haapsalu) of the Revel frontier guards brigade*

*The family of Alexander III:* (right to left) *Grand Duke Georgi,*
*Grand Duchess Xenia, Tsesarevich Grand Duke Nicholas, Maria Feodorovna*
*(embracing Grand Duke Mikhail) and Alexander III (in armchair holding*
*Grand Duchess Olga). St Petersburg. 1888—90. Photograph by Levitsky*

## Empress Maria Feodorovna

Maria Feodorovna (1847—1928) — Marie Sophie Frederike Dagmar until her adoption of Orthodoxy — daughter of King Christian IX and Queen Louise of Denmark, and wife of Alexander III lived one of the most dramatic lives of anyone to wear a crown in Russia. Soon after her betrothal to Alexander II's heir Grand Duke Nikolai Alexandrovich, she lost her fiancé to tuberculosis. Having assumed the title of Tsesarevich, the Emperor's second son, Grand Duke Alexander Alexandrovich, carried out his dead brother's last wishes by himself becoming engaged to the young Danish princess in 1866. The eighteen years of their marriage, for all that Alexander III was an outstanding family man, were no happy dream for Maria Feodorovna. Attempts to assassinate her father-in-law followed one after another and had an extremely bad effect on all the large royal family, but first and foremost on her as wife of the lawful heir to the Russian throne. In 1870, a month short of his first birthday, her second son, named Alexander in honour of his grandfather, died. After her husband's death, when the bitter epithet "Dowager" was added to her magnificent title of Empress, she entered the hardest phase of her life. Her eldest son's marriage brought her no great joy. She did not get on with his wife Alexandra Feodorovna and that undoubtedly also affected her relationship with Nicholas.

Many who knew Maria Feodorovna were of the impression that it was extremely hard for her to bear the fact that the reins of government of the immense country were in weak and uncertain hands, and that her own son — often incapable of mastering a situation and taking the proper decision — was contributing in no small degree to the great power's slide towards the abyss.

In 1899 she lost another son, Georgi, at the age of twenty-eight. The heir presumptive, since Nicholas then had no son to follow him on the throne, died of tuberculosis. When in 1904 the long-awaited Tsesarevich Alexis finally did arrive, it was for her, probably, a source of far more alarm and grief than joy. But the really stunning blows came in the years 1917—20. After her son's abdication, Maria Feodorovna took her leave of him, as it turned out forever, and departed for the Crimea on 21st March 1917. There one terrible piece of news after another reached her — the deaths in turns of her son Mikhail, then of Nicholas with all his family and other Romanovs.

In April 1919 Alexander III's 72-year old widow, her daughters Xenia (with her own children) and Olga left Russia forever when they boarded the British cruiser *Marlborough*, sent especially by the Dowager Empress's sister, Queen Alexandra of England. Maria Feodorovna and Olga went on from London to Copenhagen, where they took up residence in one of the wings of the palace of her nephew Christian X. Maria Feodorovna's financial position was extremely difficult: she had no real funds of her own and her nephew was not particularly generous. When at his mother's request King George V granted her a pension of 10,000 pounds a year, it made her feel much better. Her life was already drawing to a close, however, and she died in Copenhagen in 1928.

*Empress Maria Feodorovna, wife of Alexander III. St Petersburg. 1881.*
*Photograph by A. Pasetti*

Alexander III. Photograph autographed "Sasha".
Krasnoye Selo. 1883. Photograph by Levitsky

Alexander III. St Petersburg. Early 1880s   →

Alexander III and Empress Maria Feodorovna with
their children in the garden: (left to right) Grand Duke
Tsesarevich Nicholas, Grand Dukes Georgi and Mikhail;
(first row) Grand Duchess Xenia, Maria Feodorovna,
Grand Duchess Olga and Alexander III. Gatchina. 1888

*Alexander III. 1880s*

*The children of Emperor Alexander III: (left to right) Grand Dukes Nicholas and Georgi and Grand Duchesses Olga and Xenia. St Petersburg. Early 1880s*

While travelling from Yalta to Moscow on 17th October 1888 the imperial train crashed near the small town of Borki. The cause of the accident was discovered to be the fact that the heavy carriages were being pulled by two goods locomotives, more powerful than passenger ones, at excessive speed (the goods engines were designed to operate at a lower speed). The rocking was so great that one locomotive left the rails and the entire train fell down an embankment, crippling several people. There is a widespread legend in accounts of the event that Alexander III used his immense physical strength to hold up the collapsing roof of the carriage and thus saved his wife and children. In reality the royal family, who were in the dining car at the time, remained uninjured only because the walls there buckled inwards and prevented the roof falling.

Investigation of the causes of the accident was carried out by the noted lawyer Anatoly Koni who travelled from St Petersburg especially for that purpose. A short time after the incident Admiral Possiet, the Minister of Communications, was obliged to tender his resignation, as was the Chief Inspector of Railways, Baron Cherval (who, incidentally, had himself suffered a broken arm in the accident). For the man who was to become Minister of Communications, then Minister of Finance and Chairman of the Council of Ministers, Sergei Witte, the same incident, however, gave impetus to his breathtaking climb up the ladder. Shortly before the crash, in his position as manager of the South-Western Railways, he had submitted a report to the Minister of Communications which contained a warning of the potential dangers of pulling the heavy imperial train at high speeds on the Russian railways with their lighter rails, wooden sleepers (in contrast to the metal ones used in Europe) and sand ballast (stone chippings were used everywhere abroad).

*Site of the derailment of the royal train between Taranovka*
*and Borki stations. 17 October 1888*

*Painting-icon depicting the rescued royal family during the derailment*
*at Borki (formerly in the Cathedral of St Isaac of Dalmatia).*
*St Petersburg. 1913*

*Alexander III with generals during the patronal festival of the Life-Guards*
*Preobrazhensky and Grenadier Regiments. Krasnoye Selo.*
*Early 1890s*

*Alexander III watching manoeuvres:* on the right *(looking through*
*field-glasses) Grand Duke Nikolai Nikolayevich (senior), Inspector-General of*
*Cavalry;* (first from left) *Tsesarevich Grand Duke Nicholas Alexandrovich;*
(second from left) *Grand Duke Vladimir Alexandrovich. 1888*

*Welcoming guests from Russia — Emperor Alexander III and his family
in the port of Copenhagen. Copenhagen. August 1889*

*Members of the Russian Imperial family as guests of King Christian IX of Denmark:*
standing *Emperor Alexander III (centre, in a light-coloured suit),*
*Grand Duke Nicholas Alexandrovich* (on his left), *Christian IX* (fourth from left);
seated *Maria Feodorovna* (second right) *and her son*
*Grand Duke Mikhail Alexandrovich* (to her right).
*Copenhagen. August 1889*

*Members of the House of Romanov during a foreign visit:* standing,
upper row (from left) *Grand Dukes Sergei Mikhailovich and Nikolai Nikolayevich*
*(junior);* second row *Grand Dukes Konstantin Konstantinovich* (third),
*Nicholas Alexandrovich* (fifth), *Vladimir Alexandrovich, Georgi Mikhailovich,*
*Dmitry Konstantinovich and Piotr Nikolayevich;* seated, third row    →
*Grand Duchesses Xenia Alexandrovna, Maria Pavlovna, Elena Vladimirovna*
*and Alexandra Iosifovna, Alexander III, Grand Dukes Alexei Alexandrovich*
*and Pavel Alexandrovich;* seated, fourth row *Grand Dukes*
*Cyril Vladimirovich, Mikhail Alexandrovich, Boris Vladimirovich*
*and Andrei Vladimirovich. Late 1880s*

*Alexander III* (middle row, second from right), *Maria Feodorovna*
(upper row, second from left) *and their children, Grand Dukes Nicholas*
(bottom row, first from left) *and Georgi* (middle row, first from left),
*Grand Duchess Xenia* (middle row, third from left), *Grand Duke Mikhail*
(middle row, first from right) *and Grand Duchess Olga* (standing, centre)
*during a visit to King Christian IX of Denmark* (standing left).
*Copenhagen. Late 1880s*

*Bronze sculpture of an aurochs set up in the Bialowieza reserve to commemorate Alexander III's hunting there. Bialowieza. 1894*

*Alexander III hunting. Late 1880s*

As it had been for their ancestors, hunting was an important pastime for the royal family and one which they took very seriously. Among their favourite places for hunting was the dense forest at Bialowieza in Poland which was home to the largest and strongest of European animals — the aurochs — weighing on average some 40 poods (655 kilogrammes). Hunting these creatures demanded special preparations and a large number of people. A detailed description of this has survived in literature. In 1846 D. Dalmatov wrote: "...a battue of between 1500 and 2000 peasants and guns is assembled, it covers an area of forest from 2 to 5 square versts, where advance reconnaissance has discovered the presence of adult aurochs. If during this they come upon a herd of cows with young calves, the keepers remove them from the drive beforehand. To be as sure as possible of holding the aurochs in, they light fires all around and keep them burning until the end of the hunt. The military governor-general of the region nearly always participates in the hunt with a large number of units and lovers of the sport, for whom they make a particularly elevated booth hidden with firs and other tree branches. They decide on a given number of shots and mark them on the trees which the hunters have no right to leave. The other peasants and shooters should have guns with blank cartridges. When everything is ready, a shot is fired as a signal for the drive to start..."

→

*Alexander III and Maria Feodorovna in a carriage in front of a hunting-lodge. Spala, Poland. 1894*

→

*Members of the Imperial family and their retainers out hunting:* seated, first row *Grand Dukes Georgi Alexandrovich and Nicholas Alexandrovich, Grand Duchess Olga and Grand Duke Mikhail;* second row *Grand Duke Vladimir Alexandrovich* (second from left), *Maria Feodorovna and Alexander III. Poland. 1894*

*Alexander III with his retinue taking a drive in a forest.*
*September 1894*

*Collage: The Royal House of Europe:* second row (from left)
*Grand Duke Nicholas Alexandrovich* (third), *Grand Duchess Alexandra
Feodorovna* (fourth); third row (first), *Grand Duke Mikhail Alexandrovich*
(second), *Grand Duke Georgi Alexandrovich* (third), *Alexander III* (fourth)   →
*and Maria Feodorovna* (fifth); fourth row *Grand Duchess Xenia Alexandrovna*
(first), *Grand Duke Alexander Mikhailovich* (second); fifth row
*Grand Duchess Alexandra Georgiyevna, wife of Pavel Alexandrovich* (seventh),
*Grand Duke Pavel Alexandrovich* (eighth)

Group photograph of members of the Danish royal family:
Empress Maria Feodorovna of Russia (seated, second left) *and her father*   →
*King Christian IX* (next to her). *Denmark. 1895*

*Members of the Russian Imperial family during their visit to England:* standing, first row up (from left) *Nicholas II*(first), *Alexandra Feodorovna*(second) *and Grand Duchess Maria Pavlovna* (fifth); third row up *Grand Duke Pavel Alexandrovich*(second), *Grand Duke Sergei Alexandrovich*(sixth), *Grand Duchess Elizabeth Feodorovna*(ninth); *seated Kaiser WilhelmII* (first)*and Queen Victoria* (second). *Windsor. 1890s*

# *Grand Duke Georgi Alexandrovich*

Grand Duke Georgi Alexandrovich (1871—1899) was the second son of Alexander III and, after his father's death and his elder brother's accession as Nicholas II, he was heir to the throne. He suffered from lung disease for many years and died on his own estate of Abas-Tuman in the Caucasus.

*Grand Duke Georgi Alexandrovich. 1894*

*Grand Duke Georgi Alexandrovich*
*and Grand Duchess Olga Alexandrovna on a terrace. Peterhof. 1896* →

*Palace of H.I.H. Tsesarevich Grand Duke Georgi Alexandrovich* →
*at Abas-Tuman. 1895*

## Grand Duchess Xenia Alexandrovna

Fate proved kinder to Alexander III's daughters than to his sons. Their lives were hard, but long, despite the terrible losses of those dear to them, and they died natural deaths in one and the same year, 1960: the older one, Xenia, at Easter, the younger, Olga, shortly before Christmas.

Grand Duchess Xenia Alexandrovna (1875—1960), "an undoubtedly exemplary woman in all respects" as Witte described her, was married in 1894 to Grand Duke Alexander Mikhailovich (Sandro), a grandson of Nicholas I and thus her first cousin once removed. Alexander III did not like her chosen bridegroom and probably gave his consent because he felt his own time running out. Nevertheless, this union was a successful one. They had seven children — six boys and one girl, the eldest, Irina, who as the wife of Prince Felix Yusupov became truly world famous through her indirect involvement in the scandal surrounding the murder of Rasputin.

During the First World War Xenia Alexandrovna, like the other female members of the royal family, took part in relief work. In Petrograd she took charge of a hospital for the wounded and convalescent. After the revolution she and her whole family went with her mother to the Crimea, where for some time they found themselves under guard. To a large extent their survival depended on the chance fact of the rivalry between the Yalta and Sebastopol Soviets which made those bodies unable to come to a straight decision on having them shot. Grand Prince Alexander Mikhailovich was, however, inclined to — somewhat ironically — attribute his own deliverance to the foresight of Grand Prince Piotr Nikolayevich, who on his estate at Diulber to which the Sebastopol Soviet moved them had constructed a real fortified "Bluebeard's castle".

In 1919 Xenia Alexandrovna left the Crimea on the British cruiser *Marlborough* together with her children, mother and sister, beginning the life of an emigré that was to last more than four decades.

*Grand Duchess Xenia Alexandrovna. 1880s*

*Grand Duchess Xenia Alexandrovna. St Petersburg. 1893* →

*Grand Duchess Xenia Alexandrovna and Grand Duke
Alexander Mikhailovich. The Crimea. 29th October 1897.
Photograph by Grand Duke Georgi Mikhailovich (in the family album
this photograph bears the inscription:* Own Gates*)*

*Grand Duchess Xenia Alexandrovna and Grand Duke
Georgi Mikhailovich. The Crimea. 1897. Photograph by Grand Duke
Alexander Mikhailovich*

*Grand Duke Alexander Mikhailovich with his wife
Grand Duchess Xenia Alexandrovna on board a yacht cruising
in the Gulf of Finland. Peterhof. 1896*

*Grand Duchess Xenia Alexandrovna and a group of courtiers
on a meadow in the park at Gatchina. 1896*

*Grand Duchess Xenia Alexandrovna and Grand Duchess
Olga Alexandrovna on the porch of the dacha in Livadia. 1897*

*Grand Duchess Xenia Alexandrovna relaxing in the park. Peterhof. 1896*

*Grand Duchess Xenia Alexandrovna with her children, Irina, Andrei*
*(seated on the sofa), Feodor (standing) and Nikita (being held).*
*St Petersburg. 1900*

*Group of participants and sponsors of the International Light Industry
Exhibition:* seated (left) *Grand Duchess Xenia Alexandrovna.
St Petersburg. 1902—03. Photograph by K.K. Bulla*

*Grand Duchess Xenia Alexandrovna, her husband
Grand Duke Alexander Mikhailovich and their child-
ren, Irina, Andrei, Feodor, Nikita, Dmitry and Rostislav.
St Petersburg. 1905*

## *Grand Duke Mikhail Alexandrovich*

For the period of a few years from 1899 to 1904 (between the death of his brother Georgi and the birth of Nicholas's son) Grand Duke Mikhail Alexandrovich, the fourth child and youngest son in Alexander III's family, was the heir to the throne. His relationship with the Tsar and Tsarina was far from easy, since they were profoundly displeased by his marriage to a woman who had twice been divorced — Natalia Sergeyevna Sheremetevskaya-Mamontova-Wulfert, the daughter of a well-known lawyer who acted for the rich and influential Riabushinsky family. Despite having in the opinion of his mother, Maria Feodorovna, even less will power and character than Nicholas, in this instance Mikhail displayed enviable firmness of purpose, withstanding many noisy family rows and arguments on the score. The result was that he practically abandoned court circles and his dealings with his brother became forced.

Having been a guards officer from 1898 to 1911, Grand Duke Mikhail commanded the Caucasian Native Cavalry Division during the First World War. At the end of February 1917 he found himself in Petrograd when it was gripped by disorder. He went into what amounted to hiding at the home of his friends the Princes Putiatin at 12 Millionnaya Street. The telegram he sent to Nicholas on 1st (14th) March is evidence both of his common sense and his feeling of responsibility for the fate of the country. "Forgetting all that has passed, I ask you to take the new course indicated by the people," he pleaded. "In these alarming days, when all of us Russians are suffering so much, with all my heart I send you this advice, dictated by life and by the moment, as a loving brother and a loyal Russian."

After Nicholas abdicated in his favour Mikhail felt it impossible to take autocratic power into his hands and signed a document leaving the resolution of that question to a future Constituent Assembly.

From the spring of 1917 he lived in Gatchina Palace and after the October Revolution he was granted permission to "live freely" in Russia as plain Citizen Romanov. In February 1918, however, he was exiled to Perm by a decision of the Petrograd Soviet and together with those who accompanied him — his chef, chauffeur and personal secretary — installed himself right in the city centre in some rooms of the Hotel Royale. In the early hours of 13th June 1918 he was arrested by a group of workers, driven out of the city and shot.

*Grand Duke Mikhail Alexandrovich. St Petersburg. Early 1900s*

# Grand Duchess Olga Alexandrovna

Grand Duchess Olga Alexandrovna (1882—1960) was the youngest child of Alexander III and the only one to be born "in the purple" — when Alexander was already Emperor. Of the other children she was closest to Grand Duke Mikhail, the four years' difference in their ages proving no real hindrance to their friendship. She absolutely adored her father and his death was the first real blow in her life.

In 1901, at the age of nineteen, Olga became the wife of the Duke of Oldenburg in North Germany, but they did not make a good couple. A reckless card-player, her husband had only that one passion in life and the frequent rows this provoked between him and the old Duke made her time at the palace in Oldenburg a torment.

Her subsequent fate was decided when she met an officer of Her Majesty's Own Cuirassiers Regiment, Nikolai Alexandrovich Kulikovsky. She managed to avoid waiting for the end of the seven-year "trial period" the Emperor had declared and in Kiev on 4th November 1916 in the presence of the Dowager Empress, her brother-in-law (Xenia's husband) Grand Duke Alexander Mikhailovich, officers of the Akhtyrsky Regiment and nurses of the Olga Alexandrovna Hospital they were married and held a wedding banquet.

Modest, sincere and simple-hearted, in the eyes of Teliakovsky, the Director of the Imperial Theatres, Olga Alexandrovna "differed strongly from the other members of the royal family" and in general "little resembled" a grand duchess and sister of the Emperor: "she totally ignored all forms of etiquette... Quite often she went out alone, on foot, dropped into shops, sometimes visited the theatrical college in the mornings... She wrote letters not in the manner of official decrees, as others in the royal family did, but in the most regular way, and, when some request or other had been carried out, she was sincere and cordial in her thanks and excused herself for the trouble she had caused." She was capable of arriving at the theatre having left her gloves at home or of clumsily losing her slipper at a ball. Her gifts shone in other situations. She could draw splendidly, maintained a school on her country estate, created a hospital in which she herself worked, studying under a doctor, and then using the experience she had gained she set off for the front as a nurse and was awarded the St George Medal for the bravery she displayed there. In emigration in Denmark after the revolution she managed to turn her home near Copenhagen into the real centre of the Russian colony. Olga Alexandrovna "was in contact with the whole world, carrying on extensive correspondence with old friends, with officers of the Corps of Guards, members of the escort, cuirassiers, members of the Akhtyrsky Regiment, the Imperial family's huntsmen and many others," her son Tikhon recalled. "The Grand Duchess was honorary chairman of a

number of emigré organizations, mainly of a charitable kind. At that time her artistic talent was appreciated too and she began exhibiting her paintings not only in Denmark, but also in Paris, London and Berlin. A significant proportion of the money acquired in this way went to charity." During the Second World War Olga Alexandrovna continued to help Russians — both emigrés and prisoners-of-war. After the German defeat she unsuccessfully tried to avert the tragic fate of the Cossacks and other persons who were handed over to the Soviets. Then, accused by the Soviet side of aiding and abetting enemies of the people, she considered it prudent to move on to Canada where she died, two years after her husband.

*Grand Duchess Olga Alexandrovna. Abas-Tuman, Kutaisi Province. 1896*

*Grand Duke Mikhail Alexandrovich and Grand Duchess Olga Alexandrovna*
*on the deck of a ship at sea. 1887*

*Dowager Empress Maria Feodorovna with her younger children,*
*Grand Duke Mikhail and Grand Duchess Olga. Libau. 1897.*
*Photograph by K. Schulz*

*Grand Duke Mikhail Alexandrovich* (left) *and Grand Duchess Olga*
*Alexandrovna on the deck of a ship. Sevastopol. 1890*

*Grand Duke Mikhail Alexandrovich* (left) *by the shore of*
*the Gulf of Finland. Peterhof. Early 1890s*

From what Sergei Witte observed Alexander III loved his son Mikhail most of all. "All the Emperor's children," he wrote, "... I won't say were afraid of their father, but they were shy with him, sensing his authority. Mikhail Alexandrovich was virtually the only one who behaved completely freely with his father." To support these words the memoirist cited an incident at Gatchina which he heard about from Mikhail's valet. During one of their morning walks, when Misha was particularly mischievous, the Emperor squirted him with water from a hose for watering the flowers. The young Grand Duke was evidently quite infuriated by this and decided to get his own back. He picked his moment and emptied a whole hand-basin of water over the Tsar's head. "The only one who could play such a trick on Alexander III and get away with it was his Misha, because if anybody else had done it, he would have been dealt with good and proper," Witte concluded.

*Alexander III* (third from left) *and Grand Duke Mikhail* (second)
*by the walls of an ice fortress. Gatchina. 1894*

*Grand Duchess Olga Alexandrovna with sailor bodyguards. Peterhof. 1896*

*Grand Duke Mikhail Alexandrovich in the park at Gatchina. Early 1890s*

*Grand Duke Mikhail Alexandrovich relaxing on the lake. 1898*

*Grand Duke Mikhail Alexandrovich and Grand Duchess Olga*
*Alexandrovna playing croquet. Peterhof. 1896*

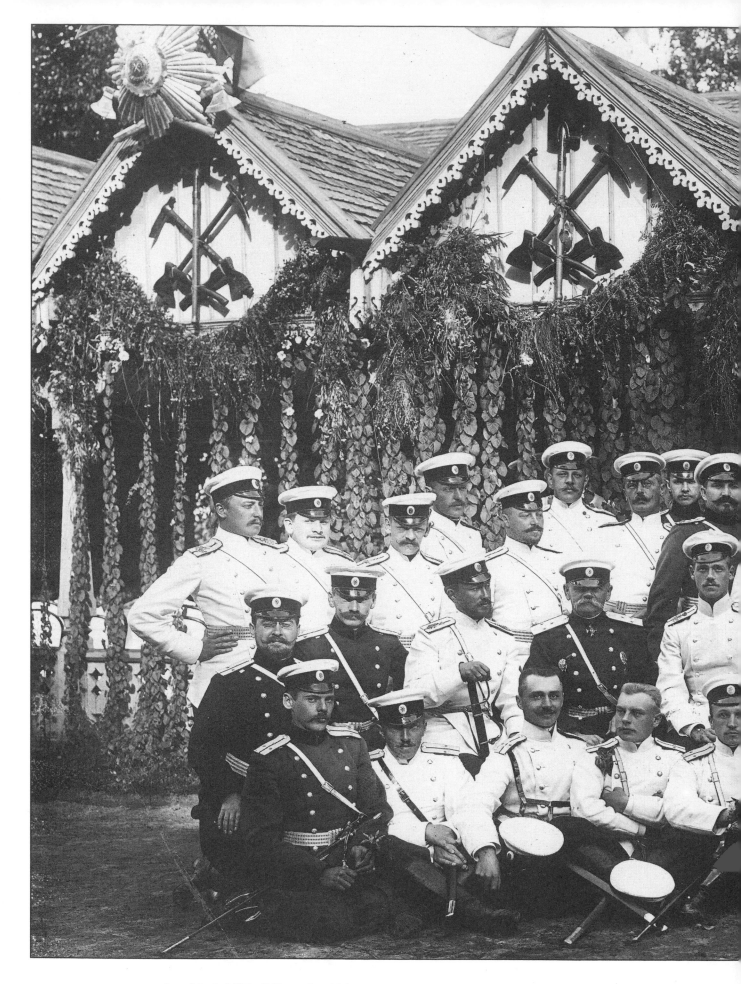

*Grand Duke Mikhail Alexandrovich* (second row, fifth from left)
*with a group of officers of the Life-Guards Sapper Battalion during his stay*
*at summer camp. Krasnoye Selo. 1904*

*Side façade of H.I.M. Own Anichkov Palace. St Petersburg. Ca. 1913*

*Façade of His Imperial Majesty's Own Anichkov Palace viewed from the garden. St Petersburg. Ca. 1903*

# PAGES
# FROM A LIFE

---

*When a man weak by nature is entrusted with*
*a great task, he can do nothing but feel insignificant*
*and oppressed by the back-breaking burden.*

ALEXANDER BLOK,
*Notes on Hamlet. 1901*

*Grand Duke Tsesarevich Nicholas Alexandrovich. Livadia. 1890s*

THE IMPRESSIONS OF CHILDHOOD ARE, AS IS well known, the strongest and most memorable. To a significant extent they determine our entire inner world and influence our psychology. Often it is these very "childish fears" and "naive fancies" which are the true motivation behind much of our action and behaviour.

Viewed from the outside Nicholas's childhood was an enviably happy and secure one. He grew up in a caring home with parents who truly loved him, always aware of their interest and concern. He could play with the best toys and beloved pets. The majority of his wishes were fulfilled, and those around him went along with his whims. And ahead of him he had an absolutely incredible future — autocratic power over the greatest empire in the world.

However, almost from the cradle the world was divided into two in his childish consciousness — the quiet, peaceful world of his family and, surrounding his home, an outside world, sinister and terrible, any contact with which carried a potential threat. And in many ways the roots of Nicholas's coming tragedy — as emperor and as a man — can be found here: chosen by fate itself to communicate with this other world, called upon to see to its prosperity and good order, and regarding this earthly destiny of his as God-given, he feared this world, genuinely found it hard to communicate with it and tried whenever possible to avoid unnecessary contact with it.

Something of this feeling of constant danger must have been passed onto him while he was still in his mother's womb. In the two years before his birth (on 6th May 1868) his mother Princess Dagmar who had arrived from the calm of Denmark struggled to accustom herself to the realities of life in a strange and bewildering country, where in that time alone two attempts on the life of her royal father-in-law were made. When Nicholas was eleven, again bullets flew and bombs exploded around his grandfather with increased regularity. This had to leave its mark on a boy already able to grasp fully the events themselves and their effect on those around him.

We can only guess what the word "revolutionary" meant to him, after the horrendous explosion in the Winter Palace — after all, he could easily have imagined himself and his family in the imperial dining-room at the fateful hour of six o'clock on 5th February 1880. We shall never know what words or vow went through his mind when taking his leave of Alexander II, after his grandfather had been mutilated by the "People's Will" bomb. That incident doubtless played no small role in his fate.

He would experience such feelings again only during the most powerful upsets in his life. Ten years later, when he learnt of the death (at the age of 21) of his young aunt, Alexandra Georgiyevna, the Greek princess who had become the wife of Grand Duke Pavel Alexandrovich and was dearly beloved by all the family, he wrote in his diary: "Since 1st March 1881 I have not lived through such a day." He would remember that fateful day, its details still imprinted on his mind, even in distant Tobolsk in the last year of his life, when, no longer Emperor, but plain Citizen Romanov, he wrote: "The thirty-eighth anniversary of grandpapa's death. At 2 o'clock we had a requiem held here. The weather was the same as then — frosty and sunny..."

After Alexander II's assassination the general atmosphere of fear and uncertainty was heightened by repeated attempts to revive the spirit of the "People's Will" in new terrorist organizations which appeared one after another. Strict security measures when travelling, a strengthening of the guard at Gatchina Palace, rare trips into the capital and a narrow circle of acquaintances formed the background to the daily life of the future Russian Emperor, a background further darkened by the fact that his mother, Maria Feodorovna, often had a less than adequate understanding of what was happening. She was truly convinced that behind all the troubles in the country lay the "nihilists".

A home background of this kind was largely responsible for the fact that Nicholas developed a strong aversion not only to the opponents of autocracy themselves, but also to practically any idea or demand that arose from the liberal-minded section of society. He was probably even psychologically unable to comprehend the fact that, as the famous journalist Vlas Doroshevich observed, the very realities of life in Russia placed bombs in the hands of those who would far rather have held a pen. It was for precisely this reason that when in January 1895, practically three months after his accession, he met the representatives of the nobility, the *zemstva* and the towns who had gathered in the Nicholas Hall of the Winter Palace, he expressed himself in words which dashed the hopes of many and seemed to some simply a "spiteful trick":

"I am pleased to see representatives of all estates who have journeyed here to profess their loyal sentiments together. I believe in the earnestness of these sentiments, that have been inherent in every Russian since time immemorial. But I know that recently in some rural assemblies the voices have been heard of people carried away by senseless daydreams of the representatives of the *zemstva* participating in the business of domestic administration. Let all be appraised that I, dedicating all My efforts to the well-being of the people, shall preserve the principle of autocracy as firmly and steadfastly, as it was preserved by My unforgettable late Parent."

This speech by the young Emperor was neither empty words, nor a dutiful tribute of filial love. All his subsequent actions served to prove his adherence to the political course set by Alexander III. He had before his mind's eye two examples: the tragic demise of his grandfather, murdered, by an irony of fate, as if in repayment for his liberalism, and the truly Christian death of his firm, decisive father, and even at this stage he made his fully conscious and, it would seem, final choice. But the paradoxical aspect of the situation was that the unshakeability of mediaeval autocracy was no longer being proclaimed by a simple peasant-like tsar, but by an enlightened and fairly cultured man with a European education, who had received a decent schooling at the hands of first-class teachers.

Nicholas's studies began when he was nine years old under the watchful eye of his royal parents and in accordance with a programme worked out for the next twelve years. He first received eight years of education at home, basically following a grammar-school curriculum, with the difference that the "dead" classical languages — Latin and Ancient Greek — were replaced by political history, Russian literature, the fundamentals of minerology, botany, zoology, anatomy and physiology; increased attention was devoted to the study of modern languages — English, French and German (although he never did in fact master the last). From the beginning in 1877, Alexander entrusted supervision of his son's studies to the former head of the infantry college Adjutant-General Danilovich.

At the age of seventeen the heir-apparent passed on to the study of "the higher sciences" following a mixed programme of courses from the General Staff Academy and the faculties of economics and law at the university. This originally lasted four years and was then extended for one further year. His tutors and teachers included noted scholars, recognized authorities in their field: I.L. Yanyshev, who lectured on canonical law in connection with the history of the church and also on the main aspects of theology and the history of religion; Ye.Ye. Zamyslovsky, who expounded on the extremely broad subject of political history; one of the leading economists of his time, the Russian Minister of Finance in 1881—86, Academician Nikolai Bunge, taught Nicholas statistics and political economics; Alexander Blok's grandfather Nikolai Beketov, an Academician and founder of the Russian school of physical chemistry, gave him a course in general chemistry. The general management of the Tsesarevich's education was entrusted to the "first adviser of the Tsar", who had in the past also been his teacher — Konstantin Pobedonostsev, who besides this, also took upon himself the giving of courses in jurisprudence, public, civil and criminal law.

Nicholas's team of instructors in military affairs was no less outstanding. He was taught strategy and military history by the military theoretician and Infantry General Genrikh Leyer, editor-in-chief of the eight-volume *Encyclopaedia of Military and Naval Sciences* and the four-volume *Review of the Wars of Russia from Peter the Great to the Present Day*. Lessons in fortification were given by the military engineer General Cesar Cui, a great scholar of fortifications, but better known as an outstanding musician and composer, one of the five members of the "Mighty Handful". The course in military statistics was the work of Infantry General Nikolai Obruchev who was a professor at the General Staff Academy and an honorary member of the St Petersburg Academy of Sciences. Nicholas was taught about "the training of troops for battle" by Infantry General Mikhail Dragomirov, a divisional commander in the last Russo-Turkish War, now head of the General Staff Academy and a great military tactician. Besides these, the Tsesarevich received courses in the art of warfare (given by A.K. Puzyrevsky), tactics (P.K. Gudima-Levkovich), surveying and topography (O.E. Stubendorf), artillery (N.A. Demyanenko) and military administration (P.L. Lobko).

In order to gain a practical knowledge of the basics of regular service and military life Nicholas

*Grand Duke Tsesarevich Nicholas Alexandrovich in infantry uniform. St Petersburg. 1887*

spent two annual camps with the Life Guards of the Preobrazhensky Regiment, rising in rank from subaltern to divisional commander. After this he had two summer seasons as platoon, and then troop commander in His Majesty's Life-Guards Hussar Regiment, and finally one more season in camp in the ranks of the artillery.

A curious feature of this process of schooling was, as a present-day expert in teaching might say, the lack of feedback. None of the scholars invited to teach the heir to the throne were permitted to ask him questions in order to assess how he was assimilating the material (a great contrast with the regular examinations his grandfather was given), so his specific areas of knowledge remained a mystery to his teachers. To judge by Count Witte's observations, even Pobedonostsev spoke of his pupil only in extremely vague terms and feared more than anything that the Emperor's youth and inexperience might lead him to fall under some bad influence.

The writings in Nicholas's own diary which contain mention of his studies, as a rule do nothing more than establish his timetable, without shedding light on which subjects he might have preferred or enjoyed: "*3rd January [1890]. Wednesday.* Got up early and managed to do some reading... Lessons with Puzyrevsky... *4th January. Thursday.* Lessons with Leyer... *10th January. Wednesday.* Lessons with Puzyrevsky... 11th January.Thursday... Lessons with Leyer, very nearly fell asleep from tiredness..."

Moreover, approached with a less than open mind, these jottings can easily give rise to an image of a lazy, negligent, young man, with no particular talents or great interests, with a taste only for drinking-bouts, binges and other unseemly diversions. "Got up at 1/2 past 10," he wrote, for example, the following day, 12th January 1890, "I am certain that I have been struck with a sort of illness — lethargy, because no matter what they do they cannot wake me. Received Lieutenant Mashkov who has spent two years in Abyssinia. Went skating without the Vorontsovs. After a snack we went to the Alex[andrinsky] T[heatre]. There was a benefit performance for Maria Savina, *The Poor Bride.* Went to Petya's for supper. We got good and drunk and quite enjoyed ourselves."

Yet in those same early months of 1890 we can find many laconic entries in Nicholas's diary which might easily be taken as evidence of his breadth of outlook, inquisitive nature and more: "We looked round Count Sheremetev's museum of ancient writings"; "At 2 o'clock there was a rehearsal of Tchaikovsky's new ballet *Sleeping Beauty.* Nothing to say about the production and performances"; "After yesterday's talk with Papa about my forthcoming sea trip I thought about it all day!"; "Read in the historical journals"; "Read a lot. After breakfast alone I drove to the State Council. The session lasted 1 1/4 hours", an so on.

We have an extremely interesting assessment of the Emperor's intellectual level left us by one of the most perspicacious men of the age Anatoly Koni. In his memoirs he noted with reference to Nicholas II: "My personal conversations with the Tsar convince me that this man is undoubtedly intelligent, if one does not consider the extension of intelligence to be reason as a capacity of grasping the totality of phenomena and situations, and not that of developing one's own thought alone in a single exclusive direction. I might say that of the five degrees of mental capacity in man: instinct, common sense, intelligence, reason and genius, he possessed only the middle one, and, perhaps, unconsciously the first. By the same token he was not narrow-minded or lacking in education. I personally saw an edition of *Vestnik Yevropy* (*European Herald*), half its pages separated with the paper-knife, and in conversation he showed such an interest in literature, art and even science and a knowledge of the outstanding events in them, that meetings with him, as say Colonel Romanow, in ordinary life might not have been a wholly uninteresting experience..."

A similar assessment of Nicholas II was made by someone who knew him well, Count Sergei Witte, who suggested that the Emperor possessed "the average education of a Guards colonel from a good family", which is not so bad if we recall that in its time the Russian army uniform was worn by Cui, who has already been mentioned, Pestel and his fellow Decembrists, Lermontov, the surgeon Pirogov, the revolutionary idealists Lavrov and Kropotkin, and many, many more. Nicholas always struck Witte as an inexperienced, but not unintelligent, "extremely well brought up young man", whose rearing concealed all his inadequacies.

Reading the great many statements on this subject made by Nicholas's contemporaries, one forms the impression that, were some ordinary

*The Russian battleship* Memory of Azov *on which the Heir Tsesarevich Grand Duke Nicholas Alexandrovich made a round-the-world cruise. 1900s*

subject of the empire being described, he would even be taken for educated and intelligent; however, for the first person in the state, and that moreover in the twentieth century, this was already clearly not enough. Sadly, however, Nicholas was to a great extent not a statesman, but simply a man. Even two years before his accession to the throne, Alexander III was absolutely amazed at a suggestion that he appoint Nicholas chairman of the committee for the construction of the Transsiberian Railway: "But he's still just a boy; his judgements are completely childish: how can he be the chairman of a committee?" The Tsesarevich, we should note, was at this time twenty-four years of age.

This parental opinion that Nicholas was still "not a man, but a boy" was justified on the whole. This comes across in full measure from his own writings. Here, as an example, are some diary entries made when the heir-apparent was in his twenty-second year.

*"30th January. Tuesday.* I'm simply tired of getting to bed late every night, but there's nothing to be done about it. Again six guests. After breakfast went to Committee of Ministers. Session lasted 1 1/2 hours. Straight from there to the skating-rink. There was potato [many researchers take this word to mean the "girl-friends" of Nicholas and his companions — *The authors*] and Olga for tea. After an early snack we drove to the *African Woman*. It was a benefit for Kondratyev... Went splendidly. Supper at the Sheremet. Listened to balalaikas.

*"13th February. Tuesday.* Began to learn my little part in *Eugene Onegin*, a tiny production in Ella's th., Obolenskys for lunch. At 1/2 past 2 we drove to the itinerant exhibition at the Academy of Sciences. I liked it less than I did last year. Skated in a strong wind, a thaw set in today. Drank tea with potato. The Sheremetevs were with Mama this evening.

*"3rd March. Saturday.* The fuss over *Eugene Onegin* ended with me driving to Bergamasco and being photographed in both costumes with Tatyana in a lot of poses. Came back slightly late for lunch: Alix and Uncle Pavel (on duty). We worked at the rink. Drank tea with potato. At 7 we went to the all-night service. After dinner drove to Uncle Sergei's. Played badminton with auntie, all the winners got presents. I ended up with 6. Drank tea till one.

*"4th March. Sunday.* Got up late, flicked through the papers. Walked to liturgy and had lunch with music. At 3 o'clock Anti, Sandro, Sergei and potato arrived. Built a fortress, played with a big ball, punctured it and got terribly soaked. At 1/2 past 7 family dinner. 1/2 past 9 we drove to the 8th naval corps of guards, where there was singing by real primitive gypsies — excellent. Played roulette for a while at Sandro's. I won 6 roubles and came home at one.

*"14th March. Wednesday.* At 11 o'clock drove to the court stables where I saw all the saddle-horse section. In the riding-school they were exercising Papa's horses and mine. At lunch: Auntie Olga, Uncle Misha and the Obolenskys. We strolled in the garden, and looked at Nevsky Prospekt through the railings for something to do. Had a snack with Sandro who is on duty with the Guards detachment. Played badminton. I won every time — 7 matches in a row. We had snacks."

Aiming to increase his heir's erudition and political horizons Alexander decided to send him on a long sea voyage, for which the Baltic cruiser *Memory of Azov* was specially fitted out. Nicholas was accompanied on the cruise by his brother Georgi (who soon had to return, however, because of an acute lung condition), Prince Bariatinsky, who was entrusted with command of the whole expedition, Prince Nikolai Obolensky, a Horse Guards officer (subsequently a

*Japanese temple. Illustration for the* Voyage of the Heir and Tsesarevich *by E. E. Ukhtomsky*

*The Heir Tsesarevich Grand Duke Nicholas Alexandrovich arriving at the royal palace in Bangkok. Illustration for the* Voyage of the Heir and Tsesarevich *by E. E. Ukhtomsky*

general in His Majesty's household, attached to Empress Maria Feodorovna), Cavalry Officer Prince Kochubei, who later held the rank of adjutant-general and headed the Chief Administration of Domains, and Volkov, an officer in the Life Guards who was destined to become a general of the royal household and the head of

His Majesty's office. When they called at Athens during the voyage, they were joined by George, the heir to the Greek king, whom friends called "Georgie". The future editor and publisher of the *St Petersburg Gazette* Prince E.E. Ukhtomsky left us a detailed, vivid and colourful account of the expedition in the splendidly illustrated three volumes of *The Voyage of the Heir and Tsesarevich* which came out immediately after being censored by Nicholas himself.

The points of call chosen for the voyage, which began on 28th October 1890, were highly exotic — Greece, Egypt, India, Ceylon, Singapore, Java, China and Japan. Practically everywhere these high-ranking visitors stopped, they were met by genial hosts happy to display their national treasures, sights and generous hospitality.

In contrast to Ukhtomsky who kept a real chronicle of events and recorded, alongside a mass of ethnographical, political and historical sketches, his own personal impressions and assessments of what he saw, Nicholas's diary entries for this period give practically no indication of his own feelings, nor of his attitude towards the political systems or cultural heritages of the lands which he visited. Just once, when he was in Delhi, he gave vent to his prejudice: "It is unbearable to be surrounded by the English again and to see red uniforms everywhere."

In other places he simply set down what were in his opinion the main events of the day. When the party left the cruiser to travel up the Nile on a relatively small yacht, he noted the occasions when their vessel was grounded, when they proceeded by land, on foot or riding donkeys, and their visits to temples. *"17th November. Saturday. On the Nile. At 6 'clock we moved on and by lunch, i.e by 12 o'clock we stopped in Luxor. We walked to look at one temple, then rode donkeys to the Temple of Karnak. Astonishingly huge. Drove to our consul's and drank coffee there. After dinner we set off secretly to watch the almahs dancing. It was better this time, they undressed and got up to all sorts of tricks with Ukhtomsky. 18th November. Sunday. On the Nile. We rose at 6 o'clock and took the ship's boats across the Nile. Travelled by donkey to the tombs of the pharaohs and looked at the two most interesting of them. We crossed a pass on foot and walked on down to a temple where we had lunch. After looking at the colossus of Memnon we came back to the yacht at 4 o'clock. At 7 o'clock we went to our consul's; dined with him*

*The Heir Tsesarevich Grand Duke Nicholas Alexandrovich
visiting the King of Siam. 1891*

Arab-style, i.e. with fingers. Visited the almahs again. Drank a bit at the Hotel Luxor and poured some drinks into our consul. *20th November. Tuesday.* On the Nile. Left the surroundings of Luxor early and arrived in Aswan at two. It's strange to be on the edge of the tropics. The temperature was worthy of it. A batallion of negroes in the guard of honour. Took the railway around the first Nile Cataract. Set off in boats to look at it. Arabs were going swimming. Visited the temple on the island of Philae. Wandered round the bazaar in Aswan — bought ourselves some things. There was something like retreat and illuminations."

When the voyage was nearing its end, the *Azov*, by now feeling the strain of many months at sea, set course for the Land of the Rising Sun. Her holds and cabins were filled with foreign gifts and Eastern tributes. But some "souvenirs" would not go down below and had to be found room out in the open, and it was these which caused the sailors the most trouble. A whole menagerie was sailing back to Russia.

On 15th April the seafarers caught their first sight of the Japanese coast. "The pink summits of mountain chains rise in front of us above a horizon shrouded in a radiant haze," Prince Ukhtomsky wrote. "Now its closer, bluer, more distinct: it's Japan! Cliffs and thick vegetation on both sides. The long narrow bay that provides access to Nagasaki is so unique and decoratively beautiful with the ridge of shadowy heights that hangs above it, that at first it even seems artificial, as if you are not seeing it all with your own eyes, but looking at a picture brought from the Far East on a superbly lacquered box or tray, or some other luxury from that part of the world which shows a typical Japanese landscape."

However, gloom was soon cast over this glowing impression by an unfortunate incident which not only interrupted the voyage, but also left its mark for ever in Nicholas's memory. The event took place in the small town of Otsu exactly a week before the Tsesarevich's twenty-third birthday. After visiting the temple in that town Nicholas, Bariatinsky, Kochubei, Obolensky, the Greek Prince "Georgie" and others accompanying him made the return journey by rickshaw. The sight of this young, somewhat unruly group of Europeans probably infuriated the local policeman Va-Tsu, who did not hesitate to take "all available measures" to restore the order that was in his opinion lacking. "At that time," Nicholas recorded in his diary, "I received a weak blow to the right side of the head above the ear, turned round and saw the vile features of a policeman, who raised his sabre against me a second time holding it in both hands. I could only shout out 'What are you about?' and jump away over the jinriksha to the pavement."

The Tsesarevich's life was effectively saved by somebody preventing the second blow from falling — the foolhardy Georgie, who, in Count Witte's words, was inclined "to actions such as might not serve as an example for grand dukes and princes". Nicholas valued his intervention. Almost half a year later, when setting off to meet his parents in Fredensborg, he made an uncharacteristically sharp entry in his diary: "I am absolutely furious at the rumours that have reached me, that Bariatinsky permits himself to continue saying, that it was not Georgie who saved me at Otsu, but the two rickshaw-men. I don't understand what he hopes to achieve by that, to shield himself (who has accused him of not acting?) or to blacken Georgie's name; but what's the point? — in my view its plain impertinence!"

Nicholas was taken urgently to the governor's residence where he was bandaged. Judging by the fact that he had to keep the bandage on for three weeks and was left with a permanent scar on the top of his forehead, the wound must have been quite serious. And it is not surprising that that day — *29th April 1891* — which, as Nicholas put it in his diary, "by the Grace of God ... ended happily" was marked every year by the royal family with a service of thanksgiving for his deliverance. A full five years later, when already Emperor and fully caught up in the preparations for his coronation, Nicholas wrote: *"29th April. Monday. Otsu.* After a stroll we went to the service in the red drawing-room; gave hearty thanks to God for the deliverance which He granted through Georgie's hand in Japan..." Subsequently many believed that these very events were the cause of his persistent hostility towards Japan and the Japanese.

With careful examination it is not difficult to discover in practically any life a whole series of key moments, which are not only destined to recur, but also to some extent or another play a "fateful" role in the life of a person. Researchers believe they have found a number of such points in Nicholas's life. These include the Tsesarevich's first "encounter" with Japan from which he did not emerge unscathed and the incidents during the coronation which he himself took to be a bad omen. At the moment of taking the crown in the Assumption Cathedral, as he went up to the sanctuary to receive the sacrament of chrismation, the jewelled chain supporting the Order of St Andrew the First-Called unexpectedly tore from his cloak and fell at his feet. Many also saw the terrible catastrophe at the height of the popular festivities on Khodynka Field as presaging worse to come.

By a striking coincidence the dynasty, which had its origin in the Ipatyev Monastery in Kostroma, where on 21st February 1613 Mikhail Romanov was proclaimed tsar, ended just over three hundred years later in Ipatyev's house in Yekaterinburg, and, from a purely legal point of view, the person left next in line to the throne was also a Mikhail (we shall have more to say about this later). Painstaking biographers counted the number of steps down to that basement room in Ipatyev's house where Nicholas and his family were shot and arrived at the figure twenty-three — almost the length of his reign, which was broken off in its twenty-third year.

Fate seems also to have predetermined Nicholas's marriage to the daughter of Grand Duke Ludwig IV of Hesse-Darmstadt, and granddaughter of Queen Victoria — Alice Victoria Helen Brigitte Louise Beatrice of Hesse. After adopting Orthodoxy in 1894 she took the name Alexandra Feodorovna, but was always known to those close to her as Alix. Alexander III had taken a dislike to her in the early 1890s and she had been ruled out as a potential bride for the heir to the throne. Nevertheless, in 1894 the event did take place, which was apparently preordained to happen.

George Buchanan, the British ambassador to Russia, who had known Alexandra well in her youth (he had been her brother's *charge d'affairs*), observed that she was "a beautiful girl, though shy and reserved... Her face was a very striking one, with, at times, a sad and pathetic expression — an expression which Koppay has reproduced to the life in the portrait which he painted soon after her marriage. I remember remarking when

*Alix of Hesse, the future Empress Alexandra Feodorovna. Darmstadt. 1888*

*Grand Duchess Elizabeth Feodorovna. 1880s*

I first saw an engraving of this picture, that there was something in it that suggested the idea of impending tragedy."

Count Witte, who first saw the future Empress at the time of Alexander's funeral, also had an impression of beauty. This was, however, somewhat marred by a permanent angry or sour, as many remarked, look on her face. Later, Anatoly Koni, produced a wonderful pen-portrait of her, which still contained reference to the same characteristics: "One could not say that the superficial impression she produced was favourable. Despite her wonderful hair which lay like a heavy crown on her head and large dark-blue eyes beneath long lashes, there was something about her exterior that was cold, even repellent. Her majestic stance gave way to a maladroit bending of the legs resembling a curtsey at greeting or parting. When she was conversing or grew tired, her face became covered in red blotches; her hands were red and fleshy."

Chance had nothing to do with Alix's move to Russia. From the time of Peter the Great it had become established tradition within the ruling dynasty to select wives for the Russian princes predominantly among the families of the German kings, princes and dukes. There was a very simple reason for this. According to prevailing standards, an heir could only marry a princess of the blood, and, fragmented as it was into scores of tiny states, the land of Germany offered a tremendous selection of royal brides, far exceeding that in all the rest of Europe. While Peter the Great heeded only his own wishes when making his second marriage to Martha Skavronskaya (later Catherine I), his successors paid much more attention to dynastic considerations. The Romanovs of later years were, from a genealogical point of view, probably strictly speaking 9/10 German rather than Russian. We should, however, note that it is scarcely possible to speak of any of the royal houses of Europe in terms of nationality, since dynastic marriages had long since mingled all their original bloodlines. For this reason the term "German" princess should be regarded as a fairly provisional one. The bride of future Emperor Peter III (the son of Anna, one of Peter the Great's daughters

*Grand Duke Sergei Alexandrovich with Grand Duchess Elizabeth Feodorovna. 1884—87*

from his second marriage, and Duke Karl Friedrich of Schleswig-Holstein-Gottorp) was German princess Sophia of Saxe-Anhalt-Zerbst, who became famous in her own right as Catherine the Great. In his turn her son Paul I married first Wilhelmina of Hesse-Darmstadt (who took the name Natalia Alexeyevna) and then, after she died childless, Sophia of Württemberg (Maria Feodorovna). Their eldest son, Alexander I, took as his wife Louise of Baden-Baden (Yelizaveta Alexeyevna), his brother Nicholas — Caroline of Prussia (Alexandra Feodorovna). The latter's successor Alexander II, as we have already seen, was married to Maria of Hesse-Darmstadt (Maria Alexandrovna). Alexander III stepped somewhat out of line by marrying the Danish Princess Dagmar (Maria Feodorovna), yet she too was half-German, her mother having been Princess Louise of Hesse.

These links with the ruling families of Germany extended throughout practically the whole House of Romanov, as is easily seen looking no further than Nicholas II's close relatives. Alexander II's sister Maria Nikolayevna married Duke Maximilian of Leuchtenberg. Another sis-

*Staircase in the palace of Grand Duke Sergei Alexandrovich (41 Nevsky Prospekt). 1903*

*Dining-room in the palace of Grand Duke Sergei Alexandrovich. 1903*

ter, Olga, became the wife of King Friedrich Karl of Württemberg, while a third, Alexandra, espoused Landgrave Friedrich Wilhelm of Hesse-Kassel. Of their Grand Duke brothers, Konstantin Nikolayevich took Alexandra of Saxe-Altenburg as his bride, Nikolai Nikolayevich (the Elder) took Alexandra of Oldenburg, and Mikhail Nikolayevich — Cäcilia of Baden. In the next generation, Nicholas II's own uncle, Alexander III's brother Vladimir Alexandrovich married Maria of Mecklenburg-Schwerin and Maria Alexandrovna became duchess to Duke Alfred Ernest of Saxe-Coburg, while only Pavel Alexandrovich married a Greek princess.

Grand Duke Sergei Alexandrovich, the seventh child in Alexander II's family, had married Alix's sister Elizabeth of Hesse (Elizabeth Feodorovna) as early as 1884. It was thanks to these two factors — tradition and close family ties with the Russian royal house — that Alix could number herself among the acquaintances of the young heir to the throne Nicholas Alexandrovich. He met her quite often when visiting her sister, his aunt and was soon captivated by her. On 20th August 1890 he wrote in his diary: "My God! How I feel like going to Ilyinskoye [Grand Duke Sergei Alexandrovich's estate near Moscow — *The authors*], Victoria and Alix are staying there now; otherwise I won't see her this time and I'll have to wait a whole year, and that's hard!!!" And again, a week later: "I have been thinking a lot about whether they'll let me make a trip to Ilyinskoye after the manoeuvres or not." By this time he was already seriously concerned with the question of possible marriage to Alix.

Nicholas's diary entry for 21st December 1891 is an unusually long one for him in which he gave vent to his dreams and feelings of love: "In the evening in Mama's rooms the three of us, with Aprak, discussed the family life of the present young generation in society; this conversation unintentionally touched the most sensitive chord in my heart, touched on the dream and the hope by which I live from day to day. A year and a half has already gone by since I spoke to Papa about it in Peterhof, and since then nothing has changed, either for the worse or for the better. My dream is one day to marry Alix of H. I have long been in love with her, but more deeply and strongly since 1889, when she spent six weeks in Petersburg! I resisted my feelings for a long time, trying to deceive myself into believing that my cherished dream could not be realized. But when

Eddy quit or was refused, the only obstacle or gulf between her and me is the question of religion! There is no other hurdle besides that one; I am almost convinced that our feelings are mutual! Everything is in the will of God. Trusting in His mercy, I look to the future calmly and resignedly."

A month later he again came back to this question. On 29th January 1890 he wrote in his diary: "When I talked with Mama this morning, she made several hints regarding Helène, the daughter of the Count of Paris, which put me in a strange position. It sets me at a fork in the road: I myself want to go the other way, but it seems Mama wishes me to follow this one! What's to come of it?"

1894 was a year of upheavals in all aspects of Nicholas's life. Already in January of that year Alexander III caught a chill which, in the doctors' opinion, developed into influenza with complications and gave the family their first real concerns about his state of health. After some time the Emperor recovered outwardly and, it seemed, returned to his accustomed mode of life, yet questions which had been regarded as of secondary importance now took on a particular urgency. In the first instance Alexander gave his blessing to his daughter's marriage to the husband of her choice, Grand Duke Alexander Mikhailovich, for whom he had a patent dislike. And Nicholas's fate was decided in just the same way. This time his father did not interfere with his wishes and agreed to the marriage with Alice of Hesse, bearing in mind, on the one hand that it is easier to marry as heir to the throne than as emperor, and on the other that the sooner the Tsesarevich married the greater was the likelihood of the birth of a son. Moreover at that point in time there were no other suitable brides in Europe and thus no great choice to be made.

By early April the Tsesarevich was ready to set off for Coburg accompanied by a glittering retinue which included his three uncles, Vladimir, Sergei and Pavel, Their Majesties' chaplain Yanyshev, who was to convert the future Empress to Orthodoxy, and a female teacher by the name of Schneider, who had been given the task of teaching Alix to read and write Russian (the Princess did not speak the language, and at first did not even understand the entries in Nicholas's diary which she had ready access to).

A lively role in the solemn ritual of matchmaking was played by Alix's grandmother, the British Queen Victoria, who had travelled from

London specially for the occasion, and by Kaiser Wilhelm. To the general satisfaction the formal betrothal took place on 8th April, four days after the Russian party arrived in Coburg. "A wonderful, unforgettable day in my life," Nicholas wrote in his diary that evening, "the day of my betrothal to my dear, darling Alix. After 10 o'clock she came to Auntie Miechen [Maria, wife of Grand Duke Vladimir] and, after a chat with her, we talked between ourselves. Lord, what a trouble has slipped from my shoulders; what a joy we have succeeded in bringing to Papa and Mama! I have been walking around all day as if in a trance, not fully conscious of what exactly was happening to me! Wilhelm sat in the next room and waited for us to finish talking with uncles and aunts. Now Alix and I have just been to the Queen and then to Aunt Marie's, where the whole family were all over us from joy. After lunch we went to Aunt Marie's chapel and attended a thanksgiving service. Then we all set off for Rosenau, where a ball was arranged for little baby "Vee" on the occasion of her birthday! I wasn't in the mood for dancing and I walked and sat in the garden with my fiancée! I can't even believe I have a fiancée. Came back at 1/4 past 6. There were already a heap of telegrams. Dinner was at 8. We drove to see the illuminations, then went upstairs for a court concert. The Bavarian Regimental Strings played superbly. In the evening we sat together again in our drawing-room."

And the next morning the newly-engaged Tsesarevich was woken by a musical concert performed beneath his windows by the Queen's Dragoon Guards. The festivities continued. Morning coffee with Queen Victoria was replaced by a formal commemorative photograph, a gala lunch at the Queen's and another court concert. Telegrams of congratulations arrived in a continuous flood and Nicholas barely managed to find the time to answer even a portion of them.

The relatives of the pair began gradually to part for home. The first to leave Coburg was Wilhelm with more urgent matters to attend to. By 11th April Uncle Vladimir and Aunt Miechen were also gone. A fairly measured and fixed daily round became established consisting of tea-drinking, lunches and strolls, photography and church services, performances of plays and music, broken, if at all, by fairly short trips in the

surroundings of Coburg. It was as if the season had been especially ordered. The whole of Coburg and Alix's home town of Darmstadt, which they also visited in this period, was literally buried in greenery and flowers; the lilac was already in blossom and its fragrance (not in the least tainted by exhaust fumes, since this was still only the threshold of the motor-car age) was quite astonishing.

Two weeks flew by like a single day. On 20th April Alix left for Darmstadt and then on to England. The Tsesarevich was left pining as a month and a half of separation lay ahead of them. Memories of her troubled him at every step and even the weather, which "got better, as if on purpose" brought him no joy. "I wandered alone through places that were now known and dear to me," he wrote the day they parted, "and collected her favourite flowers, which I sent in a letter to her in the evening." And that same evening, after making his excuses to his relatives, Nicholas began his journey back to Russia.

Yet, despite having come home, in his thoughts he was thousands of miles away. Not a day went by without the betrothed couple exchanging tender missives. In June, with his father's consent, Nicholas set off on the imperial yacht *Polar Star* for Britain, where Alix was staying. On the return voyage he stopped to visit his grandparents in Copenhagen and thus had the opportunity to learn more about life not only at the British court, but also at the Danish one.

The annual military camps broke up on 2nd June, and the following day Nicholas, accompanied by Dmitry Golitsyn and Yanyshev, took the small steamer *Alexandria* from Peterhof to Kronstadt, where the *Polar Star* was waiting for them already under steam. This voyage was to last one and a half months and Nicholas would return with a great many impressions. The trip was recorded in photographs and on the pages of the Tsesarevich's own diary, which are dotted with entries written in English by his bride-to-be.

Ten days before Alexander III's death, the Tsesarevich's fiancée arrived in Simferopol, and travelled on to Livadia where the family were staying. Her presence greatly brightened Nicholas's life at this difficult time. In these final days his thoughts and feelings were torn between his dying father and Alix with whom he spent the greater part of his spare time and whose health apparently also gave him quite some concern. Many of his diary entries provide evidence of this.

*Grand Duke Tsesarevich Nicholas Alexandrovich with his bride Alix of Hesse. Coburg. 20th April 1894*

As with any human being, joy and sorrow were close neighbours in Nicholas's life. On 14th November 1894, exactly two weeks after Alexander's body was brought to St Petersburg and transferred with all due ceremony to the Peter and Paul Fortress, the marriage of Nicholas II to Alexandra Feodorovna took place. Since the court was still in mourning, the celebrations were not particularly grand, still from early morning the streets of the capital were jammed with crowds of people. The Emperor, dressed in the uniform of a hussar and accompanied by his brother Grand Duke Mikhail, left the Anichkov Palace at about eleven o'clock and rode past the troops lining all the section of Nevsky Prospekt to the Winter Palace. At ten past twelve the wedding service was held in the Great Church of the palace, with Grand Dukes Sergei, Cyril, Mikhail and Georgie acting as supporters. Then the couple moved to the Malachite Hall, where they were presented with a huge silver swan as a present from all the royal family. After this the Emperor and the young Empress, who had quickly managed to change, boarded a coach harnessed in the Russian manner with a postilion and set off for the Kazan Cathedral past the cheering citizens. As Nicholas noted "there were swarms of people on the streets — we could barely get through!" The culminating moment of the whole ceremonial was when they were met in the courtyard of the Anichkov Palace by a guard of honour drawn from the Life-Guards Uhlan Regiment and the Dowager Empress gave the newlyweds the traditional welcome with bread and salt in their apartments.

At first the young couple stayed in the Anichkov Palace, where two more rooms, newly furnished, were added to the four Nicholas had previously occupied so they would not be cramped. A week after their wedding Nicholas and Alexandra drove to the Winter Palace, inspected its rooms together with the Empress's older sister Elizabeth Feodorovna and settled all questions about the furnishing of their new apartments.

Not only the Winter Palace, "boarded up" during Alexander III's reign, was now given a new lease of life, but also the cheerful town of Tsarskoye Selo (15 miles south of the capital) to which the young Emperor transferred his actual residence. "Words cannot describe," Nicholas wrote, "what bliss it is to live as a couple in such a fine place as Tsarskoye!"

We can get some ideas of the life of the imperial couple at this time from the memoirs of Count Alexei Ignatyev, which, besides giving a description of various court rituals, also contain interesting observations and impressions about Their Imperial Majesties. The young count's first direct encounter with the royal family took place in the Alexander Palace in Tsarskoye Selo in 1895, when he and the other members of the senior classes of the College of Pages were formally promoted to the rank of Pages of the Chamber and presented to the Tsar.

"In the middle of a large room crammed with flowers and full of the scent of noble spirits," he wrote, "in a lightgrey crepe-de-chine dress stood a tall, slender blonde beauty. I was supposed to be the first to go up to her and kiss her outstretched hand; but either she did not raise her hand in time, or I out of confusion did not bow low enough, in any case the kiss remained in mid-air, and I noticed that her face had become covered with unattractive red blotches and that embarassed me even more. I had great difficulty in making out the barely audible phrase in which she said in French that she was very pleased to meet us.

"For several months then this woman was for me 'my Empress'. Not a week went by without them sending us in full uniform to Tsarskoye Selo where we were met by a driver and footman in golden tricorns with a court coach that was pulled by two magnificent matched trotters. Inside the palace a footman in a hat with an ostrich-feather plume brought us to the hall, where the ladies of St Petersburg high society gathered to present their grown-up daughters to the Empress.

"After a few minutes the Empress's private chamberlain, the handsome greying scented Count Gendrikov, went with us to the drawingroom we already knew; at that first time we kissed the royal hand and together with Gendrikov accompanied 'Her Majesty' to the hall where we did the rounds of the Empress's guests. This was the full extent of our duties. And they were roughly the same at the palace ceremonies, what were known as the 'royal appearances', to mark the New Year, the Blessing of the Waters at Epiphany, Easter morning service, the great ball at the Winter Palace and so on. For all events of this nature the royal family, up to and including the Prince of Oldenburg, gathered ahead of time in the Malachite Hall of the Winter Palace and left it in pairs — a lady and a gentleman — according to seniority, in other words in order of succession;

*Nicholas II. Photograph with a dedication: "In memory of two good years!!! Nicky." St Petersburg. 1894*

this resulted in the Tsar's cousin Boris Vladimirovich processing in an ordinary cadet's uniform ahead of the venerable Field-Marshal of the Russian Army, Mikhail Nikolayevich, the Tsar's great uncle. This giant of a man with a greying beard and a ruddy grey nose was the younger brother of Alexander II and knew whole generations of military men in St Petersburg. In the last years of his life he would sit by a low floor window in his palace and was greatly pleased when passers-by noticed him and saluted.

"The rear of the column of 'royal dignitaries' was brought up by Prince Louis-Napoleon, a cousin of Napoleon III of France, commander of the uhlans, who walked alone with the pale blue sash of the Order of St Andrew the First-Called over his shoulder. In Russia some twenty to thirty of the highest state officials were given this order, but members of the royal family of both sexes were invested with it at birth.

"The first couple — the Tsar and Tsarina — were followed by their pages and the duty generals and aides-de-camp, the other couples by their personal pages; each of the grand dukes' wives and the unmarried royal daughters had her own page attached to her for a whole year, the boys' school results deciding who went to whom.

"The column processed slowly through all the halls of the Winter Palace, receiving the bows of the high officials and guards officers who had driven to the palace for the royal appearance. The ladies admitted to the palace wore court dresses in the form of stylized Russian sarafans and *kokoshniki* [traditional headdresses].

"Nobody had any dark presentiments in that winter of 1895—96: we all excitedly awaited the best from the new, young Tsar, and were delighted by his every gesture, looking on this, if not as the start of a new era, then at least as a break with the Gatchina way of life established by Alexander III..."

Nicholas was one of the youngest rulers of the Romanov dynasty, particularly when compared to those of the last hundred years. This fact inevitably had both positive and negative aspects to it, but the latter were, in retrospect, far more numerous. In contrast to his father, who had possibly been less well prepared and educated, the new emperor above all lacked authority within his own family. While publicly according him the signs of respect demanded by ceremonial and etiquette, his older relatives, and this applied primarily to his uncles, continued to look at him in informal situations not as the Tsar but as a young man or even a boy. It seemed no time at all since Grand Duke Vladimir Alexandrovich had in front of outsiders taken the mischievious heir to the throne and his brother by the ears, only yesterday that Pobedonostsev acting as domestic tutor had been explaining simple truisms to him. Only some two years ago he had been capable of deriving immense satisfaction from dashing round the darkened rooms of his palace with Count Sheremetev, and today, by the will of circumstances, he had been set above all of them, without any grounds but the purely formal for feeling himself superior. Incidently, he was probably himself aware of this to some extent. Addressing members of the State Council in the Anichkov Palace two weeks after his accession, he said: "May God help me to bear the burden of service to the state, *laid on Me prematurely...*" [Our italics — *The authors*]. And his own private thoughts were practically the same — on the last day of 1894 he wrote: "It was hard to stand in church with the thought of the terrible upset that took place this year... for me it was the worst that happened, the very thing I had feared all my life. Together with such irreparable sadness the Lord also rewarded me with a happiness I could not even have dreamt of — He gave me Alix."

In the initial period after Nicholas's accession many at court noted a sharp increase in the influence of the grand dukes on the policy of the state. Piotr Vannovsky who was War Minister and later became Minister for Public Education even, in his own words, made hints to Nicholas on this account and reminded him of the firm hand shown by his father Alexander III who had managed to restrict the grand dukes' visible influence on policy which had also been a feature of the reign of *his* father, Alexander II.

From the very beginning the young Tsar had around him helpers and advisers from among the ranks of his "most august" relatives. First and foremost these were Grand Duke Mikhail Nikolayevich, younger brother of Alexander II, chairman of the State Council; his father's brother Alexei who was Admiral-General; his sister's husband Grand Duke Alexander Mikhailovich (Sandro) who aspired to the same post at the head of the navy; and another of his father's brothers, Sergei, Governor-General of Moscow, whose influence was all the stronger for his being married to Alix's sister Elizabeth Feodorovna (Ella). We must add to this list the eldest of the late Emperor's brothers Grand Duke Vladimir Alexandrovich, his wife Auntie Miechen and their numerous sons (the "Vladimiroviches"); Grand Duke Konstantin Konstantinovich and his wife Yelizaveta Mavrikievna; and the most "military man" in the whole imperial family Grand Duke Nikolai Nikolayevich (the Younger) known as Nikolasha. Behind each of them there were certain forces and circles and a veritable spider's-web of intrigues was constantly being woven about the new Emperor in an incessant struggle for influence. The only person outside the royal family to enjoy great authority and complete trust with Nicholas was the Chief Procurator of the Senate, Konstantin Pobedonostsev, who, in contrast to the others, was permitted access to the Tsar whenever he considered it justified.

Over the years Nicholas's ties to the grand dukes and their families became weaker. Only the family of Konstantin Konstantinovich and

*Konstantin Pobedonostsev. St Petersburg. Early 20th century*

"The Emperor will remain Pobedonostsev's pupil to the end of his days," the former Minister of Agriculture Alexander Krivoshein once told Maurice Paléologue. Reflecting on this statement the French diplomat wrote: "Indeed, it was to none other than the Chief Procurator of the Most Holy Synod — a close associate of Alexander III — that Nicholas II owed all his moral and political baggage. An outstanding lawyer, a theological scholar and fanatical champion of Orthodoxy and autocracy, Pobedonostsev brought to the defence of his reactionary views an ardent faith, ecstatic patriotism, a profound and immutable conviction, a broad education, a rare force of argument and finally — what seems a contradiction — utter simplicity and a highly fascinating manner and way of speaking. Autocracy, Orthodoxy and *narodnost* — these three words summarize his complete programme, and he pursued its implementation with exceptional severity and a superb contempt for any aspects of reality which intruded in on him. As was to be expected, he condemned the "new spirit", democratic principles and western atheism. His persistent influence, renewed daily, left its indelible stamp on Nicholas II's pliant brain."

Yelizaveta Mavrikievna remained really close almost to the end. As British Amdassador George Buchanan observed: "In the isolation of Tsarskoye the Imperial family led a simple domestic existence, which excluded outsiders from penetrating into their happy family circle."

Alexandra Feodorovna brought substantial changes to Nicholas's life — she had troubles with her legs and was unable to ride or to play tennis and badminton; walks were a torment to her and she often took to a carriage even for short distances. She spent much time sitting at home and now and then, especially during her pregnancies, the doctors advised her to restrict her movements. Nevertheless Nicholas accepted all this without a murmur and, moreover, had no feeling of it being an imposition on himself. He could push his wife for hours in a bath chair around the garden or park.

She was, in contrast to all the others whose effect on Nicholas may have been strong but did not last, the only person whose influence remained constant throughout practically all his reign. "Dear boy! I love you, o so tenderly and deeply," she wrote in his diary on 15th October 1894 while still his bride-to-be. "Be firm and make Doctor Leyden and the other gentleman come to you every day and tell you how they find him [Alexander III — *The authors*], and also all the details of what they find it necessary to do for him, so that you are always the first to know. Then you will be able to persuade him to do what's needed. And if the doctor needs something, let him come straight to you. Don't let others be put first and you left out. You are Father's dear son and must be told all and asked about everything. Show your own mind and don't let others forget who you are. Forgive me, lovy!"

Instructions of this kind from her, becoming ever more categorical with time, would accompany Nicholas all the rest of his life. "As early as the late 90s," Koni wrote, " I heard talk from Ye.A. Naryshkina about her various *faits et gestes* aimed at inculcating the idea in her husband that as autocrat he had the right to do everything, unhindered by anything or anybody." That this was indeed the case is easily confirmed from the correspondence of the imperial couple in later years too.

"Thank God, our Emperor is an autocrat and should remain so, as you are doing — only show more force and decisiveness," Alexandra Feodorovna wrote to Nicholas on 7th September 1915. "You are master and sovereign of Russia, Almighty God set you in place, and they should all bow down before your wisdom and steadfastness," she repeated in a letter two days later. "Be Peter the Great, Ivan the Terrible, Emperor Paul — crush them all," she demanded of her royal husband on 14th December 1916. And even right before the end of the monarchy, on 25th February 1917, when the events of the revolution were already running their course in the capital, she addressed Nicholas stressing insistently: "Above all exercise your will, my dear."

Massive pressure from all sides coupled with his own lack of competence gave rise to a whole complex of negative emotions in Nicholas: shyness, uncertainty, a sense of depression and the like. The hardest moments for him came when he had to talk with people he did not know, or barely knew, and when he was obliged to speak in public. Psychologically he seems to have yearned for a solitary, "private" life, screened from outsiders. Here again his diary provides a great deal of confirmation: "It's easier to work when there aren't strangers close by, whose presence only increases the burden weighing on me." "At 12 o'clock I received all the members of the State Council — again I had to speak." (The records show that on that day, 2nd November 1894, Nicholas addressed no more than five sentences to the assembled company...) "At 1/2 past 3 received the whole retinue, again had to say a few words" (two sentences); "... received a mass of deputations ... had to talk with each of them!"; "I was full of terrible emotions before going into the Nicholas Hall to the deputations of the nobility, *zemstva* and urban communities, whom I gave a speech..."

The young Emperor's first official speeches proved more than modest, not only in volume, but also in style and content. Even taking into account Koni's observation that the collection of Nicholas II's speeches published in 1906 does not give a true impression of them ("they were so bleached and curtailed in passing through a peculiar form of censorship"), it is hard to accept that they were in reality much more interesting, unless the state officials had set themselves the deliberate goal of discrediting the Tsar in the eyes of the public. In the mouth of another person these speeches would more likely have been called remarks rather than extended monologues. The surprise with which they were received by many who had gathered specially to hear them is therefore understandable. "I thank you, gentlemen," he told, for example, the generals and adjutant-generals of His Majesty's household on 3rd November 1894, "in the name of my dearly beloved Father for your true and honest service to Him. I ask you to transfer to me those sentiments of devotion and love which you had for Him." Almost a week later, on 11th November, in the presence of the Minister of Justice and his fellows the Tsar addressed almost the same words to the senators and Chief Procurators of the Senate: "Gentlemen! In the name of my late Father, I thank you for your work. I am certain that under me too the Senate will be governed in its activities only by the truth and law."

On occasions when his words were intended to convey some proposal for action he made use of texts that had been compiled for him earlier. During his "famous" speech on 17th January 1895 notes prepared by Pobedonostsev lay in his lambskin hat. Emotion, however, caused the Emperor to get his words mixed up and he pronounced "dreams of participation by the representatives of the *zemstva* in the administration of internal affairs" to be not "unsubstantiated" (in other sources "unrealizable") as was written, but "senseless", and this was quite enough to make the speech "historic".

Finding himself at the helm of such an immense unwieldy state as the Russian Empire, Nicholas was obliged from the earliest days of his

reign to plunge himself into the unknown world of official life. From the very outset he tried to establish a very strict working routine, which thanks to his pedantic nature did not prove particularly difficult to maintain. He practically never without serious cause broke the rules he had set himself — to acquaint himself personally with the great quantity of files delivered to him. He had no secretary, as is usually the case with senior figures of state, nor even an office assistant; he made use of the services only of the officer of the day or an aide-de-camp. While reading documents, something that took up a lot of his time, he was in the habit of making his knowledge of the contents evident with marginal notes, which ranged widely from simple interjections such as "You don't say!" to whole figures of speech, like "Too many cooks spoil the broth" or "There's a black sheep in every family". But the language of most observations ("right", "agreed" and so on) is extraordinarily reminiscent of the dry, clipped army parlance, and this, incidently, also found its way into the diary, which the Em-

*Nicholas II* (right) *and King Victor Emmanuel III of Italy out hunting. Italy. 1900*

peror kept with an enviable constancy, like a log, a mere record of events, weather conditions, the time he got up, ate or went to bed.

Nevertheless, as far as can be judged from the reminiscences of those who knew him reasonably well and from his own writings, neither the great questions of politics, nor the actual running of the state in all its many aspects held any attractions for him. It seems he looked on his duties like a diligent pupil who regularly did his homework, but was always glad when the teacher was ill or the class went on an outing or some upset made it possible to escape from lessons. Nicholas II was emperor out of duty and circumstances, and not by vocation. "Walked and rode a bicycle around the garden. There was little to read [reading usually meant looking through state papers — *The authors*] and so I spent a wonderful time till dinner with dear Alix." "A day of rest for me — no reports, no audiences at all." "... It's a shame that work takes up such a lot of time that I would so much like to spend alone with her!" "It's inexpressibly pleasant to live quietly, not seeing anyone — a whole day and night just two of us."

Having embarked on his reign and on matrimony at almost the same time, he undoubtedly felt burdened by his high duties, and strove by nature after the quiet pleasures of a family life which had far more meaning and more capacity to bring him joy than the affairs of some ministry or committee. Domestic details, right down to minutiae — "were busy with arranging things, hanging pictures and photographs on the walls in the new room..." — can now be found in every diary entry, while more than coldly and grudgingly, without emotions or feelings, he writes about matters vitally important for millions of his subjects and touching on the prime concerns of the state — the land of Russia, whose "master" he literally termed himself in the census form of 1897. At the same time his diary contains a great many remarks which convey his true passions and interests: "The evening was free, they sent fewer papers and so I managed to catch up on my favourite reading, the historical journals"; "Read a new French book about Napoleon's time on the island of St Helena"; "I had the evening free, read for pleasure"; "Read until dinner, in the evening out loud to Alix the continuation of Countess Golovina's most interesting memoirs from the time of Catherine and Pavel Petrovich"; "We all looked together at back numbers of a fashionable magazine for the 30s, 40s and 50s with extremely funny stories."

Of course, not all the Russian monarchs subordinated their life to the interests of state in the way Peter I, Catherine II or Alexander I did. There were fewer still who felt themselves unsuited for the throne, and only two who in point of fact voluntarily declined the crown. While Nicholas II's brother, Mikhail, might have been put off by the near *fait accompli* of the breakdown of the empire, the other heir and Tsesarevich, living a century earlier, simply preferred to live at peace with himself. Paul I's second son Konstantin — successor to his brother Alexander I since that emperor had no legitimate offspring — by his divorce from Juliana of Saxe-Coburg (Anna Feodorovna) and his marriage to the daughter of an ordinary Polish nobleman effectively deprived himself of all rights to the Russian throne, yet, more than that, he officially confirmed his renunciation of the crown, showing clearly that the choice he made in favour of the family hearth was a quite conscious one.

It would seem unlikely that the thought of taking a similar step ever entered Nicholas's head, even if he did sense a contradiction between his inclinations as a man and the post he occupied. He was absolutely in the grasp of the idea that the tsar was God's appointee and, having been handed the crown by the father he honoured, he intended to pass it on, whole and stable, to his son and heir.

For Nicholas the family was far more important than it normally is, for even the most loving, but successful and self-assured person. It was for him a salvation and consolation and an escape from the heavy burden that lay on him from the moment of his accession to the throne. Nicholas continued, as it were, the healthy tradition established by his father, and remained all his life a loving and faithful husband and father. After his marriage the "potato" that had amused and excited him remained only a memory. He broke off forever the ties with the delightful prima ballerina Mathilda Kschessinska that were at one time the talk of all St Petersburg. He began spending his leisure hours differently too. The jolly gatherings with fairly inoffensive pieces of fun and plenty of drink were abandoned for the company of his young wife, and soon that of his children too.

This by no means implies any fundamental change in his nature or character. No one can doubt that the family occupied by far the most important role in his life in his childhood and in his youth as well. And that not only because the people with whom he was constantly in contact and whom he loved were in the main his close relatives — parents, brothers, sisters or aunts — but also because, more than anything else, in his thoughts, as is evident from his diaries, he was usually with them.

It is remarkable that on a day we have already mentioned, 12th September 1891, when Nicholas was himself deeply affected by the news of the death of his aunt Alexandra, his own sense of profound loss did not prevent him from feeling real compassion for those who had especially loved the young Greek bride of his uncle Pavel Alexandrovich. "When I went upstairs to greet Papa and Mama," he wrote then at Fredensborg, where he and his parents were visiting his grandfather and grandmother, "I learned the fateful news that dear, unforgettable Alix was taken from us in the night! I could not imagine that it had happened for real, it all seemed like some bad dream. God! what Uncle Willy, Auntie Olga and especially poor Uncle Pavel must be feeling and how they must be suffering. I can't look at Georgie, Nicky and Minnie without crying. Yes! It's all over! How terribly the Lord has displayed His wrath to us. Nevertheless, blessed be His will!.. At 3 o'clock there was a requiem for her. The whole day we wandered like ghosts through the rooms and the garden. The little Italian [the future King Victor Emmanuel of Italy, who was of quite small stature — *The authors*], having called at Fredensborg at such an inopportune moment, set off for Copenhagen after lunch... It is decided that tomorrow we will leave for Moscow, the Greeks as well! We had a family dinner in our dining-room. Who could have imagined just a month ago when we arrived here, that we would so unexpectedly have to leave this dear place, where we had earlier always found peace and the joy of a real family life. Everything is in God's will!"

His tenderness of feeling extended beyond his relatives to people close to the family whom he had got used to over the course of his life and regarded as his "own". "A very sad day," runs an entry written two months later on 7th November, for example, "today at 3 o'clock we lost one of our best friends and a person most devoted to Papa and Mama — Obolensky. A real loss that will be hard to make up! I can't convey the regret and sadness I felt when I learned of his death! A man whom we all knew from earliest childhood, whom we back then christened 'Rabbit' and loved more than a relative — and suddenly he's no longer with us! Poor, unhappy Aprak. No, absolutely, this 1891 has been a year of the most difficult trials for those of us left alive... In the course of the day we heard of the deaths of two more people we know — Letnikovsky, Sandro's former tutor, and Count Rediger, Uncle Alexei's adjutant. So, three departures in one day! — And at what could not have been a more inappropriate moment young Prince Albrecht of Württemberg arrived here today from Odessa with the official notice of the death of the old king and the accession of the new one; as if we didn't know about it anyway!"

Nicholas II is often accused of being cruel and heartless towards the people around him. And to a great extent this is indeed justified. There really was much that he quite simply did not feel, and, for all his very good education, he was lacking a knowledge of people, intuition, and on occasion even purely human tact and common sense. As we have already seen, he showed himself in the worst possible light on the day of the tragedy at Khodynka. Nicholas proved equally incapable of catching the spirit of the times or of comprehending his own people, imagining them to be something far removed from what they were in reality. Often too he made incorrect judgements about people on whom not only the fate of the empire depended, but also his own very life and well-being. An almost copy-book example of this aspect of him was the fact that the Emperor failed to attend the funeral of Interior Minister and Chairman of the Council of Ministers Piotr Stolypin — after that leading figure in the government had been fatally wounded in the Kiev Opera Theatre in Nicholas's presence and had devoted what was literally his last look to his monarch, lifting his dying hand to make the sign of the cross over him.

It was generally known that Nicholas harboured no great sympathy for his "strong" prime-minister and, even more than that, felt oppressed by his "figure" as if it threatened to push him into the background. Even so, the fact that the Emperor did not pay his last respects to the man who had served him and the country

*Piotr Stolypin, Minister of the Interior, Chairman of the Council of Ministers, with his daughter by the Yelagin Palace. St Petersburg. 1907*

loyally and truly, in the end effectively laying down his life for being his minister, not only wounded and insulted the relatives of the deceased, who had been thorough quite a lot during the years of the terrorist "hunt" for Stolypin (suffice it to mention the consequences of the explosion at his dacha), but seemed indecent even to outside observers.

Nicholas might well not have liked Stolypin; his retirement might only have been, as was suggested, a matter of time. In general that is completely naturally — it is not possible to like everybody or to empathize with everyone. Not even if you are the Tsar. In this sense it would obviously have been hypocritical for Nicholas to attend the funeral service, but the centuries-old accepted standards of human relations require each of us to observe the rules of decency, or if it can be put in that way, to practise hypocrisy in different ways dozens of times a day.

Although for the most part a man of duty, in his relations with other people Nicholas on occasion blithely disregarded this duty, subordinating it to his own wishes. In any case, when another Minister of the Interior, Vyacheslav Plehve, was also murdered his reaction was totally different. On 15th July 1904 Nicholas wrote:

"In the morning P.P. Hesse brought the grave news of Plehve's murder, by a bomb thrown in St Petersburg across from the Warsaw Station.

"We decided to kill Stolypin whatever it might cost," said O. Klimova, who participated in preparing the assassination attempt, "and since we were certain that those who were to carry it out would not be admitted to the ministry premises, we made up projectiles of especial strength, each weighing 16 pounds, which were to completely destroy the structure of the dacha. Of course, in doing so, we could not help but be aware of possible accidental victims, in light of the fact that on 12th August the minister would be receiving people. Although the decision to sacrifice outsiders caused us much agonizing, bearing in mind all the consequences of Stolypin's criminal activities, we considered it unavoidable."

After leaving the landau in which they had driven up to the dacha, three maximalist Social Revolutionaries carrying briefcases made for the entrance hall. Noticing that the officer who had arrived had a false beard, a member of the guard dashed to tear the briefcase from him. At that moment all three shouted "Long live freedom! Long live anarchy!" and simultaneously hurled their briefcases in front of them. The resulting explosion killed 32 people and injured 22 (many of them crippled for life). The terrorists perished; the minister himself remained unharmed.

*Stolypin's dacha on Aptekarsky Island damaged by an explosion. St Petersburg. 12th August 1906*

Viacheslav Konstantinovich von Plehve was Director of the Department of Police from 1881 to 1884 and Assistant Minister of the Interior for the next decade. From 1902 he held the post of Minister of the Interior and Head of the Corps of Gendarmes. Plehve had hardly taken up his new position, or as Vlas Doroshevich wrote, sat down "on the blood-spattered chair of the Minister of the Interior" (his predecessor Sipiagin had been killed by Social Revolutionary terrorists) when he promised in an interview with the correspondent of the Paris newspaper *Le Matin*, that "there will not be a single further political murder in Russia", since the epidemic of such deaths, in his opinion, resulted from a lack of police, and he intended to considerably increase their numbers. However, after two years of intensive work, the new minister was also fated to become a victim of terror. His life was cut short by the explosion of a one-pound bomb thrown by the Social Revolutionary Yegor Sazonov. The act took place on 15th July 1904 on Izmailovsky Prospekt near the Obvodny Canal in St Petersburg and left the terrorist himself seriously wounded.

*Viacheslav Konstantinovich Plehve, Minister of the Interior, Chief of the Corps of Gendarmes. St Petersburg. 1902*

*State officials and a crowd of the curious in front of the Warsaw Railway Station at the site of Plehve's assassination. St Petersburg. 1904*

Death was instantaneous. Apart from him the coachman was killed and seven people injured, including — seriously — the commander of my company of the Semionovsky Regiment Captain Ivetinsky. In such a short time I have lost two so devoted and useful servants! [The second was the Minister of the Interior Dmitry Sipiagin who had recently also been murdered — *The authors.*] Such is His Holy Will!.." And three days later he and his mother went to the Interior Ministry on the Fontanka Embankment in St Petersburg for Plehve's funeral service and as he noted: "... all the sad circumstances reminded me of Sipiagin's interment at the same place."

But, as we have already said, with regard to his own family hearth Nicholas's behaviour was irreproachable. And the appearance of children made his domestic world even more important to him. On the days of important family events his normally ineloquent, not to say monotonous, diary takes on an unaccustomed form, full of domestic details, that are none the less interesting in their lively emotions and feelings.

"A day I shall always remember," he wrote on 3rd November 1895, when his first daughter was born, "in the course of which I had much to endure! Already at one in the morning dear Alix began having pains, which would not allow her to sleep. All day she lay in bed suffering strong torments — the poor thing! I could not help feeling for her. About 2 o'clock dear Mama arrived from Gatchina; together with Ella we stayed all three of us by Alix's side. At exactly 5 o'clock we heard a baby crying and all breathed relief! God has sent us a daughter and at christening we called her Olga! When all the upset had passed and the horrors had finished, I entered a simply blessed state from what had happened! Thanks be to God, Alix came through the birth well and was in good spirits in the evening. Ate late in the evening with Mama and, when I went to bed, I fell asleep on the instant!"

The next day's entry is also mainly filled with sensations that were new to him: "Although Alix slept little in the night, she felt fine. Today I watched our daughter being bathed. She is a big baby, 10 pounds in weight and 55 centimetres long. I almost can't believe it's our child! Lord, what happiness!! At 12 o'clock the whole family arrived for the thanksgiving service. Breakfasted alone with Mama. Alix spent the whole day lying in the mauve room for a change of air. She felt fine, the little one too. Masses of telegrams!"

The rest of the children in the family were born at intervals of approximately two years: a second daughter Tatyana on 29th May 1897, Maria on 14th June 1899, Anastasia on 5th June 1901 and, finally, a son, Alexis, on 30th July 1904. Each new baby increased the alarm of the parents and their whole family about the appearance of an heir. Alexandra was under great psychological pressure because of this: the task which she was effectively called upon to perform as the legitimate spouse of the Emperor seemed beyond her — one after another she gave birth to daughters. Being by nature a very diffident person, inhibited to a pathological degree, who might come out in red blotches or convulsively pinch her lips at the slightest blunder, she felt this "inadequacy" so keenly that gradually her inferiority complex and obsession with the idea of a boy child grew into a genuine psychological disorder.

One consequence of this was the Empress's false pregnancy which became generally known and gave rise to a great deal of talk (an amnesty for prisoners was even expected to follow the birth of a heir). She not only felt the usual physical symptoms, but even put on weight. Appparently a certain part in this episode was played by a French occultist, a former pork butcher from Lyons, later a medical assistant, who had at one time been prosecuted by the police for charlatanism. He was installed in the room next to the royal bedroom so that his "charms" could bring about the birth of a son. Monsieur Philippe (Vachot), was undoubtedly a striking and colourful character possessing remarkable hypnotic powers. A real spiritualist, he even summoned up the spirit of Alexander III who gave his son instructions on the management of the country. He soon gained some influence over the Empress, at least, she treated him with sincere confidence and placed her hopes on him. "Our friend Philippe," she wrote to her husband, "gave me an icon with a little bell which warns me when evil people are around and prevents them coming closer to me."

Philippe was far from being the first strange character to appear at the royal court. Even before him, all sorts of people had been invited there, many of whom we might today call rather vaguely exponents of the "paranormal". There was the Austrian Schenk, another Frenchman Papuce as well as home-grown "enchanters" — the pilgrim Darya Osipovna, the fortune-teller

*Reproduction of the painting* Emperor Nicholas II and Empress Alexandra Feodorovna Beside the Bed of the New-Born Heir. *1904*

"Barefoot" Matrena, the holy fool Mit'ka Kozelsky, Antony the Wanderer and several more.

The birth of a son and heir is a solemn event in any established family. In a royal household it is a matter of state importance. In the present case, when there could not but be serious doubts about the health of the Empress and every successive pregnancy brought new complications, the long awaited occurrence which happened on 30th July 1904, came as a happy relief for all concerned.

"An unforgettable great day for us," Nicholas's diary entry reads, "in which we have so clearly been visited by the Grace of God. At 1/4 past 1 this afternoon Alix gave birth to a son who has been named Alexis [in honour of the seventeeth-century Russian Tsar Alexei or Alexei Mikhailovich Romanov — *The authors*]. Everything went remarkably quickly — for me at any rate. In the morning I visited Mama as usual, then took a report from Kokovtsev and Klepikov, an artillery officer wounded at Wafangkou (Telissa), and went to join Alix for lunch. She was already upstairs and half an hour later the happy event took place. There are not the words to thank God sufficiently for this consolation He has accorded us in this year of sore trials. Dear Alix felt very well. Mama drove over at 2 o'clock and sat with me quite long before meeting her new grandson for the first time. At 5 I drove to the service with the children, all the family gathered there..."

On the thirteenth day after the birth, 11th August, the important ceremony of the boy's baptism took place. He had, incidentally, already been entered in the rolls of the guards units (on 4th August their commanders came to thank the Emperor for this sign of honour and trust). At half past nine the golden coaches lined up outside the imperial home at Peterhof and the grand procession set off escorted by hussars and senior Cossacks. This event marked the "coming out" of Nicholas's eldest daughters Olga and Tatyana who, together with Grand Duchess Irina Alexandrovna, the daughter of the Tsar's sister Xenia who was about the same age, and other children coped with their duty and stood through the long service. The chief godparents who received Alexis from the font were his grandmother Maria Feodorovna and his great uncle Alexander II's son Grand Duke Alexei.

At last the country had an heir to the throne in the person of the Emperor's own son (prior to this the heir and Tsesarevich had been Grand Duke Georgi, and, after his death, Grand Duke Mikhail). This happiness did not, however, last long. On the morning of 8th September to his parents horror the boy began bleeding from his navel which had not yet fully healed. The flow of blood continued intermittently until evening and then recurred for several days. This was the first indication of the fateful, incurable disease of haemophilia, which the child had inherited through his mother from his great-grandmother, the British Queen Victoria. It is a peculiarity of this disease that it is passed on through healthy mothers only to their male offspring. The best doctors, Korovin and the surgeon Fedorov, were urgently summoned to attend the child, they were more or less powerless to do anything and limited themselves to applying dressings. The fate of the heir was thus left in the hands of God and a tragic outcome was only a question of time — there were then few sufferers from this disease who lived to see their twenty-first birthday.

Alexandra Feodorovna — the woman who shared the throne with her husband in the most difficult years for Russian autocracy — was far more deserving of simple human sympathy than of the various, at times absurd accusations, that were in fact her lot. Not only her demise was terrible, but the whole of this part of her life, which she spent in constant alarm and expectation of the possible death of her son. It is enough for any normal human being to "try the situation out for size" on himself or his near ones, so as to see clearly that in such a case all thoughts and feelings would in one way or another be subordinated to the one all-absorbing anxiety and that it would be impossible to demand fully rational actions and a proper grasp of reality from someone already unhealthy and psychologically unstable, as the Tsarina was.

She herself sometimes painted a picture of her depressed state in her letters: "My head aches every day..."; "I get dead tired: my heart aches and is dilated..."; "at times I feel I just can't go on, and then I get tipsy on heart drops..."; "there is such a weight on my heart, such a sadness..."; "I came home and then I couldn't stand it — I burst into tears, prayed, then lay down and smoked to set myself right...". Frequent attacks of hysteria alternated with severe bouts of gloomy melancholia, which had a grim effect not only on Nicholas, but on the whole household, especially their daughters.

In one of her letters to Rasputin Grand Duchess Tatyana acknowledged this directly: "... O, if you knew, how hard Mama's illness is for us to bear."

From our position today we can say with certainty that Alexandra Feodorovna's unhealthy psychological state was open to definite medical diagnosis and required the most intensive attention and treatment. Be that as it may, the Russian and foreign doctors — Dranitsyn, Fischer and Grotte — who examined her could see perfectly clearly that the Empress of Russia was a person with a serious illness.

The documentary book *The Murder of the Russian Imperial Family*, published in Paris in 1925 (its author, Nikolai Sokolov, was a former legal investigator for the Omsk circuit court and had in March 1919 been entrusted by the White leader Admiral Kolchak with discovering the facts surrounding the killing of Nicholas II, his family and other members of the house of Romanov in the Urals), includes testimony by Mrs Zanotti, a former lady-in-waiting at the Russian Court, who was very close to and fond of the Empress and

had been at her side practically all the time. According to her evidence: "The Tsarina was suffering, it seems to me, from hysteria. In the last years she was not the same as she had been earlier... What it was that fuelled the Empress's hysteria, I can't tell you... Doctor Dranitsyn and Doctor Fischer who treated the Empress might tell you that... A few years ago the Empress was complaining of her heart, went to Nauheim and consulted Doctor Grotte. Grotte did not find any heart disease. It seems to me, he discovered some nervous disorders and insisted on a completely different regimen. Fischer then found the same thing with Her Majesty. He even made a secret report to the Emperor about the Empress's illness. Fischer predicted with exact precision what would then begin to happen with the Tsarina. In particular he indicated treatment not of her heart which was evidently healthy, but of the nervous system. But the Empress found out about Fischer's report. He was dismissed and Botkin was summoned."

In accordance with Alexandra Feodorovna's wishes Doctor Yevgeny Botkin did become her household physician. While paying due honour to his fine qualities as a man, who had paid for "his profound devotion to the royal family with his life", Sokolov also came to the convincing, in our opinion, conclusion that "he had neither sufficient will, nor sufficient authority, to take his patient in hand. It was not a case of the doctor winning over her, on the contrary — this patient beat the doctor... In the last resort, Botkin too was obliged to acknowledge the truth. During the period when they were imprisoned at Tsarskoye Selo he once came out of the Empress's room totally overwhelmed and went to Gilliard's room. The latter asked him what was the matter. Botkin did not reply, collected his thoughts, and then said out loud: 'Now I, as a doctor, cannot consider Her Majesty quite normal'."

Nevertheless, as we know, the treatment vital in such cases was lacking. It is hard to say to what extent Nicholas realized the seriousness of his wife's illness, but it would seem he was aware of everything. In any case the Emperor's attitude to his wife remained impeccable and he did his best to shield her from much that might have been the cause of further suffering.

Yet, at the same time, he did not undertake anything which might have improved her state of health. But it is fairly easy to explain why the Empress did not receive any special treatment.

Everything that occurred in the royal house was liable to become an object for talk and gossip not only among their numerous relatives, but also in the widest public circles. Unflattering rumours about Alexandra Feodorovna's madness were already creeping around the country, and to invite psychiatrists or neuropathologists would have amounted to a confirmation of such conjecture, which would hardly have bolstered the authority of the autocrat or the power of the state itself. It was already sufficient that the Tsesarevich's serious illness was almost common knowledge.

Alexandra Feodorovna's constant fear for her son, the hope of the possibility of a "miracle cure" and her acute need for some point of moral support in her life laid a heavy mark on her and encouraged already very profound religious sentiments. Her very first contributions to Nicholas's diary show that she was literally crammed full of religious homilies and maxims, constantly aware of her dependence on divine providence, and even conducted by it in her daily life. The agonizing vacillations that before her marriage had accompanied her decision to adopt Orthodoxy gave way to both a zealous participation in the new rites and rituals, and a sincere, if not fervent, striving to give herself fully to her new religion.

Yet her Orthodoxy was a complex and not completely clear combination of Russian religious ritual, mystic teachings and spiritualist searchings. It rested to a large extent not on the authority of the official Church, an institution which seemed to her to be far from perfect (here too the influence of Western Protestant ideas could be felt), but on the spiritual strength of outstanding personalities, of anchorites, elders and preachers. This is the reason behind her great enthusiasm for the figure of a Russian monk of the late eighteenth and early nineteenth centuries, the Venerable Serapfim of Sarov, the confessor and spiritual mentor of the nuns of the Diveyevo Convent near Sarov. Even

*Nicholas II holding an icon of St Seraphim of Sarov giving parting encouragement to Grand Duchess Anastasia Nikolayevna's 148th Infantry Caspian Regiment before its departure for the front in Manchuria. Peterhof. 1905*

in his own lifetime he had had no small number of highly placed admirers and patrons, including Nicholas I's wife, Alexandra Feodorovna, and Alexander II's, Maria Alexandrovna.

Evidently, these German princesses raised in European traditions were attuned to the cult of the Virgin preached by Seraphim, a cult not typical of Russian Orthodoxy in the nineteenth century, which was borne up by such masculine symbols of religion as images of Christ, ascetic monks and pious holy princes. Not the least of the reasons for the Empress's interest in Seraphim was that he was noted for his ability to help women suffering from infertility with his prayers. Alexandra Feodorovna's insistence led, even in the face of objections by Pobedonostsev, the Chief Procurator of the Most Holy Synod, and many Church officials, to a ceremony for the translation of the Venerable Seraphim's relics at the Sarov Monastery and his canonization in 1903.

It is remarkable that during this ceremony the Tsar, in contrast to the other grand dukes and high officials who took turns, carried the coffin with the sacred relics of the elder the whole time, and the Empress, despite her poor state of health, stood throughout the service of canonization which lasted more than four hours.

The reports of numerous miraculous cures brought about by the healing holy springs close to the Sarov Monastery which appeared quite frequently with photographs in the press, as well as being spread by word of mouth, prompted Alexandra Feodorovna together with her sister Elizabeth Feodorovna and her sister-in-law Olga Alexandrovna to wash in the sacred waters of the Sarov spring. The birth of a male heir a year after this event was for Alexandra Feodorvna and Nicholas the final proof of the Venerable Seraphim's might and ability to work miracles. It was no chance, therefore, that icons depicting him were used to bless the troops setting off for the front in the Russo-Japanese War, that his icon also decorated Nicholas's study and that his personal items were kept in the cathedral at Tsarskoye Selo.

The Empress was not alone in her faith, the Emperor too was deeply and sincerely religious. This shines through their correspondence and in their attitude to everyday squabbles and joys. A favourite place for both of them was the secluded church of the palace at Tsarskoye Selo which was not open to outsiders and where they were able to be alone with their thoughts and feelings. Their constant close contact enabled them to influence each other in spiritual matters as well. During their stay in Moscow in the spring of 1900 as preparations were underway for the Easter celebrations, Nicholas wrote to his mother: "I never knew, that I was capable of reaching such heights of spiritual rapture as those which the present Lent has revealed to me. My present feeling is much stronger than the one I had in 1896, which is quite natural. Now I am so calm and happy, and everything here inspires to prayer and brings conciliation to the soul."

The forms in which this religiosity expressed itself, however, their somewhat demonstrative and overt character gives grounds for thinking that this was determined not least by political reasons. We should look, it seems, in the same light on his attempts, still more persistent than those under his father, to revive old Muscovite customs and traditions. As we have already noted, this showed itself in full measure during the coronation ceremonies in Moscow in 1896. And four years later the "white-stone" capital became the centre for no less grandiose, carefully conceived and orchestrated Easter celebrations. As a special account of the Tsar's arrival in April 1900 said, the monarch had come to Moscow "at the sacred behest of our own history", to celebrate Easter "in close unity with the loyal and devoted Orthodox people and in spiritual communion, as it were, with the distant past... with that past when Moscow was capital city, when the Tsar and the Patriarch of Moscow lived here, when the life of the first capital, particularly in Lent, was an uninterrupted and unbending fulfilment of the rules of the Church, and when the example in such life was set by the Tsar of Moscow himself."

The imperial couple spent all of Holy Week visiting Moscow churches, reading religious and historical books, and in the night of Easter they took part in the ceremonial procession from the Kremlin Palace to the Church of Christ the Saviour, in the company of high state and Church figures. The Emperor, as usual, processed in the military uniform of the Preobrazhensky Regiment, but Alexandra Fedorovna wore a richly embroidered *kokoshnik* on her head and an old Russian white dress with precious stones and pearls. For her this was not simply some fancy-dress costume. She tried as far as ever she could to realize her imagined picture of the Russian national type, character and traditions. Dismissing at a later time the numerous reproaches addressed to the Empress for her pro-German sympathies, the French ambassador to Russia Maurice Paléologue wrote that "Alexandra Feodorovna neither in her soul, nor in her heart has ever been a German... In 1878 at the age of six, she lost mother and from that time usually lived at the court in England. Her upbringing, education, intellectual and moral development were absolutely English. Still today she is an Englishwoman in her appearance, in her manner, in her well-known primness and puritanism, in the implacable and martial sternness of her consciousness, and, finally, in many of her intimate habits. This, by the way, is the limit of what has remained with her of her westren origins. In essence she has become completely Russian... I have no doubt of her patriotism. She fervently loves Russia. And how could she not be tied to this second homeland of hers, which for her encompasses and embodies all her interests — as a woman and a wife. When she came to the throne in 1894, it was already known that she had no love for Germany and Prussia in particular; in recent years she has felt a personal loathing for Kaiser Wilhelm and she lays the blame on him 'for this terrible war'. When she heard about the burning of Louvain, she exclaimed:'I blush to have been a German!'."

Of course, it was not easy for Paléologue to evaluate Alexandra Feodorovna's degree of "Russianness". Those who accused her of not knowing and not understanding Russia were not so far wide of the mark. She tried as hard as she could to understand the country, but this was a near impossible task for a European, who had come to know the Russian language and Russian traditions only as an adult and had not absorbed from childhood the national atmosphere and the special culture, completely dissimilar to the Western, of this immense land. Nicholas himself by blood, by education and by upbringing was, it might seem, just as European, but, in contrast to his wife, he had grown up in the country and proved by all manner of parameters (patriarchal, tenor of life conservatism, religiosity, indecisiveness, negative attitude to democracy and so on) to be a highly typical Russian character.

It is curious, however, that the very act of crossing the borders of Russia was enough to affect Nicholas strongly. This was reflected in his very dress — "there" he became a real gentleman with the obligatory cane, bowler hat, tie and suit with a European cut, while not a single photograph exists of the Emperor in such a "get-up" at home — but the greater change was in his manner of behaving. It was as if he shrugged off his heavy burden of responsibilty and the officiality that went with his rank, and became for a time a private person, travelling around Europe or simply enjoying a holiday.

Buchanan had come across the Russian Tsar in Darmstadt, when he was attached to the court there, long before he was appointed to his post in Russia. They met several times at the local tennis club, where Nicholas came to play, and then he was granted a private audience. The Briton recalled their conversations as being quite free and unconstrained on the subjects of politics, tennis, and Nicholas's hunting achievements, the Tsar mentioning an incredibly high number of deer, bison, wild boar and, particularly, pheasants which he had supposedly bagged.

How great then was Buchanan's surprise when, appointed British ambassador to Russia, he found here what were for him staggering antiquated mediaeval traditions.

"When, ..., on the eve of my first audience I received a telephone message from Tsarskoye saying I was to remain to luncheon, I naturally imagined that I was to lunch with the Imperial family. I was, however, mistaken, as at the conclusion of my audience I was taken off to lunch with the household. I said nothing at the time, as I felt that it hardly became a new-fledged Ambassador to be too punctilious.

"In the following year, on being invited to Tsarskoye to present to Their Majesties the members of the recently arrived British delegation, I was once more constrained to lunch with the household in spite of my having tried to excuse myself. As my colleagues and I had agreed not to accept such invitations in future, I thought it time to protest. As soon, therefore, as the luncheon was over I spoke to the grand master of the ceremonies. He had, I said, placed me in an embarrassing position. I had come to the palace in my official capacity as His Majesty's Ambassador, and he must know as well as I did that under such circumstances it was contrary to all etiquette to invite me to lunch with the household." Nevertheless, this protest clearly changed nothing. Lunches with the imperial family did not come about, but from now on it was open to the disgruntled ambassador at any moment to forego the conversation of the courtiers and return to St Petersburg on the train which was waiting specially for him (!) in Tsarskoye Selo.

Yet at this same time, as if to embody or give substance to the idea of the unity of the Russian Tsar and his people, Nicholas tried in his own way to make public contact with simple people, first and foremost with peasants, since they were, as he saw things, the bearers of the true "Russian spirit" and the soil in which autocracy was rooted. And while in the early part of his reign Nicholas met only representatives of the higher section of the peasantry — elders and elected deputations, he himself, it would seem, gradually began to favour public conversation with the simplest and most ordinary members of the estate. The image of a caring "peasants' tsar" was created by more than just the part Nicholas played in such meetings, which were arranged as if to deliberately spite the Europeanized aristocracy and the liberals who nursed ideas of democracy and a constitution, or in simple acts of public worship or visits by the Tsar to agricultural exhibitions and his acquaintance with the plough and the field. The pages of official publications carried extensive spreads of photographs of such subjects, while official historiographers and publicists were unstinting in their praise for his diligence and zeal. "Not one matter concerning the peasant ploughman," the Tsar's biographer, professor and member of the imperial household, General A.G. Yelchaninov wrote, "went through without the active participation of the Tsar." In every way possible emphasis was given to the prevalence, even in the Emperor's tastes, of everything Russian and simple, right down to his favourite dishes, which were supposed to include *borshch,* sucking pig, kvass, pancakes, *kasha* and the like, although a Russian peasant could not even have imagined the delicacies that really did feature every day on the artistically designed royal menu which was itself at times a real work of art.

In Russian history one can judge the orientation of a particular monarch towards the West or the East, even by what would seem such a secondary matter as the cut of people's clothes. The first westernizer to cram the broad Russian soul into a narrow European waistcoat was, of course, Peter I. Paul I too managed to express his sympathies through the introduction of Prussian-style dress in the army. Over the nineteenth century, in general, Russian military uniforms did not differ significantly from European ones (this is particularly noticeable in battle paintings where at times the layman would be hard put to distinguish to which particular army curassiers or hussars belong in the hand-to-hand fighting of, say, the campaign of 1812).

A new move towards using national traditions in military costume began, as we have noted, with the reign of Alexander III. Nicholas wholeheartedly continued this trend. And one of the few variants of his own everyday dress (besides an ordinary soldier's cloth blouse with a colonel's shoulder-straps) was the simple Russian-style shirt buttoning at the side of the collar, tied at the waist and loose wide trousers, tucked into short shagreen boots with crumpled tops.

Like his father before him, Nicholas encouraged the development of an old Russian style in architecture as well. His reign saw the construction of the Alexander Nevsky Cathedral, dedicated to the memory of Alexander III, which the architect Alexander Pomerantsev built onto the Training Council of the Most Holy Synod, copying an old cathedral in the historic town of Borisoglebsk. In Tsarskoye Selo the entire "Feodorovsky Town" appeared with a tsar's cathedral in seventeenth-century style and palaces, one of which soon became the home of the Society for the Regeneration of Artistic Rus; it enjoyed the favour of the Tsar and court circles and thus took on the nature of a state, monarchal institution. In Alexandra Feodorovna's home town of Darmstadt the Church of Mary Magdalene was constructed in the traditional style of cathedrals in the ancient Yaroslavl or Rostov principalities.

These pro-Russian tendencies reached their apogee in the last years of Nicholas's reign. In the jingoistic fervour of 1914 the name of the northern capital of the Russian Empire was hastily changed from St Petersburg to Petrograd (in contrast to Soviet times, the renaming of towns was not customary in pre-revolutionary Russia). Then in 1916 the Emperor came up with the absurd idea of eliminating foreign terms from Russian legislation, and D.A. Koptev, the Secretary of State to the State Council, was actually entrusted with this responsible task.

It seems that even in terms of pure appearance Nicholas began over the years to more closely correspond to the image he strove after. While in his youth he looked without exaggerating like a dashing aristocratic hussars officer with an excellent bearing, by the time he was a mature man little remained of this. Mikhail Lemke, the

*Nicholas II with members of his family leaving the Church of Our Lady of Feodorovo (Feodorovsky Sobor). Tsarskoye Selo. 28th April 1913*

historian and publicist, noted in his staff diary on 16th October 1915: "Today I was able to take a close look at him... The Tsar is not handsome, the colour of his beard and moustache is tobacco-yellow. peasant-like, his nose is fat, his eyes stony..." Many of Nicholas's customs and manners also matched his appearance. He took a genuine pleasure in engaging in such simple chores as sawing or chopping firewood, or any other physical work in the open air. He was hardy by nature and enjoyed long walks.

Hunting was an inseparable part of his leisure time, something Nicholas had developed a taste for back in his childhood, during the traditional trips with his father to the preserve at Bialowieza or Spala, where for several weeks the royal family and the usual escort of grand dukes engaged in cheery picnics in the lap of nature, hunting drives and strolls through the forest with guns on their shoulders. It is curious to learn that the women played a very direct part in this hunting, and Nicholas's mother even arranged her own hunting trips ("At 1/2 past 7 Mama drove off on her own hunt," the Tsesarevich wrote, for example, on 11th September 1890. "We, though, went off almost to the other end of the world, and hardly bagged a thing all day..."). Subsequently, after Alexander III's death, such extended "hunting seasons" became almost a thing of the past, yet the Emperor did not lose his passion and tried to use any opportunity to go hunting even in the suburbs of St Petersburg. "It was a wonderful sunny day, 4°. above zero... quickly changed into hunting gear and set off for the station," Nicholas noted in his diary on 11th January 1904. "All the participants were already

*Nicholas II in his room in the hunting-lodge. 1894*

*Members of the Imperial family returning from the hunt. Bialowieza. 1894*

*The royal hunt. Beaters standing by killed deer. Spala. 1894*

*The royal hunt. Cart with killed deer. Spala. 1894*

waiting there and I travelled with them to Gatchina. Took lunch on the way. There was a battue in the pheasantry. I thoroughly enjoyed the magnificent weather and the spring-like day. The hunting was very successful: in all we bagged 879 things. My tally was 115: 21 partridges, 91 pheasants, a white hare and two rabbits..." A week later we find a similar note: "... went off on the railway with Misha and with other hunters to Ropsha, where we arrived about one in the afternoon. The hunt was in the same pheasantry and turned out very successful. Total kill: 489. My tally: 96 — 81 pheasants and 14 partridges and a white hare..."

Nicholas was also fond of pastimes with a scientific or technical element to them. These included an undying love for motor cars and motor boats, and also a real passion for photography, which lasted many years. He was also the personal patron of the aviation club which appeared in St Petersburg shortly after the turn of the century. Yet Nicholas himself and all the imperial family had a very cool and distrustful attitude to another technical invention — cinematography. We know that on a report informing him that someone had scattered leaflets from the Russian Social Democratic Labour Party at one of the cinemas, he wrote: "I have pointed out more than once that these cinematographic sideshows are dangerous establishments. The scoundrels might get up to God knows what there, since people, I'm told, flock there to watch any rubbish. I don't know what to think up against such shows..." At the same time royal documentary reels, a genre in which the St Petersburg photographer Drankov had become particularly successful among Russian cinematographers (he filmed *The Departure of the King of Sweden*, *The Meeting of the Sovereign Emperor and King Edward VII of Britain at the Revel Anchorage* and other events), were viewed with some interest and even enjoyment by the august family. Later, when he was at Stavka with the Tsesarevich, the Tsar went to evening film shows in the officers' club (he declined to have a room specially equipped for his own private viewing).

Nevertheless, the favourite leisure activity for Nicholas and his family remained reading, in part even out loud to each other. The Emperor had a personal library next door to his study to which new publications from home and abroad were constantly being added. When he moved or went on a journey his library invariably accompanied him. General Yu.N. Danilov recalled that the head of the royal library, S.A. Shcheglov, issued up to twenty books a month for the Tsar to read.

As far as was possible the Tsar's family tried to be together. Even the very smallest members were taken to many official events — formal ceremonies, parades, the unveiling of monuments, the laying of foundation stones, church services to mark some important event and so on.

The theatre was an important element in the life of the imperial family. Both the Emperor and the Empress, and incidentally many other members of their family (which included quite some few real theatre-lovers), were more than well-disposed towards this institution. The imperial theatres enjoyed the particular favour of these high-ranking patrons — private establishments were visited very rarely — and their preference in the majority of cases was for opera or ballet. Visits to the theatre began with the ballet for the children of the Tsar and the grand dukes. At first they would attend matinées during the Christmas holidays or Shrovetide, and gradually going on to evening performances.

The Tsar usually visited the theatre in the middle of winter, in autumn and spring he almost never went there. At first he was nearly always accompanied by Alexandra Feodorovna, but following the birth of their son she began to attend considerably less often. As the former director of the imperial theatres Telyakovsky recalled "the last time she attended was in 1913 for a gala performance to mark the 300th anniversary of the House of Romanov, but she sat through only one act of the opera *A Life for the Tsar* and drove away."

An established ritual accompanied the Emperor's visits to the theatre. The director was usually informed of the sovereign's intentions by telephone, and as much as an hour before his arrival the palace security took up positions from the entrance right through to the stage and the royal box (in the majority of imperial theatres there were two or three of these on the side, adjoining the stage, and a central one, which would be occupied by members of the royal retinue and court officials; the Emperor took a seat in these only for gala performances, in the Mariinsky Theatre the actual Tsar's box was considered to be the lower left-hand one by the stage). Then footmen arrived from the Winter Palace bringing tea-things and refreshments, with which they would lay two tables in the royal box during the first act — one for cold drinks, one for tea. "The table with drinks had a layout established once and for all," Telyakovsky remembered, "a bowl of fruit, a bowl of the court confectionary and a bowl of biscuits, as well as a plate with sandwiches. Then a bottle of red Bordeaux, a bottle of red Madeira, a bottle of Seltsers water and a jug of some drink. On the tea table, which was also covered by a white tablecloth, there were several plates with fruit bread, pastries and rusks. Tea was brought already poured into cups when the Emperor gave the order. They usually drank tea in the first or second interval, and then in the following one they were brought a tray of ice-cream, fruit or dairy, on glass dishes. At the same time as tea was being served in the Tsar's foyer, the same trays with ice-cream and tea were taken by the court servants to the central box for the royal entourage, to the minister's box, if he and his guests were in attendance, and to the director's box. After the last interval the tea table was cleared, but the table with drinks was left until the sovereign's departure. All this procedure, once it had been established, was always carried out precisely and in exactly the same manner."

On entering the theatre the Emperor was always met by the chief of the city police in his dress uniform with all his medals. He usually greeted him and shook hands with him. The director of the theatre waited for him on the landing of the staircase in the near-uniform of evening dress with the obligatory white tie. It was Nicholas's habit to smoke a cigarette with him before the curtain went up. It is noteworthy that if the sovereign was more than five minutes late the performance was supposed to start without him. If, on the other hand, he arrived early then he did not as a rule go into the box, but stayed in the royal foyer, which in both the Mariinsky and Alexandrinsky Theatres was very plainly decorated. In the Mariinsky Theatre the white gloss-painted walls of the foyer were hung with a single picture of one of the theatre's ushers, and on the table stood a round copper ashtray about a pound in weight, which Alexander III, trying his strength, had bent into an oval and a bronze clock.

In contrast to the majority of the grand dukes and duchesses, the Emperor and Empress were fond of serious works, including Wagner's *Ring* cycle, particularly *Götterdämmerung* and *Siegfried*, and also *Tristan and Isolde*. Nicholas invariably watched all performances to the end. In the intervals (the length of which would be agreed with the Emperor) the whole royal family would assemble in the royal foyer without special invitation. Etiquette was far less strictly observed during Nicholas II's reign than in the time of Alexander III and proceedings in the foyer were usually very lively, not inhibited by the presence of the Emperor. The grand dukes conducted themselves in a more than democractic manner: they permitted themselves to sit while he was standing, smoked a good deal to the displeasure of the grand duchesses who vainly tried to disperse the smoke with their fans or handkerchiefs. Alexandra Feodorovna suffered especially from this, while Maria Feodorovna on the contrary stood up for the smokers, all the more so as since her husband's death she had taken to smoking heavily herself, frequently ordinary cigarettes without a holder. Not the least of the motives for this behaviour was a certain degree of hostility towards her daughter-in-law with whom she never formed close relations. Court journals of a later period contained evidence of an almost complete rift between the two imperial households. Maria Feodorovna appeared in Tsarskoye Selo only on formal occasions and never stayed more than a very short time. Nicholas in turn visited the Anichkov Palace mainly on his own and only exceptionally in the company of the Empress.

The outbreak of the Russo-Japanese War put an end to the imperial couple's visits to the theatre. The realities of life ran contrary to Nicholas's own inclinations and strivings, changed his existence and demanded that he pay ever more attention to the interests of the state and of the people as a whole. While at the beginning of his reign two hours of work could seem like a long time to Nicholas, as he himself candidly wrote, in the 1910s more and more space in the diaries is taken up with entries (albeit no more than bare records of the facts) about numerous audiences, reports and sittings or information about military actions during campaigns, somewhat reducing even his reports of domestic affairs.

For Alexandra Feodorovna, however, the opposite is true. Having originally taken some part in public activities as the chairman of the board of guardians she had founded in the charitable workhouses, with the birth of her son, she became wholly absorbed in her family problems

and she divorced herself finally from all such matters and occupations, striving only to maintain an influence on questions of high politics.

The reader may be surprised that in the majority of photographs reproduced in this book the Emperor is shown in military uniform. It looks as if he never took it off. But there is far more than chance at work here. At the same time as he took a university course, Nicholas followed a course of the General Staff Academy and he was both by education and in his heart more of a military man than a civilian. With his highly pedantic and painstaking attitude towards his duties, he evidently had an inner yearning for military precision and a regulated life.

In the first months of Nicholas's reign Alix's uncle, the Prince of Wales, future King Edward VII, arrived in St Petersburg for a short visit. Turning familiarly to his niece at one of the dinners, he remarked that in profile her husband reminded him of Emperor Paul I. This opinion spoken out loud did not please either Alexandra Feodorovna or Nicholas, although the distant resemblance noted by this relative went further than just outward appearance. It would indeed seem that of those who succeeded to the Russian throne, only his great-great-grandfather Paul had such a taste for military trappings, ceremonial, marches, parades and practically endless drill sessions.

In contrast to those of his predecessors who were crowned generals, Nicholas, because of his early accession, had no time to rise to higher military rank. By the prevailing legislation the Emperor retained the same rank as he had had when Tsesarevich and thus Nicholas II was a colonel to the end of his days, something which he did not, incidentally, feel as much of a burden. By tradition all members of the imperial family were enrolled at birth in one or even several regiments, and also became patrons of military colleges, cadet corps, artillery brigades and batteries, guards regiments and ordinary ones. As well as being included in the rolls of life-guards regiments — the 2nd Her Imperial Majesty Sovereign—Empress Maria Feodorovna's Own Tsarskoye Selo Infantry Regiment, the Grodno Regiment, the Life Guards of the 2nd Artillery Brigade and the 3rd His Majesty's Infantry Regiment — Nicholas II was also patron of two mili-

tary colleges, the 1st Cadet Corps, the Life Guards of the 1st Artillery Brigade, the 1st and 6th Batteries of the Life Guards of the Horse Artillery, the Life Guards of the Engineering Batallion and sixteen further regiments.

Tsesarevich Alexis, Nicholas's son, extended his patronage to a more modest number of military units, which, nonetheless, included the military college named after him, the Tashkent Heir and Tsesarevich's Own Cadet Corps, four life-guards regiments and the 4th Battery of the Life-Guards Horse Artillery. On the other hand his name was included in the rolls of far more regiments, batallions and so on than was his father's. In the imperial family even the women were patrons of different regiments and were expected to dress up in military uniform and take part in regimental ceremonies.

In general the Russian Empire had long had the appearance of a military-police state with regulation clearly evident in all spheres of life. Literally everything exuded this, including the countless peaked caps, greatcoats and uniforms which were worn not only by military officers, the police and the gendarmerie, but also by civil servants, students and even very young grammar school pupils. The *Table of Ranks* which had begun in Peter the Great's reign was still operating at the beginning of the twentieth century. It not only divided the whole of society up into the great and the small, but also allocated every person a place determined by the standards for his given estate and extended even to the system of education. Perhaps only in Prussia was the role of the army and the military traditionally as great and esteemed as in Russia.

The place accorded to the army in the schedule of Russian priorities can easily be gauged by looking, for example, at a printed directory of St Petersburg for 1899, the fifth year of Nicholas's reign. The information about the military department and the army appears immediately after the section on the imperial family, and only after it come the court staff, the State Council, the Committee of Ministers and separate ministries and administrative institutions. It is also a remarkable fact that the departments of the military and the navy were housed in what were architecturally some of the finest buildings in St Petersburg — the latter in Andrean Zakharov's Admiralty, without which it would be impossible to imagine the city, the former in the General Staff Building which brilliantly completed the

*Nicholas II in the uniform of H.I.M. Life-Guards Hussar Regiment. St Petersburg. 1910–14*

*March-past by soldiers of the Life-Guards Pavlovsky Regiment at a review on the Field of Mars. St Petersburg. 1903*

ensemble of Palace Square and included the architect Carlo Rossi's celebrated arch. Even down to the present day, the central part of the city is adorned with the magnificent edifices that once housed military academies, colleges, cadet corps, riding schools and regimental barracks.

Every day no matter what the weather or the season, units of the life guards of the Izmailovsky, Pavlovsky, Preobrazhensky, Semionovsky and other regiments marched through the city on their way to do guard duty at the Emperor's residence and other government institutions, forming an inseparable part of the St Petersburg landscape.

"Since the route from the barracks of the Izmailovsky and Semionovsky regiments, as well as those of the Naval Guards Corps, to the centre of the city lay along our Nikolskaya Street and on along Morskaya," the famous artist Alexander Benois, who was the same age as Nicholas, recalled, "we saw those soldiers every day, sometimes in big detachments, sometimes in small ones, and without fail the guards of the Winter

*Nicholas II and Alexandra Feodorovna leaving the Evangelical-Lutheran Church of St Peter after the requiem for the German Empress. St Petersburg. 6th August 1901*

*The patron of the Life-Guards Cuirassier Regiment, Dowager Empress Maria Feodorovna with her daughter, Grand Duchess Olga Alexandrovna at a parade of the regiment. Gatchina. 1904*

Palace drawn from one or the other of those regiments would pass by on their way there and back. Besides this, a considerable part of the St Petersburg garrison would leave along our street in the spring when going off to the camp near Krasnoye Selo. Then I could get my fill of looking at all sorts of very striking, choice uniforms. Finally, for the May parade the Gatchina Cuirassiers and the Cossacks appeared in St Petersburg, and they all rode their wonderful horses in step past our windows to the sound of their bands."

It is not surprising then that so much importance was attached to military festivals. A favourite sight for St Petersburgers were the ships of the Baltic Fleet decked in colourful flags after they had sailed up the Neva and dropped anchor by the Winter Palace and the Admiralty. Particularly striking were the magnificent and vivid annual spring parades which had reached their peak under Alexander II. These reviews of the troops of the capital's garrison marked "an awakening from a long winter sleep".

During the time of Alexander III, who, as we know, was a very poor rider and even afraid of horses (Baron Fredericks, at that time in charge of the court stables, complained that "it is terribly difficult to find a horse for the Emperor or to persuade him at all to mount any new horse"), the military parades on the Field of Mars ceased. There were no mounted trooping the colour ceremonies in the Mikhailovsky Riding School and the manoeuvres at Krasnoye Selo which the

Emperor followed sitting on a chair or standing lost their former glory.

Immediately on succeeding to the throne, Nicholas II revived the tradition of Alexander II, his magnificent grandfather. Every year, in the very centre of the city, on the Field of Mars with its highly suitable covering of sand, military festivities were resumed — the opening of the summer season. The royal tent was pitched in advance on the edge of the Field of Mars, close to the Neva and in front of the palace of the Prince of Oldenburg. Beyond it, open stands were put up along the whole length of the Summer Gardens for spectators, a great many of whom were ladies sporting spring outfits in keeping with the latest Paris fashions.

One of these royal reviews — already the second of Nicholas's reign — took place shortly before his coronation on Monday 15th April 1896. The following day the capital's newspapers vied with each other in reporting the event. The parade was commanded by His Imperial Highness, the Commander in Chief of the Forces, Grand Duke Vladimir Alexandrovich (Nicholas's uncle). Other members of the Imperial family also participated: the Most August Inspector General of Cavalry Grand Duke Nikolai Nikolayevich, Grand Dukes Konstantin Konstantinovich, Pavel Alexandrovich and Dmitry Konstantinovich, Duke Georg of Mecklenburg-Strelitz, Cyril Vladimirovich and his brother Boris. At exactly eleven in the morning the Emperor and Empress, riding in an open carriage, reached the commandant's post. Nicholas wore the uniform of the Life-Guards Chasseurs Regiment and the sash of the Order of St Andrew; Alexandra Feodorovna had an exquisite snow-white dress on. After greeting the Grand Dukes and the retinue Nicholas mounted a horse, while the Empress took a seat with Princess Maria Pavlovna and Grand Duchess Xenia Alexandrovna in an open phaeton drawn by a line of four white horses each with a rider. The Emperor listened to the Commander in Chief's report and then rode along the six ranks in which the troops were formed up. He greeted each unit and after the last returned to the Royal Tent which stood on the troops' right flank. This marked the start of the main event.

"After the inspection," General Count Alexei Ignatyev wrote in his memoirs, describing events of which he had been a direct participant, "the Tsar stopped in front of the royal box with only a trumpeter from his own escort — in a scarlet tunic on a grey horse — behind him and a little to one side. Two scarlet stripes formed by the two Cossack *sotnias* [hundreds] of the escort opened the march past of troops... The escort was followed by a batallion from the Pavlovsky Military College, setting the pace, then came a composite batallion, with the corps of pages forming the first company, their helmets bringing back memories of a long forgotten age. Then there was a break — the band of the Preobrazhensky Regiment marched out to the centre of the field and the march past by the guards began. They marched in company columns known as Alexander Columns, a survival from the Napoleonic period... The artillery followed the foot-soldiers, their exemplary teams of strapping, well-fed horses cathing one's eye. They were matched for colour in a pure Russian manner: the first battery on chestnuts, the second on greys and the third on black horses. After a minute's pause on the far side of the field by the Engineers' Castle a golden mounted mass appeared, glittering as it moved in the sun. Our First Guards Cuirassiers Division was advancing at a steady pace..."

At the end of the march past, all the cavalry formed up in a line of columns by Tsaritsyn Street and on a command from their most august Inpector General this mass of horsemen many-thousand strong threw up clouds of sandy dust as it hurled itself at a gallop towards the royal tent, stopping dead ten paces from the Emperor. Following this and after thanking those who had taken part in the parade, the Emperor and Empress withdrew to Prince Oldenburg's palace.

The festivities were coming to an end and the soldiers and officers went back to their barracks. Ahead of them lay the daily routine of army life. On one of the warm days in May the guards regiments would set off for summer camp at Krasnoye Selo to the south-west of the capital. They were led in the main by young officers since the remainder had left for spa towns or their own estates. Shortly before the arrival of the Emperor and the grand dukes, Krasnoye Selo and the Pavlovskaya Sloboda, where the horse guards were billeted on the peasant farmers, were completely transformed. The palace police appeared, as did the mounted guards gendarmerie in their smart light blue uniforms, troops arrived and so did wonderfully dressed ladies. The dusty highways were watered several times a day from barrels specially fetched on one-horse carts. The lanes between the houses of the senior military men and the grand princes palaces were carefully strewn with sand. There were fragrant flowers everywhere, and for these weeks Krasnoye Selo resembled some idyllic suburban corner.

The "Main Camp" consisted of numerous rows of white tents which extended for some seven kilometres on the slope down to the River Ligovka, while across the river there was the Advance-Guard Camp for the infantry and the military colleges. The officers installed themselves in cottages painted to match the colour of the uniforms of the relevant guards regiment which stood beyond the tents in the green of a birch grove. Behind the camp, for its whole length, stretched shooting ranges equipped for all distances, while the cavalry regiments usually occupied the same villages within a ten-kilometre radius of the Training Ground.

The great manoeuvres, which ended the annual camp, were attended by the Emperor and his presence was of major importance to all those taking part. The gentlemen officers moved at this point from their well-appointed dachas to the comfortable officers tents which were sometimes covered with expensive eastern carpets. Peasant carts were used to transport all the goods and chattels attendant on the officers — including kitchens, chefs, regimental silver and crockery. The end result was that campaign tents were turned into something like miniature palaces, where by candlelight, like in the city, delicate food was served with wines and champagne.

The arrival of the Tsar turned the camp into a grand high society occasion, the culmination of which were the Kransoye Selo horse-races. It would have been considered sacrilege to attempt to change these and they were described notably in *Anna Karenina*. With striking precision, down to the last detail, Leo Tolstoy recreates an episode from this dramatic and gripping spectacle:

The races were to take place on a large four-verst long elliptical course in front of the pavilion. Nine obstacles were constructed on course: a stream; a large, two arshin tall, blank barrier right in front of the pavilion; a dry ditch; a water-filled ditch; a steep slope; an Irish bank (one of the most difficult obstacles) consisting of a rampart covered with brushwood beyond which, invisible to the horses, there was a ditch as well, so that an animal had to clear both obstacles or kill itself; then there were two more water ditches and a dry one — and the finish was opposite the pavilion. But the races began not on the circuit, but 100 sazhens away from it, and at this point there was the first obstacle — a dammed up stream three arshins wide which the riders could opt to either jump or wade.

Some three times the riders lined up, but each time somebody's horse broke away early, and they had to start again. The expert starter, Colonel Sestrin, was already beginning to get angry when finally he shouted for the fourth time: "Go!" and the riders started.

All eyes, all binoculars were turned on the gaily-coloured group of jockeys while they were lining up.

"They're off! They're running!" rang out from all sides, breaking the expectant silence.

And small groups and lone walkers began to rush from place to place to get a better view. The knot of riders that had formed in that first minute became strung out and you could see how they approached the stream in twos and threes and one after another. For the spectators, it seemed as if they all jumped together, but for the riders there were seconds of difference that meant a great deal to them...

The great barrier stood straight in front of the royal pavilion. The Tsar, and all the court, and a crowd of people all looked at them — at him [Vronsky — *The authors*] and Makhotin who had got a length ahead, when they came up to the Devil (as they called the blank barrier). Vronsky felt these eyes turned on him from all directions, but he saw nothing apart from the ears and neck of his horse, the earth dashing up to meet him and the rump and white legs of Gladiator, beating rapid time in front of him and remaining always the same distance away...

The Emperor presented prizes to the winners of the races in specially constructed pavilions, right by the stands. It was not just jockeys, however, who pitted their talents against each other, although they were, of course, the "élite". During the camps genuine, and no less entertaining, "tournaments" were arranged between those skilled in the boiling of cabbage soup and porridge, for which purpose hollows were dug on the slopes of the Duderhof Hills to take the kettles. The winners here were decided by the secret vote of a jury of sergeant majors. The winners and the best marksmen also received their souvenir prizes from the Emperor's own hand.

After the races everybody took off in troikas, pairs or cabs to the Krasnoye Selo theatre, where the leading role in the ballet was played by Kschesslinska, who was admired at once by all three of her successive most august lovers — Nicholas II himself, his young uncle Sergei Mikhailovich and the younger brother of the future pretender to the throne Cyril, the still very youthful Andrei.

On the following day all the company that had been in the theatre assembled shortly before sunset at the church of the main camp, where a 'ceremonial retreat' was to take place. The annual camp had finished and trains full to the point of overflowing took all the officer class back to the capital, while life in Krasnoye Selo went into suspension until the next spring...

Nicholas had taken part in these annual military events even earlier, while still heir to the throne, getting a taste of life in the field in accordance with his father's wishes. Like the other young officers the Tsesarevich was obliged to sleep in a tent, to take part in training, manoeuvres and inspections, to shoot, to take his turn on duty and so on. The majority of his time was not occupied, however, and was spent in playing billiards and roulette, boating, fishing, hunting, merry gatherings round the table in the company of other officers, clay-pigeon shooting, listening to gypsy music and visiting the theatre. One season was more or less identical with another and contributed little in the way of variety. From 1890 another delight was added to the military fun and the martial camps took on a rather romantic aspect. This was the beginning of Nicholas's infatuation with one of the most brilliant ballerinas of the Mariinsky Theatre, Mathilda Kschessinska.

"At 11 o'clock supper began. With gypsies, the friendly conversation continued until 6 in the morning," he recorded, for example, in his diary for 6th July 1890. "Arrived in Kaporskoye when the regiment had already left, with trepidation I galloped to Staro Skvortsy where the regiment was bivouacking. A brigade from the 2nd battery was in action against the 1st Brigade. The attack was taking place on the Training Ground. Slept till 1/2 past 5. After dinner we drove to the theatre. I am absolutely taken with Kschessinska, the second. Supper at Uncle Vladimir's. *19th July...* At 4 I came back to Kaporskoye accompanied by the singers on horseback. Slept till 1/2 past 11. After lunch played billiards with Krupensky. It rained all day, so I didn't leave the house, apart from lunch and dinner times. At 9 o'clock we began playing roulette here. Had a splendid evening until 1/2 past 12. Lost 30 roubles. *20th July...* At 1/2 past 9 went through a rehearsal with the squadron for the parade at the foot of the hill. At 1/2 past 12 rode for lunch to the horse-guards to mark the 25th anniversary of Papa being entered in the regimental rolls. An appropriate quantity of liquid was taken after lunch. We had dinner at the Trubetskois and went from there to the theatre... Supper at Uncle Valdimir's. *22nd July...* Rose at 6 o'clock and went off for a hunt near the village of Mar'ino. In 2 1/2 hours bagged 17 black grouse and a young pheasant. Came back to Kaporskoye for lunch. Did the ceremonial march. Uncle Sergei paid a visit. Watched the 37th Division from the tower as it marched complete through our village. At 1/2 past 7 dinner in Telez with Gorbunov, extraordinarily jolly. Listened to a choir of wandering gypsies in their tent. *29th July...* At 10 o'clock rode into Krasnoye for Liturgy. The family took lunch alone in the garden tent. At 2 there were the customary races, which went off without incident. At 6 o'clock the Krasnoye Selo races took place: fast and successful. After a substantial snack at the Horse Guards drove to the theatre. Returned to Kaporskoye at 12 o'clock. Took supper on the Hill with Spaniards, gypsies and Little Russians. *31st July. Tuesday.* Yesterday we went through 125 bottles of champagne. I was duty officer for the division. At 10 o'clock set off with the squadron to the Training Ground. There was an exercise for all the cavalry with attacks on infantry. It was hot. Took lunch in Krasnoye. At 5 o'clock reviewed the military colleges in the pouring rain. After a snack drove for the last time to the good old Krasnoye Selo theatre. Said goodbye to Kschessinska. Supper at Mama's until one."

General Ignatyev later had the opportunity to evaluate the true significance of all these army spectacles. When a few years later in the fields of Manchuria he was obliged to rack his brains over the causes of the catastrophic defeats suffered by the Russian army, in his mind's eye "there unfailingly appeared the picture of the May parade on the Field of Mars — that wicked mockery, that criminal self-deceit and sham, which had nothing in common with war... Sadly for the Russian army this divorcing of the troops' training from the real requirements of the art of warfare occurred not only on the Field of Mars, but also on the Training Ground of the camp at Krasnoye Selo. How many times in Manchuria did we former guardsmen say, when caught in some hard action: 'Yes, this isn't your Krasnoye Selo manoeuvres!'."

The "victorious little war", with the help of which Interior Minister Plehve advised Nicholas to settle the ever growing heap of internal contradictions in the country, produced results that were completely the opposite of those imagined. For the majority in the country these events were wholly unexpected: in contrast to Turkey, with which Russia had been in conflict with varying degrees of success for many centuries on her own southern borders and later also in the Balkans, Japan — located on islands in a distant ocean — could not be compared with the Russian Empire at all, either in size, or in military might, or in level of economic development.

"The new year 1904 began fortissimo — with the crash of the war that had suddenly begun against the Japanese," Alexander Benois expressively described the mood of wide circles of educated people. "It came completely unexpected for us, for our circle. But it seemed that other circles too were not completely prepared for it — 'those who are called on to lead'. It was the first real war Russia had been involved in since 1878, but at first nobody regarded it as completey real, and almost everyone looked on it with a surprising flippancy — like some trifling from which Russia simply could not fail to emerge victorious. Imagine. Those impudent Japs, yellow-faced monkeys, and suddenly they impose themselves on such a great state as the Russian Empire with its population of over a hundred million. I and many others even had something like pity then for those 'imprudent madmen'. After all, they'll be beaten in a jiffy and nothing will be left of them, and if the war spreads to their own islands, then it's goodbye to all their wonderful art, all their magnificent culture of which I and my friends had become particularly fond in recent years...

"The Russian public did not, however, remain for long in ignorance of the true strength of this new scorned enemy...

"Gradually the situation began to change, and after the loss of the *Petropavlovsk* and the battles at Liaoyang and Mukden, after a series of withdrawals from 'positions fortified earlier' — the Japanese monkeys ceased to be funny, the Russian public recalled the martial spirit and military glories of this 'land of the samurai' and realized that they should be repulsed in a proper manner."

Among the high military leadership too there was at first no doubt in an easy victory. This even went so far that when the then Minister of War Alexei Kuropatkin at the very start of the war discussed with his predecessors the question of how many troops needed to be sent to the Far Eastern theatre, the first considered the ratio of two Russian soldiers to three Japanese to be fine, the second even thought that one Russian was a match for two Japanese!

Besides purely internal political problems, it seemed that an unlosable war like this might also satisfy Nicholas II's ambitious thoughts of extending the geographical boundaries of the empire. "Our sovereign," General Kuropatkin wrote in his diary, "has grandiose plans in his head: to take Manchuria for Russia, to go on to annex Korea to Russia. He dreams of taking Tibet too under his rule. He wants to take Persia, to capture not just the Bosphorus, but also the Dardanelles."

*Battleship* Tsesarevich *at anchor in Kiao-Chow for repairs. Port Arthur. 29th July 1905*

*Funeral of soldiers killed during the Russo-Japanese War. 1905*

*General view of mass graves after the end of the Russo-Japanese War. 1905*

However, these dreams began to crumble on their first encounter with reality. On the evening of the day the war began, 26th January 1904, the Emperor had already received a telegram from General Alexeyev reporting that Japanese destroyers had attacked the *Tsesarevich*, *Retvizan* and *Pallada* while they were lying at anchor and caused them serious damage. The following day his diary contains an entry like this: "In the morning another telegram came with news of the bombardment of Port Arthur by 15 Japanese ships and of a battle with our squadron. Minor damage was inflicted on the *Poltava*, *Diana*, *Askold* and *Novik*. Casualties were not significant. At 4 o'clock I processed through the over-filled halls to a service in the cathedral. On the way back there were deafening hurrahs! In general on all sides touching signs of a rise of spirits and of indignation with the impudence of the Japanese..."

One gets the impression that the Emperor saw his main role at this time as consisting of nothing more than to rouse the patriotic sentiments of the population and to raise the martial spirit of the troops. He spent almost the whole of 1904 on journeys about the country, visiting Belgorod, Tula, Poltava, Moscow, Kolomna, Syzran, Penza, Odessa, Romny, Birzula, Zhmerinka, Suvalki and Vitebsk, seeing off troops departing for the Far East, and in September he went to Revel to inspect the fleet. And all this time despatches, most of them bearing bad news, kept arriving: "In the morning the grave and inexpressibly sad news came," he wrote on 31st March, "that while our squadron was returning to Port Arthur, the battleship *Petropavlovsk* struck a mine, was blown up and sank with the loss of Adm. Makarov, most of the officers and crew. Cyril, slightly injured, Yakovlev — the captain, a few officers and sailors — all wounded — were rescued. The whole day I could not get this terrible misfortune out of my mind..."

The report of the surrender of Russia's main Pacific base — Port Arthur — caught up with the imperial train when it was in Byelorussia on its way from Baranovichi to Bobruisk on 21st December. "Received staggering news from Stessel in the night," Nicholas wrote as neatly as ever, "about the surrender of Port Arthur to the Japanese in the light of immense losses and disease among the garrison and the complete lack of shells. It's hard and painful, although it had been foreseen, but one wanted to believe that the army would come to the assistance of the fortress. The defenders are all heroes and did more than could have been expected. It was God's Will then!"

Conceived as a saving measure to pull the country out of a crisis, this war not only deepened it still further, but also aggravated the position of the Tsar's government which now bore responsibility for the failures in the Far East. While the beginning of the Russo-Japanese campaign saw a temporary stop in the drift towards the left in liberal circles and the manifesto on the declaration of war inspired a great flood of loyal addresses even from the rural assemblies that were suspicious to the central authorities, patriotic fervour died down and the war grew ever more unpopular in the eyes of the most varied elements of the population as Russia suffered a growing series of defeats at sea and on land. Those who had yesterday favoured the "defence of the motherland" and "civil peace" for the period of military operations, began to demand more and more insistently the conclusion of a peace treaty and the introduction of a constitutional system of government.

The government was discredited even more in the eyes of the public and the already grave situation in the country complicated still further by the events of 9th (22nd) January 1905, which became popularly known as "Bloody Sunday", when thousands upon thousands of workers set off to deliver a petition to the Winter Palace. On the advice of his government, given on the eve of the expected peaceful demonstration, the Tsar agreed to taking the strictest measures against the crowds of people carrying icons of Christ the Saviour, portraits of Nicholas himself and petitions to him with the "loyal request" to improve their lot, their lives. The guards and the soldiers of the garrison fired in salvoes, Cossacks slashed at people with their sabres on the streets of St Petersburg: on Palace Square, at the start of Nevsky Prospekt, by the Narva Gate...

Valentin Serov, a witness to this bloody tragedy, wrote to his fellow artist Repin: "Dear Ilya Yefimovich. What I was obliged to witness from the Academy of Arts on 9th January is something I shall never forget — a well-behaved, dignified unarmed crowd walking into cavalry charges and the sights of rifles — a terrible spectacle. What I heard later was still more incredibly horrific. Can it really be that the Tsar's not wishing to come out to the workers and receive their request meant that they were to be massacred? Who decided that this massacre was to occur? Nobody and nothing can wipe out this stain."

Gorky's response to these events was the furious article *Bloody Sunday* in which he recreated the dreadful scenes on Palace Square: "People dropped in twos and threes, crouching on the ground, clutching their stomachs, running somewhere, limping, clambering through the snow, and all across the snow a mass of bright red spots broke out. They spread, steaming, catching the eye. The crowd fell back, stopped for a moment, frozen, and suddenly a wild, startling howl rang out from hundreds of throats."

On the evening of that day which Nicholas had spent with his family at Tsarskoye Selo (knowing of the planned demonstration, the Emperor had left the capital as a precaution) the following entry appeared in his diary: "A hard day! Serious disturbances took place in Petersburg as a consequence of the workers' desire to reach the Winter Palace. Troops were obliged to open fire in different parts of the city, many were killed and wounded. O Lord, how painful and hard it is!.."

More than one hundred and forty thousand people took part in the peaceful procession; the

*Detachments of soldiers by the Winter Palace. St Petersburg. 9th January 1905*

total of killed and injured, including no small number of women and children, ranges, depending on the source, between 1,000 and 5,000. As a sign of their indignation at this carnage the French, British and German parliaments suspended loans to the Russian tsar; throughout Europe and America political parties, societies and gatherings of ordinary citizens sent telegrams of protest to the Russian government and expressed their sympathy to the workers of St Petersburg and the Russian people...

Nicholas himself, in a speech on 19th January 1905 to a deputation of workers gathered by the police from a number of works and factories, displayed "magnanimity" by forgiving his foolish subjects their "fault".

"I have summoned you," he said, "so that you might personally hear My words and pass them on directly to your fellows.

"The deplorable events with their lamentable, but inevitable consequences of disorder occurred because you allowed yourselves to be enticed into error and delusion by traitors and enemies of our country.

"In asking you to come and give Me a petition about your needs, they stirred you to a revolt against Me and My government, forcibly tearing you away from honest labour at a time when all true Russian people should be working together

indefatiguably towards vanquishing our persistent external enemy.

"Strikes and mutinuous gatherings only rouse the idle crowd to such disturbances as have always caused and will cause those in power to resort to military force, and that inevitably produces innocent victims.

"I know that the life of a worker is not an easy one. Much needs to be improved and set in order, but be patient. You know from your own consciences that you should be fair to your mas-

During the period of the first Russian revolution in which courts martial were operating — August 1905 to April 1906 — the death sentence was passed on more convicts than in the previous eighty years. The wave of repression was strongest in the capital. Some 7,000 people were exiled from the city, roughly 1,000 arrested, 13 newspapers and periodicals were closed, 42 print shops were stopped from working, demonstrations and meetings were banned and many trade unions were disbanded.

*Political prisoners being led from prison to be sent to the Turukhan Region. St Petersburg. 1906*

ters as well and take the state of our industry into account. But to announce your needs to Me through a mutinuous crowd is a criminal act.

"In my concern about working people I shall see to it that everything possible be done to improve their lives and to provide them henceforth with legal means to express their urgent needs.

"I believe in the honest sentiments of the working people and in their steadfast loyalty towards Me, and I therefore forgive them their fault.

"Return now to your peaceful labour, set to work with a blessing together with your fellows and may God be there to aid you."

But the blood that was shed on 9th January told heavily on the Tsar. It cried out for vengeance and vengeance came years later in accordance with the cruel ancient law that appears in the Bible as "An eye for an eye, a tooth for a tooth" (*Leviticus* 24:20). The very day after Bloody Sunday a proclamation was going around St Petersburg, produced in a print-shop the workers had seized. "To arms, comrades," it

*Group of Muscovites at the site of the assassination of Grand Duke Sergei Alexandrovich, Governor-General of Moscow, by the Social Revolutionary Ivan Kaliayev. Moscow. February 1905*

read, "capture the arsenals, weapons stores and gun-shops... Lets topple the Tsar's government and install our own. Long live the revolution, long live the constituent assembly of the representatives of the people!"

The mass arrests which began on the orders of Dmitry Trepov, appointed Governor-General of St Petersburg with dictatorial powers on 11th January, (688 people were investigated in connection with the "affair of 9th January") could not stop a wave of anti-government actions. The famous strike in Ivanovo-Voznesensk had repercussions throughout the country, while armed clashes took place in Lodz, Warsaw, Riga, Libau, Odessa and other cities. A new impulse for the revolutionary movement in Russia came with the mutiny on the battleship *Potemkin* in June 1905 and the strength of the peasant movement increased sharply, embracing a fifth of all Russian rural districts between May and August.

And at the beginning of October a general strike started across Russia which was openly political in character.

By this time the number of political murders and terrorist acts had grown considerably. But it was not these crimes in themselves that were indicative of the depth of the crisis of power so much as the attitude of the broad mass of the public towards them. As *Osvobozhdeniye* (*Liberation*) wrote in the summer of 1902, the popularity of political murders in Russia had become "a socio-psychological fact" and the death of, for example, Sipiagin, was received in very different social circles with "a strikingly unanimous delight..." The same was true of the murder of Plehve, which was seen by many as the just deserts of a man who had on his conscience the pogrom in Kishinev in 1903, the shooting of striking workers in Zlatoust and the persecution of *zemstva* activists. This comes across in full measure in the story told by S.L. Sazonov, the father of the murderer. Ashamed to look people in the eye he took a night train from Ufa, but he was recognized by chance "and people started to come into the carriage. They congratulated me, shook my hand ... you, said one, are a real father! ... Some officer and company even came up with a glass in the buffet: I drink to your health, he declared..." Kaliayev's assassination of Grand Duke Sergei Alexandrovich also met with a similar reception. Only a few days after the explosion a joke was doing the rounds in Moscow that the "something had entered the Grand Duke's brain at least once in his life".

More than any of his predecessors, Nicholas II was constantly being called upon to make a choice, and that in circumstances of the most complex social tension. Winston Churchill perspicaciously noted of the Russian Tsar: "His was the function of the compass needle. War or no war? Advance or retreat? Right or left? Democratize or hold firm? Quit or persevere? These were the battlefields of Nicholas II."

As we have already stated in the prologue, circumstances obliged the monarch to make concessions, although it went completely against his wishes and convictions. Even on the eve of signing the Manifesto of 17th October Nicholas observed: "Yes, Russia is being granted a constitution. We were few in number who fought against it. But support was not forthcoming from any quarter in this struggle, every day an even greater number of people turned away from us and in the end the inevitable happened..."

The strengthening of autocracy, as the only course consonant with the spirit of the Russian people according to the demands of right-wing conservatives, was hampered by the sharply increased influence of the revolutionary democrats and of the liberal circles who had made

*Vladimir Nabokov, one of the members of the First State Duma who were condemned to three months' imprisonment for signing the Vyborg Appeal, in a carriage at the prison gates. St Petersburg. 1908*

common cause with them in many matters. It is a curious fact that both liberals and conservatives in equal degree reminded the Tsar of the sad fate of the executed French king. In the opinion of Prince Abamelek-Lazarev, who presented Nicholas with an extensive letter substantiating the necessity for firm autocratic power, it was precisely concessions to the liberals and revolutionaries that could bring the Tsar to a repetition of the fate of Louis XVI, who "in six weeks" lost power and plunged the country into the abyss of revolution.

On the other side Anatoly Koni, for his part, tried to convince the monarch that only carrying out the promises given in the manifesto and in his speech at the opening of the first State Duma would be effective in relieving high social tension. "On this occasion a dull look from impenetrable eyes accompanied an answer that was not direct: 'Yes! It (he meant sedition, of course) happened everywhere. All states have gone through it: England too, and France...' I — Koni recalled — could hardly keep from saying: 'But there they cut off Your Majesty's head!'."

The proclamation of the Manifesto, the establishment of the State Duma and other public bodies reduced the "living space" left for autocracy and distorted its original nature — now it had become something in between autocracy and a constitutional monarchy. This situation was in Nicholas's mind almost tantamount to the end of Russia. The choice he made to copy out a passage when looking through the diary of Prince Meshchersky, one of the ideologists of monarchism, is quite noteworthy. It reads: "Whenever I find myself flirting with the idea of constitutionalism, in Russia it is prevented by Russia itself, since the first day of a constitution will be the beginning of the end of absolutism. It demands autocracy, and the end of autocracy is the end of Russia."

Having survived the critical boiling point of the revolution, sheltering behind phrases full of great promise, the forces of reaction with the Tsar at their head went over onto the offensive. Following the presentation in the State Duma of a bill by the Constitutional Democratic Party which envisaged the partial alienation of landlord's property rights with compensation, Nicholas issued a decree and manifesto on 9th July 1906 by which the Duma, which had still not in fact begun to flex its muscles, was dissolved. Deputies who objected to this decree travelled to the town of Vyborg, then in Finland, and 232 of them signed a special appeal calling on the population to "stand up" for the State Duma and "until the convocation of a popular government" (i.e. of a new Duma) not to give "a kopeck into the treasury, nor a single soldier into the army" and not to acknowledge state loans. For the most part, though, this appeal met with no response — the country was still not mature enough for parliamentarianism. Repression of the participants of the Vyborg session began: dismissal from the service, the defrocking of members of the clergy, exclusion from "noblemen's societies", arrests.

The decisive transition to reactionary policies and the reversal of course did not, however, take place until after the dispersal of the Second State Duma on 3rd June 1907 and the arrest of its Social-Democrat faction, which was even termed the "third June coup". In breech of existing legislation the Tsar's government introduced new electoral law which all but excluded workers from representation in the Duma. Legal public mass organizations were subject to repression. In the three years from 1907 to 1909 about 500 trade unions were closed down; the declared "freedom of the press" was also on the decline. This same period saw the repression of more than fifty thousand individuals (condemned to death, hard labour or prison terms, or sent into "adminstrative exile" without the judgement of a court).

In his policies Nicholas II consistently orientated himself by the "simple peasant's love for the Tsar" without taking into account revolutionary and social-democratic forces of "Europeanized society". Throughout almost all its life the Russian State Duma, a wretched likeness of European parliaments, had to endure real persecution from the government. And over the ten years of its history from the beginning up to the 1917 draft manifesto for the dissolution of the Fourth State Duma one and the same idea kept recurring with variations: "Russia has no need of speeches that disturb the soul of the people and impair our statehood, but constructive work, strengthening order in the state."

The closer autocratic monarchy came to its tragic end, the more the authorities, as if in an attempt to shield themselves from the approaching storm, organized around the country, and in St Petersburg in particular, grand celebrations to mark one anniversary after another — 200 years of St Petersburg and 200 years of Tsarskoye

*Celebration of the Bicentennial of St Petersburg. Peter I's Square.*
*St Petersburg. 1903*

Selo, 200 years since Riga's incorporation into Russia and 50 years from the reform of 1861, anniversaries of victories in the Battles of Narva and Lesnaya, 200 years since the capture of the Schlüsselburg Fortress and of Vyborg, since the Battle of Poltava, the 100th anniversary of the Battle of Borodino, 200 years of the Holy Trinity St Alexander Nevsky Lavra and 300 years of rule by the House of Romanov. More regularly there were the All-Russian temperance holidays and the days of the Knights of the Order of St George, magnificent, pompously arranged visits by eminent foreign guests, balls, ceremonies, parades, dinners... The deafening thunder of endless salutes and firework performances drowned out the distant noises of the Russo-Japanese War, the shots and cries on Palace Square and the terrorists' explosions.

These undeniably brilliant pages in the history of the Russian state were invoked to support and strengthen the authority of monarchical power in its most difficult period. The way these festivities were arranged reflected not so much a love for the historical past of the country, as a desire to glorify the present-day emperor as the con-

tinuer of the deeds of his great ancestors. Thus in the festive ceremony to mark the 200th anniversary of the foundation of St Petersburg the central place was given to a "sacred" dynastic relic: with all military honours and to the accompaniment of a series of salvoes from the guns of the Peter and Paul Fortress the "grandfather of the Russian fleet", Peter the Great's small sailing boat, was conveyed on a barge from Peter's cabin to the landing-stage by the Bronze Horseman (the monument to Peter) on Senate Square. The little vessel was saluted all along its grand progress by the modern-day ships of various types and classes drawn up in the main channel of the Neva to demonstrate the majestic power of the Russian fleet, the creation of the first Russian emperor. Everywhere in the central part of the city state flags were hanging and the Russian coat-of-arms — the double-headed eagle — was displayed, while the square around the Bronze Horseman was decorated with highly ornate wooden structures bearing the initials of the Russian emperors and the dates of their reigns.

Holidays and celebrations of this kind had one more, no less important aspect to them. They allowed Nicholas to escape for a while from the modern-day realities he found unpleasant and even repellent. A special place all of its own among this fairy kaleidoscope of festivities was taken by the famous costume ball held in the Winter Palace on 22nd January 1903 — "the last great ball". By the Emperor's desire, those attending had to dress in Russian seventeenth-century style costumes and St Petersburg society, having put off all other matters until later, was for several whole months chiefly engaged on the problem of preparing a historically accurate and natural ball dress. Grand Duke Alexander Mikhailovich, who was one of the participants, perceived this decision to hold a magnificent ball as a desire on the tsar's part to forget himself, "to return if only for one night to his family's glorious past". Yet while the courtiers played out an idyllic winter fairy-tale a "new, hostile Russia looked in through the immense windows of the palace... While we danced, workers were striking in Petersburg and the storm clouds kept gathering in the Far East."

The appearance at the imperial court of such an odious figure as Grigory Rasputin and the subsequent growth of his influence was due above all to the fact that contemporary medicine, having come to a terrible conclusion in the case of the Tsesarevich, proved impotent in the face of his then mysterious illness and this roused his parents, in particular Alexandra Feodorovna, to look for help and support from forces outside this world.

The royal couple became acquainted with Rasputin through the agency of the so-called Montenegrins — Grand Duchesses Anastasia Nikolayevna and Militsa Nikolayevna (the wives of Grand Dukes Nikolai and Piotr Nikolayevich) who had first met the *starets* (holy man) when on a pilgrimage to the Mikhailovsky Monastery and come to be on fairly close terms with him. When Rasputin told them about his ability to cure all illnesses including haemophilia, the symptoms of which he could describe quite accurately, the sisters saw a chance to help the royal family and made sure they introduced their new acquaintance to the tsar and tsarina.

It is certainly possible that Militsa Nikolayevna, an intelligent, calculating and undeniably gifted woman (she had learnt Persian especially so as to be able to read Persian mystics in the original and also published her own work *Selected Passages from the Holy Fathers*), imagining the sort of impression Rasputin might make on Nicholas and Alexandra with their mystical inclinations, reckoned on using this to increase her influence at court. However the case may be, some people in royal circles did express such suspicions. The Grand Duchess gained no more power, though, despite Rasputin becoming with time one of the most influential figures in Russia.

Rasputin's very appearance was striking and practically everyone who recalled him mentioned his extraordinary individuality and immense inner power which radiated from his stare. "Long, black, badly combed hair; a thick black beard; high forehead; a broad bulbous nose, muscular mouth," Ambassador Paléologue recorded in his diary on 24th February 1915. "But all the expression of his face is concentrated in the cornflower-blue eyes, glinting, deep, strangely attractive. His look is at one and the same time penetrating and gentle, naive and cunning, intent and distant. When his speech grows animated, his pupils seem to become charged with magnetism."

Vladimir Bonch-Bruevich who met Rasputin at the home of Varvara Ivanovna Ikskul recalled: "My attention was caught above all by his eyes: an intense and direct look, some phosphorescent light seemed to play in his eyes all the time. It was always as if he was probing his audience with his eyes, and sometimes his speech suddenly slowed, he drew out the words, lost his track as if he were thinking of something else and stared fixedly at someone, steadily, right into their eyes, and stayed like that for some minutes, all the time slurring his words in an almost unintelligible manner. Then suddenly he recalled 'who he was', became confused and hastily tried to change the conversation. I noticed that it was that fixed stare in particular which had an effect on those present, especially the women, who were terribly confused by his gaze, became quite unsettled, and then looked timidly back at Rasputin themselves and sometimes seemed drawn towards him, wanting to talk a little more, to hear more of what he would say."

It is striking that a man who had this bewitching influence on those around him, evoking a feeling of adoration in many, should, to judge by detailed descriptions of him, have created quite the opposite impression, one of revulsion. "Rasputin had a lump on his forehead," his personal secretary A. Simanovich wrote, "which he carefully concealed with his long hair. He always had a comb with him which he used on his hair which was long, shiny and always greased. His beard was almost always untidy. Rasputin only rarely

*Grigory Rasputin (Novykh) with Major-General M.S. Putiatin, a Special Envoy for the Administration of the Marshal of the Court (right) and D.N. Loman, Colonel of the Life-Guards Pavlovsky Regiment. St Petersburg. 1904—05*

By the time Rasputin appeared in St Petersburg, met the royal family and developed into an influential figure at court, he already had behind him a long and in large measure remarkable life. Born into a moderately well-to-do peasant family in the village of Pokrovskoye in the Tiumen district of Tobolsk Province, he fairly soon became notorious in his home area as a man with an ungovernable temper, extremely effusive, sly and self-assured. Rasputin was seen stealing on several occasions and once he was savagely beaten by a man from the same village (he was struck a very heavy blow on the head with a stake, causing him to bleed from the mouth and nose, and to lose consciousness), after which, according to eyewitnesses, he turned strange and even slightly stupid.

But his real transformation came as a result of a pilgrimage to the Monastery of Verkhoturye in Perm Province, which he undertook to escape a legal action brought by the local populace, not wishing to share the fate of those of his friends whose disorderly and immoral conduct had already earned them deportation to Eastern Siberia. This journey, which lasted some three months, brought about a real change in his behaviour, prompting those who had known him earlier to suggest that he was patently suffering from some psychological disorder. He completely changed his way of life: he stopped drinking and smoking, gave up eating meat and began to read texts in Church Slavonic, the liturgical language of the Orthodox Church; he cut himself off from people, prayed a lot and talked with wanderers representing various sects and dogmas, including those whom the official Church called "*khlysty*" — a sect which believed that one should sin more in order that one's salvation would be the greater. Over a period of several years he spent time at dozens of monasteries in Siberia and European Russia, and even on Mount Athos, returning each time to his native village, where a completely closed circle of his admirers formed, with new female companions.

The numbers of those who looked on him with mystical adoration and blind faith, despite the scandalous tales which followed him, grew apace, embracing people from the most varied circles and greatly increasing his reputation. "Father Grigory", as they came to call him, could in the minds of his many female followers be compared with Tikhon Zadonsky, who was the same sort of "ordinary mortal, when he walked on the earth, but then came into glory".

In an incredible manner fate impelled Rasputin into the highest court circles, making the simple Tiumen peasant the all-powerful favourite of the supreme authorities, whose whim decided the rise and fall of many statesmen. Rasputin had a tremendous effect on the Empress who saw him not only as the healer of her only son but also as a genuine oracle whose word she believed absolutely. This gave him an immense influence on all aspects of state policy under the last of the Romanovs and this influence was unflagging, despite Rasputin being compromised by numerous facts it was impossible to ignore. The St Petersburg period of his life, according to the reports of the agents who kept him under constant surveillance, was marked by ever-growing unrestrained debauchery, drinking-bouts and orgies, embroiling even highly placed figures. For the immediate royal family, however, his "holiness" and "piety", enhanced by renewed wanderings about Russia and more than one pilgrimage to Jerusalem, were not a matter for question.

On various grounds — some seeking advice or support, others out of pure curiosity — many high society ladies visited Rasputin. The Provisional Government's Extraordinary Investigative Commission established for certain, though, that members of the Tsar's and grand dukes' families were never at his home. Nevertheless, this relationship had already dealt a shattering blow to royal prestige. All attempts to separate the "*starets*" from the Emperor's family came to naught, and it was only the violent death of this man, so disastrous for the ruling dynasty, that put an end to a whole period of Russian history connected with his name.

used a brush on it. In general he was fairly clean and bathed frequently, but he wholly lacked table-manners. He used a knife and fork only on rare occasions and preferred to pick his food up from the plates with his dry, bony fingers. He tore big pieces apart like a wild animal. There were few people who could watch him doing this without disgust. His mouth was very large, but instead of teeth some kind of black stumps showed inside. When he was eating, bits of food very often stuck in his beard... In his dress Rasputin always remained true to his peasant costume. He wore a Russian shirt, tied at the waist with a silk cord, wide trousers, high boots and a long tight-fitting *poddevka-coat...*"

There can be not the slightest doubt that Rasputin possessed unique capabilities and an exceptional capacity to affect a fairly wide range of people. Given this, his completely improbable rise and a career literally unheard-of for a simple peasant from distant Siberian Tobolsk was no coincidence.

Apart from the undoubted gift of his exterior, which Rasputin himself nevertheless denied, not considering himself a hypnotist, he was possessed of colossal energy which expressed itself in the most varied ways. Material gathered by the Extraordinary Investigative Commission of the Provisional Government, which studied the history of Rasputin's ascent and influence over the royal family, shows that the passion in his nature came out in violent rages and also manifested itself in uncontrollable outbreaks of sensuality, arousing in him, by his own confession, the "prodigal devil". The testimony of a whole series of people proves that in the last period of his life he could drink and make merry from 12 noon to 4 the next morning, then go off to matins, stand through the service until 8 a.m. and, after coming home and drinking strong tea, receive until 2 p.m. the visitors who came in their thousands. His extremely strong aura or the energy which poured out of him literally drew people to him, evoking in many a passionate desire to get close to or even touch him. With his growing influence in "high society", though, Rasputin became surrounded by more and more characters who were pursuing their own highly mercenary goals.

Beyond all this, it must be acknowledged that Rasputin was purely and simply an interesting and unusual man. Suffice it to mention his walking around Russia and his repeated pilgrimages

to Jerusalem. Many have testified that he had no small knowledge of the Scriptures and was even able to interpret them. Most important of all, he undoubtedly had a lot of knowledge in the realm of folk medicine and had a gift for treating and healing people.

There are many recorded episodes which reveal just this talent of his as a healer. The ways and methods of treatment were very varied: from herbs and infusions made to Siberian prescriptions to almost shaman-like incantations and gestures. "If anyone had a bad head and was feverish," Simanovich related, "Rasputin stood behind the patient, took his head in his hands, whispered something no one could understand, and pushed the patient with the words "Be off!" The patient felt he had got better. I experienced the effect of Rasputin's incantation myself and must acknowledge that it was staggering."

It was this very ability, used by Rasputin on many occasions to help the Tsesarevich when he was in a very poor state, that formed the thread, for many years invisible, yet strong, which bound that demonic figure to the royal family.

As Major-General Voyeikov, Nicholas II's last palace commandant, recalled, "from the first time that Rasputin appeared at the sick-bed of the Heir, relief followed immediately. All those close to the royal family are well aware of the incident at Spala, when the doctors could find nothing to help Alexis Nikolayevich who was suffering greatly and groaning with pain. As soon as a telegram had been sent on Anna Vyrubova's advice to Rasputin and the reply had come back, the pains began to diminish, his temperature started to fall and in a short time the Tsesarevich was better. If you take the point of view of the Empress, his mother, who saw Rasputin as a God-fearing *starets* whose prayers helped her sick son — much should be clear and forgiven..."

Many people have spoken and written about this, including the person closest to Alexandra Feodorovna — her maid-of-honour and friend Anna Vyrubova. "When the Empress or the Tsesarevich were ill," she recalled, "Rasputin was either invited to the patient or a telegram was sent asking for his prayers. In 1911, when the Tsesarevich had internal bleeding, a telegram was sent to Rasputin asking him to pray and Rasputin calmed the Emperor and Empress with a telegram saying the Tsesarevich would live. Early in 1916 the Tsar unexpectedly returned with the Tsesarevich when they had been on their way to Stavka, because the Tsesarevich had begun to bleed uncontrollably from the nose owing to the haemophilia. When the Tsar arrived Rasputin was immediately sent for. I did not witness what happened afterwards, but from what the Tsar and Tsarina said I know that Professor S.P. Fedorov could not find any way of stopping the bleeding, that Rasputin appeared, made the sign of the cross over the Tsesarevich, stroked his head and by some miracle the bleeding ceased. The doctors who treated the Tsesarevich, Professor Fedorov and his assistant, the surgeon Derevenko, said that the Tsesarevich had hereditary bleeding due to thinness of the vessels and that he would never get over it, Rasputin reassured them by asserting that he would grow out of it. Wasn't that enough to win the faith and love of parents who loved their child immeasurably?.."

Incidentally, it was not only the case of their own child nor just widely circulating rumours that helped Nicholas and Alexandra to convince themselves of Rasputin's "omnipotence". They also happened to be immediate witnesses of his literally miraculous influence on Vyrubova herself after a railway accident as she lay close to death, unconscious with shattered legs and pelvis and a fractured skull. "When she was pulled out of the wreckage," Prince Andronnikov said, retelling under examination the story as he heard it from Yelizaveta Naryshkina, lady-in-waiting, head of the Empress's household, and, by the way, no friend of Rasputin, "the poor woman kept shouting 'Father, father, help me' (meaning Rasputin). She believed that he would help her... And that's what did happen... He dashed off to Tsarskoye Selo. When he arrived at Tsarskoye, the injured Vyrubova was surrounded by the former Tsar, the Tsarina, the whole royal family, the daughters I mean, and several doctors. Vyrubova was in a completely hopeless state. When Rasputin arrived, he bowed, came up to her and began making some kind of gestures and saying 'Annushka, can you hear me?'. And she, after not saying anything to anyone, suddenly opened her eyes..."

The royal family saw Grigory Rasputin as a man sent to them by God, a near-saint, a prophet and a man who most genuinely cared for them. This attitude comes across fully in the correspondence which passed between Alexandra Feodorovna and her daughters and the "*starets.*"

From Alexandra: "My beloved and unforgettable teacher, saviour and mentor. How painful it is for me without you. I am only calm in my heart and relax when you, my teacher, are sitting by me and I kiss your hands and lay my head on your blessed shoulders. Oh how easy it is for me then. Then I wish for only one thing: to go to sleep, to sleep for ever on your shoulders, in your embraces. Oh what happiness even just to feel your presence near me. Where are you? Where have you flown to? And it's so hard for me, such melancholy in my heart... Only you, my beloved mentor, must not tell Anya about my sufferings without you. Anya's kind, she's good, she loves me, but don't you reveal my sorrow to her. Will you be by me soon? Come quickly. I wait for you and long for you. I ask your holy benediction and kiss your blessed hands. Forever your loving, *M... (Mama)."*

From Olga: "My priceless friend. I often remember you, your visits to us and the talks we had about God. It's hard without you: there's no one to turn to with my sorrows, and how many sorrows I have. This is my torment. Nikolai is driving me mad. I only have to go into the cathedral, Sophia's, and catch sight of him and I'm ready to climb the wall, my whole body shakes... I love him... I would just throw myself at him. You advised me to proceed more cautiously. But how can I be more cautious when I can't control myself... We drive to Anya's often. Each time I wonder whether I'll meet you there, my priceless friend; oh, if only I could meet you there soon and ask for some advice about Nikolai. Pray for me and bless me. I kiss your hands. *Your loving Olga."*

From Tatyana: "My dear and true friend, when are you going to come here? Are you going to sit in Pokrovskoye for long? How are your children? How's Matresha? When we gather at Anya's, we always remember you all. How I would like us to spend some time in Pokrovskoye. When will the time come? Arrange everything quickly; you can do anything. God loves you so much. And God, in your words, is so good and kind that He immediately carries out what you think up. So come as soon as possible. Because we miss you, miss you. And Mama's ill without you. And it's so hard for us to see her ill. Oh, if you only knew how hard it is for us to bear Mama's illness. You do know, because you know everything. I give you a strong, burning kiss, my dear friend. I kiss your holy hands. Until we meet. *Yours Tatyana.*

From Maria: "My dear, kind, unforgettable friend, how I miss you. How miserable it is without you. Would you believe I dream of you almost every night. In the morning, the moment I wake, I take the Gospel you gave me from under the pillow and I kiss it... Then I feel as if it's you I'm kissing. I'm so wicked, but I want to be good and not to upset our dear, kind, good nanny. She's so kind, so good, we all love her so. Pray, my unforgettable friend, that I shall always be good. I kiss you. I kiss your bright hands. Yours forever, *Maria.*"

From Anastasia: "My dear friend, when shall we see you? Anya told me yesterday that you will come soon. How happy I shall be. I love it when you talk to us about God. I love to hear about God. I think God is kind, so kind. Pray to Him so that He will make Mama well. I often dream of you. Do you dream of me? When will you come? When will you talk to us in the nursery about God? Come quickly. I'm trying to be a good girl, like you told me. If you are always near us, I'll always be good. Till we meet. I kiss you and you bless me. Yesterday I got cross with little brother, but then made it up. Your loving *Anastasia.*"

These letters were published by the hieromonk Iliodor (Sergei Trufanov) in the book *The Holy Devil* with the obvious intention of discrediting the Empress in the eyes of the public. A one-time friend and later implacable enemy of Rasputin, Iliodor was directly involved in an unsuccessful plot to assassinate him. Alexandra Feodorovna's letter, which was confirmed as genuine by the testimony of Anna Vyrubova, is frequently produced as evidence (the only piece, though) for the existence of a liaison between Rasputin and the Empress. There is, however, not the slightest justification for talking about a relationship of that kind. Just as absurd and groundless are the numerous similar rumours that went round about Anna Vyrubova to the effect that she was the mistress of both Nicholas II and Rasputin.

This opinion was so widespread that even after the February Revolution in 1917 the Investigative Commission was forced to transfer the former maid-of-honour from the Peter and Paul Fortress, where many ministers and officials close to the royal family were being held, to the arrest room of the former Gendarmes Department, sparing her nothing short of mockery and threats against her life from the soldiers of the fortress garrison. Nevertheless, the results of the medical examination carried out on Vyrubova in May 1917 at the direction of the Extraordinary Investigative Commission irrefutably established her virginity. As Vladimir Rudnev, one of the members of the Commission, wrote "as a consequence of the failure of her marriage, A.A. Vyrubova's religious feeling became ever stronger and, one might say, started to take on the nature of religious mania. In this state Rasputin's predictions about the thorns on the path of life were for Vyrubova true prophesy. Because of that she became the purest and truest of Rasputin's worshippers, and until the last days of his

---

The hieromonk Iliodor (Sergei Trufanov) came to prominence in 1905—07 by making a series of antirevolutionary addresses and was one of the organizers of the Black-Hundred Union of the Russian People. At one time he was friendly with Rasputin and enjoyed his support, but, as a result of a quarrel with him, Iliodor was incarcerated in a monastery from where he fled to Norway. In exile abroad he published his book about Rasputin, *The Mad Monk of Russia.*

---

*Hieromonk Iliodor with the police officer E.E. Dolgushin. St Petersburg. 1911*

life, he appeared to her in the guise of a holy man, altruist and miracle-worker."

Nevertheless from the very first moment that Rasputin's star began to ascend the narrow-minded people came up with the most incredible, and often unsavoury speculations about his activities. In the Special Section of the Police Department albums of press-cuttings began to stack up, articles and paragraphs about Rasputin printed in Russia and abroad, the majority of which bore little relation to reality. The vivid imagination of contemporaries created an amazing legend about this man's boundless influence on the royal family, all but claiming that he held the fate of the Church and indeed of the very State in his hands.

As events in Russian history developed this image took on ever new details. The existing gossip that a "money-grabbing *khlyst*" (the *khlysty* were an extreme sect who believed in sinning as much as possible so that their salvation should be greater), a depraver of women and girls was living with the Empress, and, perhaps, with her daughters, and that the Tsesarevich was his son, was enhanced by rumours that he and Alexandra Feodorovna were heading a pro-German party in Russia, striving for the conclusion of a separate peace, and that through them the German command learned about "all our military plans".

His actual influence in the making of the most important political decisions was considerably exaggerated not only during his lifetime, but particularly afterwards. Nonetheless this influence was undeniably quite strong. It was through Rasputin and Vyrubova that many gained appointment to positions of state; his advice, frequently going beyond the limits of personal relations, was listened to not only by ministers, but also by the Emperor and Empress. Those who owed their posts to his protection included Vladimir Sukhomlinov, Minister of War; Alexander Khvostov and later Alexander Protopopov, Ministers of the Interior; Ivan Goremykin, Chairman of the Council of Ministers, and his successors in office, Boris Stürmer and Nikolai Golitsyn. Also considered his protégés were S.P. Beletsky, V.N. Voyeikov, P.G. Bark, I.L. Tatishchev, A.A. Rittikh, L.A. Kasso, I.G. Shcheglovitov, N.A. Dobrovolsky, G.Yu. Tisenhausen and many others. This situation gave rise to constant and ever growing discontent in circles around the Tsar and to attempts to push Rasputin aside and get him away from court.

There were various motives behind these attempts. Some wanted to be rid of an influential figure who enjoyed the unhesitating trust of the royal couple, others genuinely feared for the honour and reputation of the Emperor and his wife. A third group associated Rasputin's name with the loss of credibility of monarchical power as such, seeing him as a direct threat to the throne and to the idea of monarchy. Reports and information about the improper doings of the *starets* reached Tsarskoye Selo on many occasions.

After spending three weeks on the Empress's advice together with Rasputin in the village of Pokrovskoye, M.N. Vishniakova, the nanny of the royal children, confessed to the Alexandra Feodorovna on her return to St Petersburg that she had had sexual relations with Grigory, and incidentally related that on the journey back to the capital she had seen him at night in a compartment with another female travelling-companion, Z. Mandstet. According to S.M. Tiutcheva, a maid-of-honour, "the Empress, when she heard this story, declared that she did not believe that gossip; she saw it as the work of the forces of darkness that wanted to destroy Rasputin and forbad speaking of it to the Emperor." When the rumours nevertheless reached Nicholas and she had to explain to him what had occurred, the result was Tiutcheva's dismissal.

A similar fate overtook General Dzhunkovsky, a friend of the Minister of the Interior, who presented the Tsar with a note about the pernicious influence of Rasputin, suggesting that he was "the instrument of some association, luring Russia to its death". After granting him permission to continue his observation of Rasputin, Nicholas was soon insisting on the General's immediate dismissal.

Categorical rejection was the response to the advice of the Minister of the Court, Fredericks, and the Palace Commandant, Voyeikov, that the Tsar not receive Rasputin. Grand Duchess Elizabeth Feodorovna later related that when, after hearing of the behaviour of the *starets*, she tried to caution her sister, the Empress remarked that "she did not believe those rumours, that she considered them the slander that usually pursues people who lead a holy life..."

Rasputin was also denounced by G.I. Shavelsky, the Archpriest of the Army and Navy Clergy, who reported to Nicholas that rumours circulating in the army were undermining royal prestige. The former inspector of the Petrograd Theological Academy, Bishop Theophanes of Poltava, met the Empress and tried to explain to her that Rasputin was in a state of "spiritual self-delusion".

No royal attention was paid either to a report produced for the Emperor by Stolypin, who seems at first to have been full of goodwill towards Rasputin, at least he even asked him to the sick-bed of his daughter who had been injured in the terrorist explosion at his dacha on Aptekarsky Island. Soon, however, as a result of the information that reached him from the denunciations of police spies and the reports of the Police Department he changed his attitude sharply and demanded his removal from court. His successor as chairman of the Council of Ministers also expressed his negative attitude towards Rasputin in strong terms.

Alexander Khvostov connected his dismissal from the post of Minister of the Interior directly to his presentation to the Tsar of a summary of material compromising Rasputin. "The Emperor listened unwillingly to the report," he recollected, "went over to the window, behaved as if it was of no interest to him, but I asked him to hear me out... My dismissal followed, I think, on 2nd or 3rd March 1916..."

The attempt by the Governor of Yalta, I.A. Dumbadze, to prevail on the Tsar was no more successful. Other methods came into play. A new Chairman of the Council of Ministers offered Rasputin 200,000 roubles on the sole condition that he cease interfering in the affairs of State. Add to that numerous questions and speeches in the State Duma, strongly worded attacks in the press that must have reached Tsarskoye Selo and we can see that there were certainly more than enough voices on all sides advising caution.

The last warning to the imperial family proved to be a speech made by Vladimir Purishkevich at the session of the State Duma in November 1916. "The recommendation of Rasputin must not in future be sufficient for the appointment of the most villainous characters to the highest posts," he said. "Rasputin is at present more dangerous than ever the False Dmitry [a pretender to the throne at the turn of the seventeenth century] was... Gentlemen ministers! If you are truly patriots, go there, to the royal Stavka, throw yourselves at the feet of the Tsar and plead for him to rid Russia of Rasputin and Rasputin's men, the great and the small." But it all came to naught be-

*Vladimir Purishkevich, member of the Second and Third Dumas (representing Bessarabia Province) and of the Fourth Duma (Kursk Province). Petrograd. 1916*

Vladimir Mitrofanovich Purishkevich (1870—1920) — a member of the Second, Third and Fourth Dumas, a large landowner, monarchist and one of the organizers of the Black Hundred Union of the Russian People and later the Union of Michael the Archangel — not only set the stage for Rasputin's murder, but also played the final scene in the drama, unloading his revolver into the *starets*. He left almost immediately for the front where he was kept under secret observation by the military police. After the October Revolution he fought actively against the Bolsheviks.

cause of the deafness and blindness of the royal couple. Their feeling for Rasputin was maintained by a genuine faith in his holiness and by their boundless love for their child, whose life and health seemed to them to depend on the presence and concerned prayers of Grigory. This was the reason why, when once he had agreed to expel Rasputin from St Petersburg, after a worsening in his son's condition, the Emperor changed his decision and brought him back.

The failure of attempts to remove Rasputin from court by political means gave birth to the idea of physically disposing of him. Khvostov tried on several occasions to organize his murder, convinced that it would be received with ardent sympathy among the grand dukes. The mutual antipathy between Rasputin and the majority of members of the Romanov family was common knowledge, and Grand Duke Nikolai Nikolayevich, the former commander-in-chief of the Russian forces in the war with Germany, had sworn simply to hang Rasputin as soon as he appeared at the front.

Once Rasputin did indeed come within a hair's-breadth of death. Relationships between him and Iliodor had reached a state of extreme tension and this prompted the latter to send someone to murder him — one of his worshippers, a peasant-woman by the name of Khina Guseva. "She appeared in the village of Pokrovskoye even before Rasputin came there," his secretary Simanovich wrote. "She often visited Rasputin's house and never evoked the slightest suspicion. Once Rasputin received a telegram from St Petersburg... Rasputin asked if they had remembered to give a tip, and when he got the answer no, he hurried after the man who had delivered the telegram. Guseva was waiting for him and came up to him saying: 'Grigory Yefimovich, for the Lord's sake, give alms.' Rasputin began searching in his purse for a coin. At that moment Guseva struck him in the stomach with a knife that she had kept hidden under a shawl until then. Since Rasputin only had a shirt on, there was nothing to stop the knife going deep into his body. Rasputin ran, seriously wounded, with his belly ripped open, to the house. His intestines came out through the wound and he held them with his hands. Guseva ran after him, intending to strike him again. But Rasputin still had strength enough to pick up a log and hit the knife out of Guseva's hands with it. Guseva was surrounded by the people who came running when they heard the cries and quite badly beaten. There's no doubt she would have been lynched, but Rasputin spoke up for her. The wound proved to be very dangerous. The doctors thought it a miracle that he was still alive. He took some medicinal herbs and ascribed his recovery exclusively to them."

The real "hero" of the dénouement of the tragedy was destined to be the twenty-eight year old Prince Felix Yusupov-Sumarokov-Elston, who was by then married to the daughter of Nicholas II's sister Xenia Alexandrovna — Grand Duchess Irina Alexandrovna. The thought of killing Rasputin had come to him in November 1916 and he talked about it with one of the leaders of the Constitutional Democratic Party (the "Cadets"), the lawyer Vasily Maklakov, who prudently advised him not to employ the services of hired assassins.

After witnessing Purishkevich's ardent speech at the State Duma, Yusupov became confirmed in his intention and the following day he went round to see the deputy.

"Today, at exactly 9 in the morning, Prince Yusupov came to see me," Purishkevich wrote in his diary on 21st November 1916. "He was a young man of about 30 in the uniform of a page. I liked him very much — both his appearance with its hint of inexpressible elegance and breeding, and, most of all, his spiritual tenacity. He is obviously a man of great will and character, features that are rarely present in Russian people, especially among the aristocracy.

"He spent more than two hours sitting with me.

"'Your speech will not bring the results that you expect,' he informed me at once. 'The Tsar doesn't like it when people impinge on his will and Rasputin's importance, we must believe, is not only going to decrease, but, just the opposite, it will grow due to his total influence over Alexandra Feodorovna, who is now the *de facto* ruler of the country, since the Tsar is busy with military operations at Stavka.'

"'What's to be done?' I remarked. He gave a mysterious smile and, looking me straight in the eye, he whispered through clenched teeth — 'Dispose of Rasputin.'

"I burst into laughter.

"'That's easy to say,' I observed, 'but who will do the job, when there are no decisive people in Russia, and the government which could do it and do it neatly, is held up by Rasputin and cares for him as the apple of its eye.'

"'Yes,' Yusupov replied, 'there's no counting on the government, but people will be found nonetheless.'

"'You think so?'

"'I'm sure of it! And you have one of them before you now.'" Counting on the other's support, Yusupov unveiled his plan and found a reliable ally in Purishkevich. There and then a programme of action was drawn up and even a date set for the carrying out of the sentence. A cousin of Nicholas II, Grand Duke Dmitry Pavlovich, was recruited into the conspiracy, as were A.S. Sukhotin, a lieutenant in the Preobrazhensky Regiment, and the Polish doctor Stanislaw Lazobert. Others in on the plot included Yusupov's wife, Irina, his brother Fedor and Vasily Maklakov, who refused to take an active role in the murder (although he did, incidentally, supply Yusupov with the cyanide), but promised Purishkevich he would defend them in court.

The plan was extraordinarily simple. It was proposed to carry out the murder in the Yusupovs' palace on the Moika River in St Petersburg. Execution of it was a matter of technique; the greatest problem was how to lure the shrewd and cautious Rasputin there, especially as he was under the intensified protection of several services each independent of the others. On the orders of the Tsarina his protection was in the hands of the Department of Police and the capital's branch of the *Okhrana* security service. He was constantly accompanied (at a cost of 1,500 roubles per month, paid from the police budget) by I.F. Manasevich-Manuilov, while at his home, or wherever he was to be found, there were agents on duty allocated by the head of the Petrograd *Okhrana*, General K.I. Globachev.

The "bait" the conspirators decided to use was Yusupov's young wife Irina, since Rasputin would be unlikely to turn down a meeting with her (not being aware that she was in fact out of St Petersburg at the moment).

The carefully worked out plan ran like clockwork at first. Rasputin was evidently not afraid of Felix — although when Yusupov kissed him on meeting that day, he remarked "that's not a Judas kiss is it" and added that Protopopov had come to see him and said that people wanted to kill him — and drove round to his palace. The conspirators intended to put an end to Rasputin with a large dose of cyanide and then to dispose of his body under the ice of the Malaya Nevka River, but at this point they came across unexpected complications. Felix fed Rasputin with poisoned pies and Madeira, but to his horror the poison did not take effect instantly; some time later his guest only felt ill. There are various versions regarding this point: either Rasputin was a unique person in this regard too, or, fearing to be murdered, he managed to develop an immunity to poison by taking it in miniscule doses. It is also possible that the poisoners themselves committed an error, not considering that the cyanide might be neutralized by sweet pies and sweet wine.

One way or another, the situation obliged Felix and the fellow-conspirators, who were waiting for him upstairs, to do something urgently — so as not to let the poisoned Rasputin leave the house. It was decided to shoot him and Grand Duke Dmitry Pavlovich gave Yusupov his revolver (or, in Purishkevich's version, Yusupov took his Browning out of the table drawer). The state of those directly involved in the murder was so close to hysteria — Doctor Lazobert actually fainted — that in their recollections only the broad sweep of events remains the same, while there are many discrepancies in the details.

Inviting Rasputin into the next room to admire a sculpture of the Crucifixion, Yusupov fired almost point-blank into his side from the left. He fell with a cry to the floor and seemed by all the signs to be dead. They locked the room. Prince Dmitry, Lazobert and Sukhotin wearing Rasputin's fur-coat staged the departure of the *starets* as a further precaution.

"Some time later," Yusupov recalled, "I felt just as if something hit me. I went downstairs to where Rasputin was. He was lying in the same place, but his body was still warm. I was already on the point of leaving, but the trembling of one of Rasputin's eyelids attracted me. I bent down. Suddenly Rasputin's eyes opened. I was frozen with terror. With a sharp movement he leapt to his feet. Foam was coming out of his mouth; a roar filled the room. His fingers dug into my shoulder, reached for my throat.

"— You scoundrel! — he croaked. — Tomorrow you'll hang...

"I wanted to tear myself away from him, but I couldn't. We began to fight. Finally I managed to tear loose from his clasping hands, and he fell on the floor again, holding my torn shoulder strap in his hand. I dashed headlong out of the room calling Purishkevich.

"— Quickly, the revolver quickly! Shoot, he's still alive."

We should let Purishkevich himself take up the story now:

"Suddenly downstairs a wild, inhuman cry rang out, that seemed to me to come from Yusupov: 'Purishkevich, shoot, shoot, he's alive! he's getting away!'

"A-a-a!.. and Yusupov appeared rushing full tilt up the stairs shouting; he literally did not have a face; his splendid big blue eyes had grown larger still and were bulging out; he was only half-conscious, almost didn't see me; with a panic-striken look in his eyes he flung himself towards the door out onto the main corridor and ran through into his parents' half...

"There wasn't a moment to lose and keeping my head I pulled my *Sauvage* out of my pocket, took off the safety catch and ran down the stairs.

"What I saw downstairs might have turned out to be a dream, if it hadn't been dreadful reality for us: Grigory Rasputin, whom half an hour before I had seen breathing his last, lying on the stone floor of the dining-room, tossing from side to side, was running quickly across the powdery snow in the palace courtyard along the iron railing that gave onto the street in the same clothes in which I had seen him almost lifeless just before.

"For the first instant I couldn't believe my eyes, but the loud shout he gave in the silence of the night 'Felix, Felix, I'll tell the Tsarina everything' ... convinced me that it was him, that it was Grigory Rasputin, that his phenomenal vitality might let him get away...

"I went chasing after him and fired.

"In the still night the extraordinarily loud noise of my revolver carried through the air — missed!

"Rasputin increased his pace; I shot a second time on the run — and ... again I missed.

"I can't express the feeling of fury with myself I experienced at that minute.

"A better than decent marksman, who constantly practised on the range at the Semionovsky parade ground and hit little targets, I found myself today incapable of bringing a man down at twenty paces.

"The seconds ticked by... Rasputin was already running up to the gates, then I stopped, bit my left hand with all my might to force myself to concentrate and the shot (my third) hit him in the back. He stopped, then I took more careful aim, remaining in the same place, fired a fourth time and hit him, it seems, in the head, since he dropped like a stone face downwards in the snow with his head twitching. I ran up to him and kicked him full force in the temple. He lay with his arms stretched out in front of him, scraping in the snow as if he wanted to crawl forward on his belly, but he was already incapable of moving and only chattered and ground his teeth."

Two soldiers who were on duty in the lobby by the main entrance into the palace became chance witnesses to what had occurred and now helped to carry the body into the lobby. They were preparing to wrap it up when Felix Yusupov dashed up with a two-pound rubber dumb-bell and began in an unnaturally agitated manner to beat Rasputin about the head with it, upon which, according to Purishkevich, his victim groaned again.

... Before the day was out rumours of Rasputin having been murdered spread throughout the capital. Among the first to learn of it were members of the allied missions, who followed events in Russia unceasingly. To give an example, the information reached General Handbury-Williams, the British high-command's representative at Russian army headquarters, literally within half-an-hour while he was with Wilton, a reporter on *The Times*, in one of the rooms in the Hotel Astoria.

There was no real mystery in the matter for the St Petersburg police either. The fact that Rasputin had been invited to Yusupov's at an unusually late hour was even known to Empress Alexandra Feodorovna. She had learnt about it from Vyrubova, who had talked with the *starets* the day before. Besides this, Felix himself had driven to the house on Gorokhovaya Street to fetch him, an action that simply could not have failed to be noticed. Tikhomirov, the *Okhrana's* agent on duty at the house that night, followed the car unnoticed straight to the palace at 92 Moika Embankment and remained in the street outside. Naturally people heard the shots fired in the courtyard. When these brought the policeman Vlasiuk running, an agitated Purishkevich declared in the heat of the moment: "I am Purishkevich, a member of the State Duma. We have just killed the dog Rasputin. But you should keep quiet about it." Sent packing in such a preemptory manner the constable dashed off to fetch his superior who was not, however, let into the palace either. In only a few minutes the news of what had occurred (although the results were as yet unknown) had been passed up through the chains of command — to G.N. Grigoryev, Chief of Police for the Kazan District; A.P. Balk, the City Governor; General D.N. Tatishchev, commander of the Corps of Gendarmes; the abovementioned General Globachev; and A.T. Vasilyev, director of the Police Department.

As early as the afternoon of 17th December Yusupov was interrogated by General Grigoryev and it took the police only a short time to check and dismiss the prince's fairly naive story that after they had been drinking one of his guests had shot a dog. Analysis of the blood found on carpets in the palace proved that it was human.

In Tsarskoye Selo panic set in early in the morning. Vyrubova recorded a chronicle of the events of that day in her diary: "On the morning of 17th December one of Rasputin's daughters telephoned me. She told me with some alarm that their father had not come home after driving off with Felix Yusupov late in the evening... When I arrived in the palace I told the Tsarina about it. After listening to what I had to say, she expressed her bewilderment. An hour or two later a telephone call came to the palace from the office of the Minister of the Interior Protopopov, who informed us that during the night a policeman on duty near Yusupov's home had heard a shot fired in the house and rang at the door. Purishkevich had run out to him drunk and announced that Rasputin had been killed. The same policeman had seen a military vehicle with its lights switched off leaving the house soon after the shots... The Empress and I sat together, very despondent waiting for further news. First there was a call from Prince Dmitry Pavlovich who asked permission to come for tea at 5 o'clock. Pale and sad, the Empress refused. Then Felix Yusupov rang and asked permission to come and give an explanation either to the Empress or to me; he rang me several times but the Empress would not allow me to go to the telephone and said he should be told to send his explanation in writing. In the evening the Empress was brought the famous letter from Felix Yusupov in which he swore in the name of the Yusupov princes that Rasputin had not been at his house that evening. He had indeed seen Rasputin on several occasions, but not that evening. Yesterday evening he had held a party, a housewarming celebration, they had drunk too much and on the way out Grand Duke Dmitry Pavlovich had killed a dog in the courtyard."

The Empress sent several telegrams to Stavka, the army headquarters at Mogilev, asking Nicholas to come back urgently. To a letter already written to her husband she hastily added in pencil a summary of the events that had shocked her: "We are all sitting together — you can imagine how we feel and think — our Friend has disappeared. Yesterday A. (Anna Vyrubova) saw Him and He said that Felix had asked Him to come round at night, that a car would come for Him so

He could see Irina. A car did come for Him (an army car) with two civilians and He drove off. Last night there was a huge uproar in the Yusupov house — a big gathering, Dmitry, Purishkevich and so on — all drunk. The police heard shots fired. Purishkevich ran out and shouted to the police that our Friend had been killed... Felix purports not to have gone to the house and never to have invited Him. It was obviously a trap. I still pin my hope's on God's mercy, that He has only been taken off somewhere... I can't and won't believe that they've murdered him."

Despite the great amount of evidence pointing to it (the only thing missing was the body), there were still many who doubted Rasputin's death. When he heard the news at the yacht club on the evening of 17th December even Grand Duke Nikolai Mikhailovich considered the whole story just the latest hoax, since, as he said, he had heard talk of the death of the *starets* about ten times already and each time he "rose from the dead" more powerful than before.

Nonetheless both Grand Duke Dmitry and Prince Felix Yusupov had already been placed under house arrest on the orders of the Empress (although she was exceeding her authority in doing so). They did not dare arrest Purishkevich, who had behind him both the Duma and the monarchist organizations known as the Black Hundreds, and on 18th December he left for the front, secretly accompanied by agents of the military police.

In general, outside a fairly narrow circle of people, reaction to the event was the same everywhere: it was seen as a great blessing. The majority of British and French newspapers congratulated the Russian people on their happy deliverance from a "dark force" and "national disgrace". Most eloquently the London *Times* captioned pictures of Felix and Irina Yusupov with the words "The Saviours of Russia".

The mass rejoicing in St Petersburg was also recorded by the French ambassador Maurice Paléologue. "When they learnt of the death of Rasputin the day before yesterday," he wrote on 20th December, "many people hugged each other on the streets, and went to light candles in the Kazan Cathedral.

"When it became known that Grand Duke Dmitry was among the murderers, a crowd formed around the icon of Saint Demetrius to light a candle there.

"The murder of Grigory is the only topic of conversation in the endless queues of women waiting in the wind and rain outside the doors of butchers' and grocers' for the distribution of meat, tea, sugar and so on.

"They tell each other that Rasputin was thrown into the Nevka alive and express their approval with the saying: 'For a dog, a dog's death'.

"Another popular version: 'Rasputin was still breathing when they threw him under the ice of the Nevka [this fact was confirmed by the autopsy carried out on his body by Professor Kosorotov. — *The authors*]. That's very important because that way he'll never be a saint.' The Russian people have a belief that drowned men cannot be canonized."

Since the conspirators refused to give statements, the police were obliged to search for Rasputin's body themselves. It was only on the third day, 19th December, that their efforts met with success and then a "fateful role" was played by a clue left completely by chance. The murderers, understandably extremely nervous, had in their haste and in the darkness simply failed to notice that a galosh had fallen off Rasputin's foot onto the ice. Divers were called out and they began to carefully search the bottom of the Malaya Nevka near Petrovsky Bridge. It was not too long before they found what they were looking for. Rasputin's body was secretly taken to the Home for the Veterans of Chesme (The Chesme Almshouse) which stood five kilometres from Petrograd on the highway to Tsarskoye Selo. On 21st December he was temporarily buried, again secretly, in the park at Tsarskoye Selo (it was intended that in the spring the coffin containing Rasputin's body would be taken to his native vil-

lage of Pokrovskoye in Tobolsk Province). Very few people were present at the graveside (neither the wife nor the daughters of the deceased were allowed to take their final leave of him): the Tsar and Tsarina, the four young Grand Duchesses, Vyrubova, Protopopov, Colonels Loman and Maltsev and the court Archpriest Alexander who read the burial service.

That same day Nicholas wrote in his diary: "At 9 o'clock we drove as a whole family past the photography building and to the right to a field where we played a part in a sad picture: the coffin containing the body of the unforgettable Grigory, killed in the night of 17th Dec. by monsters in the house of F. Yusupov was already lowered into the grave. Father Al[exander] Vasilyev read the last rites after which we returned home..."

Contrary to the Empress's insistence, Nicholas II did not venture to bring the murderers to court in the face of the general approval of their deed. Members of the imperial house even approached him with a written request not to have Grand Duke Dmitry punished. Although Nicholas's attitude to what had been done is expressed in his laconic resolution on this letter: "Nobody has the right to kill" — he nevertheless had to limit himself to sending Grand Duke Dmitry to the front in the Caucasus and exiling Yusupov to his estate in Kursk Province.

On 27th December 1916 at the apartment of the industrialist Alexander Konovalov, a deputy in the Fourth State Duma who was to become Minister of Trade and Industry in the Provisional Government after the February Revolution, a group of representatives of various parties heard a speech by another member of the Duma, Vasily Maklakov. This report, which analyzed the state of Russian society on the threshold of the coming upheavals, was almost wholly devoted to the role and influence of Rasputin in the upper echelons, and also to the impression his murder had made on the country. "We deputies," he said, "are being approached from all corners of Russia not with requests, but with nothing less than demands to tell all we know about Rasputin and that period in the life of our state that will undoubtedly go down in history under his name. And faced with these demands we deputies cannot but acknowledge our duty to respond to them. But before ascertaining the full truth about this most disgraceful page in our history, we had ourselves soberly and objectively to investigate

*The body of Grigory Rasputin, who was assassinated on the night between 16th and 17th December 1916*

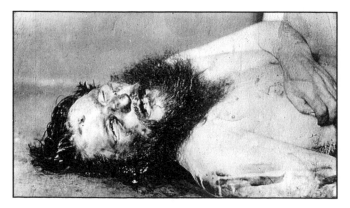

this story, to separate truth from lies, the true grain of historical truth from the flagrant legend. And a group of deputies, having the appropriate connections, have engaged in this work. They were assisted by many statesmen, high court officers, maids-of-honour and so on. The result was objective, strictly proven data and it is not our fault that this historical truth sounds worse than any slander, any unrestrained calumny, worse than some nightmare story...

"People keep talking," he continued, "about a revolution coming to a head, or, rather, one that has come completely to a head, but there are no outward signs of it yet. That might seem mysterious, and the right-wing optimists are inspired with a certainty that there will be no revolution. But there can be no denying that what is taking place now in the minds and hearts of the Russian people is the most terrible revolution that history has ever seen. It is not a revolution — it is a catastrophe: a whole centuries old concept of the world is collapsing, the people's faith in the tsar, in the justice of his power, in the idea of it being divinely ordained. And this catastrophic revolution in the innermost depths of the heart is being created not by some malevolent revolutionaries, but by authority itself, gone mad and suffering from some fatal attraction. Decades of the most intensive revolutionary work could not have brought about what has been done by the last months, the last weeks of fateful errors by authority. The supreme authority itself has doomed itself to existence in an absolute vacuum; it has deprived itself of its last points of support; it has repulsed a mass of people close to it, who were but recently its loyal subjects. Now it is no longer a powerful historical force, but the hollow, dried up trunk of an oak-tree, gnawed at by mice, and standing only by the force of inertia, until the first terrible jolt... The dynasty is setting its very existence on a card. Not destructive forces from without, but terrible destructive work within is reducing its potential natural lifespan by a good century... Reckless authority would be horror-stricken, if only it knew, could hear, what they say in the countryside and how they say it. God knows by what methods, but they immediately learnt there what every cook and doorman knows in Petrograd. And in the countryside that terrible grain of truth began to be wrapped in the improbable stuff of legend. The result is a real nightmare. The intelligentsia, trying to understand the phenomenon, though

*Boris Stürmer, member of the State Council. St Petersburg. 1913*

Stürmer is 67 years old. He is a man of less than average calibre. He has no great mind, is petty, mean-spirited, of dubious honour with no experience of affairs of state or flair for business. At the same time, though, he is not lacking in cunning. His roots are German, as can be seen from his name. He is a grand nephew of the Baron Stürmer who was the Austrian government's commissar for the surveillance of Napoleon on St Helena. Neither Stürmer's personal qualities, nor his past career in administration, nor his social status fitted him for the high role which has now fallen to him. Everybody is surprised at this appointment. But it all becomes understandable, if you assume that he is only someone else's pawn; then his non-entity and servility prove very appropriate. Stürmer's appointment is the handiwork of the *camarilla* around the Empress; his cause was taken up with the Emperor by Rasputin, with whom Stürmer has become close. This all bodes ill for the future!

*From the diary of Maurice Paléologue.
5th February 1916*

*Vladimir Fredericks, Adjutant-General, Minister of the Imperial Court and Domains, member of the State Council and the Council of Ministers. Tsarskoye Selo. 1913*

Count Vladimir Borisovich Fredericks, the Minister of the Imperial Court and Domains, had already been able to consider himself a personal friend of both Alexander II and Alexander III. The latter is supposed to have told him: "I love you as a second father, because you are always even, unchanging, and I know that I can rely on you." By his own confession — not, incidentally, contradicted by the facts — Fredericks strove to keep out of politics, avoided attending the sessions of the Council of Ministers when he could and did not seek the company of Vyrubova or Rasputin. On Saturdays he regularly gave his reports at Tsarskoye Selo and invariably stayed on for the royal lunch. Without any real grounds Fredericks was considered by the public to be one of the leaders of the "German party". In actual fact his significance, as noted in the documents of the Provisional Government's Extraordinary Investigative Commission on Rasputin and the Corruption of Autocracy, "was chiefly confined to being a support and shield for his son-in-law, the palace commandant Major-General V.I. Voyeikov..."

horrified by the sight of this breakdown, nevertheless keeps its magnanimity to the end and speaks of illness, pathology, psychosis; the countryside decides things more simply: in assessing what occurred it knows only one terrible word: treason, a betrayal of the Russian people to the Germans. That is where the horror of the impending revolution lies. This will be no political revolution which might run according to some plan, but a revolution of the anger and vengeance of the benighted lower classes, which cannot be anything but elemental, convulsive and chaotic."

Maklakov's words were undoubtedly correct — a couple of months later Russia did indeed enter the chaos and horror, to predict which one did not need to be a clairvoyant, only to look around at what was happening in the country and retain one's clarity of thought.

It is remarkable that one of Rasputin's prophesies came wholly true: that the ruling dynasty was doomed to follow him into the grave. Certainly it was far from being the death of the *starets* that brought on the collapse of autocracy in Russia. Its death sentence had been signed by the last Russian emperor somewhat earlier, when he announced to the subjects of his empire that they were at war with Germany. It was this war, or more precisely its consequences, that led rapidly to the fall by turns of the ruling houses of Russia, Austria-Hungary and Germany, those lands whose people suffered above all from the hardships and privations of the war years.

On 15th June 1914 in Sarajevo, the capital of the Austrian province of Bosnia, the Serbian-born Gavrilo Princip assassinated Archduke Franz Ferdinand, the heir to the Habsburg throne, and his wife, which soon provoked a military conflict between Austria and Serbia. Understandably this did not leave Germany and Russia indifferent since they were bound by alliances to support opposing parties in the conflict. Following the start of military operations on the Austrian-Serbian border on the evening of 17th July Nicholas II affirmed a decision to order a full mobilization in Russia. The decree to this effect was published on 18th July and at midnight Germany presented the Russian side with an ultimatum demanding a revocation of the mobilization. On the evening of 19th July 1914 Count Pourtales, the German ambassador to Russia, came to the Foreign Minister Sergei Sazonov, for an answer. When he received a refusal, he handed him a note containing a declaration of war.

The 20th July 1914 was one of the rare clear cloudless days in St Petersburg. Innumerable crowds of people of various ages and stations in life, having heard that the royal family were going to arrive in the capital, streamed down to the Neva to meet the royal yacht *Standard* coming from Peterhof, where Nicholas and his household had been at this time. About one in the afternoon the yacht entered the Neva and a steam-launch brought the whole royal family to the Winter Palace. After Their Imperial Majesties' chaplain Father Alexander Vasilyev had said formal prayers in the Nicholas Hall for God to grant victory over the enemy to the "Christ-loving triumphant Russian host", Nicholas II turned to the assembled representatives of the army and navy with a speech:

"With calm and dignity our Great Mother Russia received the news of war being declared against us.

"I am certain that with the same sense of calm we shall pursue the war, however it may be, to the end.

"I solemnly declare here, that I shall not conclude peace until the last enemy soldier has left our land.

"And I address you, gathered here as representatives of the forces dear to Me, of the Guards and the St Petersburg Military District, and, through you, all My united army, single of purpose, strong as a wall of granite, and bless it for its martial labour ahead."

Straight after this the Emperor went with the Empress out onto the balcony of the Winter Palace to the many-thousand strong crowd that had gathered on the square below, which fell as one man to its knees as he appeared and the area was filled with cries of enthusiasm and the singing of the anthem *God save the Tsar*.

The emergency order of 26th July reconvened the State Council and Duma which had been dissolved until the autumn. After a royal reception in the Council and the Duma both legislative chambers went into session and quickly approved the draft laws made necessary by the war. The rise in patriotic sentiments which occurred everywhere put an end to almost all disputes between the parties; all those who only the day before had been opponents of the government went over onto defensive positions, with the exception of the Bolshevik wing of the Social-Democratic party. The fact that Germany had been first to declare war on Russia (even if only as a formality) gave rise to an explosion of ebullient patriotism and a growth of anti-German sentiments in the country which had already been strong. As early as the 22nd July a chauvinistic crowd in St Petersburg smashed up the German embassy building on St Isaac's Square and set it on fire. The figures of Germanic warriors with horses that decorated the roof were thrown down by enraged patriots as if they symbolized the superiority of Germany over Russia and France allied against it. There were strong rumours in the crowd that these figures concealed radios to receive reports from spies in the Hotel Astoria across the square. As has already been mentioned, this madness reached its apogee when the Russian capital was hastily renamed from St Petersburg to Petrograd. Life in the country swiftly moved onto a war footing.

Life changed for the royal family as well. A legal investigator who made a study of the palace journals for July 1914 onwards produced from them a detailed description of the mode of life that was established in the Tsar's household in this period: "It was a way of life like that of a quiet, business-like middle-class family, closely tied up in its own circle, without excesses, without diversions, without deviations from the life-style established once and for all. Beyond that, it was the mode of life seemingly of profoundly religious people, who never failed to attend a single festival or pre-festival service, and who several times a year marked every in any way serious step in life with a church service. Whether it was just that the war cast its shadow even as far as Tsarskoye Selo, but the journals make no mention of a ball, great or small, not a single show, not one visit to the theatre, not one hunting-trip, not one picnic... Until lunch which was usually at about 12 o'clock, the former emperor received ministers and nobles and military officers who had announced themselves, and at this time the former empress drove out to visit one of the palace hospitals. The meetings with any one minister were not prolonged and rarely lasted more than an hour. It was in this period of the day too that sessions of the Council of Ministers under the personal chairmanship of the former emperor took place. These sessions did not last more than an hour and ended with a lunch that was laid for the ministers who had attended the session in one of the halls of the Alexander

Palace in Tsarskoye Selo. The former emperor attended such a lunch only once. After receiving people the former emperor went out for a short walk in the garden.

"At 12 noon the former emperor and empress had lunch with their children, although sometimes the former empress had lunch separately with the heir. On those occasions when the former emperor was in Tsarskoye Selo and took lunch with his children and the empress, his duty aide-de-camp was invariably invited to the meal; more often than not this was Captain Second Class Sablin, who seems to have belonged to the intimate circle of the former tsar and tsarina. On the occasions when the former emperor was with the army in action and the former empress took lunch with the children, the aide-de-camp, with extremely rare exceptions was not present at lunch. Sometimes his place was taken by one of the maids-of-honour or ladies-in-waiting, sometimes by Vyrubova. On rare occasions the empress took lunch with the wife of Captain Second Class Den — she appears to have been among those closest to the former empress and is known to have frequently visited Rasputin. Sometimes one or other of the grand dukes was present at lunch. Besides old Count Fredericks, the Minister of the Court, whose whole life had been spent at court, none of the ministers were ever invited either to lunch or to dinner. Evidently this was an honour which only those who were especially close to the family of the former emperor or had given exceptionally outstanding service could count on...

"From lunch until dinner, which usually took place at 8 o'clock in the evening, the receptions continued, and after the receptions the former emperor usually took a walk, either alone or with the children, in the garden, and sometimes he was accompanied on these walks by the duty aide-de-camp, again most often by Captain Second Class Sablin. More rarely he went out for a walk in the garden with not only the children, but also with the former empress, who on such occasions was often accompanied by Vyrubova. Sometimes the former emperor filled this period of the day with reviews of military units, visits to the wounded or calls on the Dowager Empress which he usually made alone or on Grand Duke Konstantin Konstantinovich and his wife Elizaveta Mavrikiyevna, to whom he usually drove with the former empress. In this part of the day, after receptions in her apartments, the former empress either visited the palace military hospital or went for a drive alone with the children or with Vyrubova, or drove round to her house and drank "afternoon tea" there... At 8 o'clock in the evening dinner took place; apart from the duty aide-de-camp, sometimes Vyrubova and on rare occasions one or other of the grand dukes who had driven over, there were never any outsiders. The evenings the former emperor and empress spent in the family circle. On the evening of 2nd January 1915 Vyrubova returned to Tsarskoye Selo after being injured in a train accident at the sixth verst from Petrograd, and from that date in the evening the former empress and the grand duchesses usually drove to call on Vyrubova, where the former emperor too would arrive a little later and return to the palace together with his wife and daughters."

From the very beginning of the war it had been Nicholas's intention to take his place at the head of the army. He had, however, to reckon with the opinion of a number of statesmen and appoint as commander-in-chief his uncle, Grand Duke Nikolai Nikolayevich (junior), Adjutant-General and Cavalry General. The Emperor nonetheless involved himself with the progress of the war and his life was turned into an endless series of trips to the western parts of the country, to Stavka (the military headquarters that was located first in Baranovichi, then in Mogilev) and back again — to Tsarskoye Selo. In September (from 20th to 26th) and October (from 21st to 2nd November) he visited Rovno, Brest, Osovets, Vilna, Minsk, Baranovichi, Lublin, Ivangorod, Dvinsk, Grodno and other places besides.

His Imperial Majesty's Own Train — which as a rule conveyed, apart from the Emperor himself, the Minister of War, Adjutant-General Sukhomlinov, Adjutant-General Nilov, the Palace Commandant Major-General Voyeikov, the Marshal of the Court, Major-General Prince Dolgorukov, the Emperor's own surgeon Fedorov, the Inspector of the Imperial Trains Yezhov and others — was usually followed by a train for the retinue, which contained high ranking members of the Emperor's retinue and also officers of the escort, a combined regiment, the corps of chasseurs, junior officials of the office of the Imperial Court and the Military Campaign Office, subordinates of the Palace Commandant, clerks, servants and others.

On 23rd August 1915 following the failures of Russian forces on the Western Front Nicholas II

*Alexandra Feodorovna with her daughters. Petrograd. 1915*

When the war began Empress Alexandra Feodorovna and Grand Duchesses Olga and Tatyana Niko- layevna took nursing courses and for a few hours a day worked in the hospital at Tsarskoye Selo tending the wounded. From that time, according to Gilliard's memoirs, they practically never removed their new uniform. "Her Majesty, sometimes with the Emperor, and sometimes alone with the two elder daughters," he wrote, "visited Red Cross institutions in western and central Russia. At her request many military hospitals were created and hospital trains were equipped, specially adapted to take the wounded to the rear, often very slowly because of the great distances... "She tired herself out at the beginning of the war. She expended her energy without counting the cost, with the ardour and passion which she brough to all her undertakings, and, although her health was already seriously undermined, she showed amazing endurance. She seemed to draw great support from carrying out the cause she had taken up; in it she found both a satisfaction of her need for self-sacrifice and forgetfulness of the fears and melancholy with which the Tsesarevich's illness filled her even in periods of calm."

took over as commander-in-chief. "From this date I have taken upon Myself the leadership of all land and naval forces within the theatre of military operations," ran the order sent out to the army and navy, to the text of which the Tsar had made his own addition: "In the firm conviction in God's mercy and with an unbreakable

certainty in a final victory we shall carry out our sacred duty to defend the Motherland to the end and shall not disgrace the land of Russia."

Grand Duke Nikolai Nikolayevich was appointed Governor-General of the Caucasus and Commander-in-Chief of the Caucasian army. In taking all power into his own hands, the Emperor was also assuming all responsibility for the outcome of the war, the fate of the army, and in the last resort of Russia. Once again Nicholas failed to sense where the main danger would come from and where his place should be. Even when he was present at Tsarskoye Selo, a mere twenty versts from Petrograd, he sometimes failed to adequately appreciate events in the capital — when he was far away he simply ceased keeping track of the situation, letting it slip through his fingers, the more so since the correspondence which reached him at Stavka frequently contained distorted information. As a result, trying to raise the fighting spirit of the army, he never even noticed that he was becoming an object of extremely caustic and biting mockery among a people who only the day before had been God-fearing and loyal to their tsar, yet now, on learning that he had been given the Cross of St George, passed an insulting remark around the country: "The Tsar's with George, the Tsarina's with Grigory".

There was a time when it would have been possible to avoid the threatening catastrophe and save the country from chaos, anarchy and great sufferings, but that time had already passed. History, from whose lessons the highest authority, in the person of the monarch, had not benefited, repeated itself, producing a still greater tragedy. While the cries of the wounded and dying on the battlefields of the Far East in 1904—05 had barely reached the capital, now the hot breath of war could be felt in earnest. The number of casualties, measured in hundreds of thousands in the Russo-Japanese War, now began to be reckoned in millions of dead and wounded. But the decisive factor was that again, just as ten years before, the Empire proved unable to stand up to the exhausting rhythm of war. Long before reports of the overthrow of the monarchy spread across the country, the real "revolution" took place in the trenches of the Western Front, where millions of men, often hungry, cold and ragged, without cartridges or shells, cursed their officers and generals, and at the same time also their tsar.

Some time later (in November 1917) one of the officers of the Tsar's army, Lieutenant-Colonel D.V. Focke, happened to take part, as military consultant, in the peace talks between representatives of Germany and what was by then Soviet Russia. In his memoirs Focke described his impressions of the other side of the front line. "The German party," he wrote, "was waiting for us on an area of wooden planking — a little island among the sticky mud that drowned the Russian trenches and no-man's-land. That planking is also a symbol: — We came out to meet you, but we don't want to get stuck in your mud...

"A few paces away from the planking was the parapret of a German trench, which we climbed into by means of some wooden steps. On Russian land, on the same soil, which the protracted Russian autumn had turned into a sticky bog, we entered a different world, with different rules, a different way of life, different possibilities of organizing the underground existence of the front line.

---

*Nicholas II, a Catholic priest and attendants in the area of military operations. 1915*

*Nicholas II reviewing the guard of honour of the 13th Dragoon Regiment, which held the Military Order of Field Marshal-General Münnich. Borkovichi Station. 31st January 1916*

"Nowhere did you have to bend double — the trenches were deep. You did not have to get stuck in the clay — there was a wooden floor everywhere, latticed, not holding back water. There was no danger either that water from weeks of rain would rise to your waist, making the lattices that had failed to save you from it start floating — at every pace they had a little channel to drain the trench. We walked along such a parquetted trench following wire hand-rails for several minutes, able to examine the amenities in the German positions: the walls of the trenches were lined with tin-plate, their living quarters were wallpapered and in some dug-outs they even had soft furniture and home comforts up to and including a piano. There was electricity everywhere, an astonishing abundance of light.

"I learnt that for the quarters of one division the staff have allocated 10,000 light bulbs.

"And the spirit of discipline in these clean shafts of a war, where the director generals and engineer officers direct the efforts of the worker-soldiers, is different from that with us..."

Alas, how different and, sadly, how far less positive things were on the other, Russian side. Not only in the front-line trenches, sticky with the autumn mud, where Russian soldiers "fed the fleas" and died from the lack of elementary medical supplies and drugs as well as from enemy bullets and shells, but also in the rear of the immense country, with every month the war continued, the situation became more and more critical.

By the start of 1917 the war had already been going on more than two and a half years, every day claiming many human lives and vast sums of public money. The collapse in the economy and transport, the number of unemployed and the crisis in food-supplies became ever greater. The increase in police repressions and in lock-outs by factory- and mill-owners, in particular the closure, on 22nd February 1917, for an indefinite period of the Putilov Plant, which threw 30,000 men onto the streets at once, provoked a sharp rise in revolutionary activity. A powerful wave of protests against the force used on the Putilov men coincided with the International Day of Working Women (23rd February Old Style) and the further worsening of the food-supply situation (by the beginning of February there were only ten days reserve of flour left in Petrograd). Anti-government meetings on the square by the

Narva Gate and in other working districts turned into mass rallies and demonstrations on Nevsky Prospekt and the central parts of the capital. The 23rd February, when more than 120,000 striking workers took to the streets of the city, proved to be the first day of the revolution.

From that moment events followed one another like an avalanche. The next day, 24th February, the strikes alredy affected 224 enterprises in Petrograd and 200,00 people were involved. On Saturday 25th February these demonstrations evolved into a general political strike as a result of which transport stopped, all factories and plants and places of learning closed down, and newspapers ceased appearing. Demonstrations many-thousand strong filled the streets and squares of the capital under the slogans "Give us bread!", "Down with the war!" and "Down with autocracy.". It was on this day that the first news of the events that had developed in Petrograd reached Nicholas II at Stavka. In a verbose report sent by cable General Sergei Khabalov, commander of the military district, informed him that in the preceding two days "as a consequence of a lack of bread, strikes have broken out in many works", that "violent actions" had occurred, and listed the military units which had taken part in the "suppression of disorders". The same degree of perspicacity as Khabalov was shown by Protopopov, the Minister of the Interior, who, in also informing the Emperor by cable of the course of events, indicated that the demonstrations had an "unorganized, spontaneous nature; alongside the excesses of their anti-government stance, the disorderly masses hail the troops" (probably the "quick-witted" minister took the cases of "fraternization" between demonstrators and troops which were already happening as the hailing of soldiers loyal to the regime).

Alexandra Feodorovna first wrote to Nicholas about the stormy events taking place in the capital on 24th February: "Yesterday there were disorders on Vasilyevsky Island and on Nevsky, because the poor stormed the bakeries. They smashed Filippov's [bakery] to pieces, and the Cossacks were called out to deal with them. I hope that Kedrinsky [Kerensky — *The authors*] from the Duma is hanged for his terrible speech — it is vital (martial law, state of war) and it will be an example. Everybody craves and begs you to show firmness." In her regular letter of 25th February the Empress also commented on the

events that had developed: "The strikes and disorders in the city are more than provocative... It's a hooligan movement, boys and girls running and shouting that they have no bread — simply to create excitement — and workers who prevent others from working. If the weather was very cold, they would all, probably, be sitting at home. Yet all this will pass and calm down, if only the Duma will behave well. The worst speeches are not being printed, but I think, that it is vital to punish speeches against the dynasty immediately and very severely, the more so, since we are now in a state of war." In the last of the letters quoted Alexandra Feodorovna as usual advised: "Please, go for a minute to the icon of the most pure Virgin and pray calmly for yourself, to gather strength for our family, great and small", and then she again reminded him: "Above all, do your will, my dear."

On the evening of 25th February Khabalov received a telegram back from Stavka: "I command you to stop tomorrow the disorders in the capital, which are intolerable in the difficult time of war with Germany and Austria. Nicholas." Later, when already under arrest, Khabalov said in his statement to the Extraordinary Investigative Commission that this telegram had "left him thunderstruck". "... How was I to stop them? When they said 'Give us bread' — we gave bread and it was over. But now written on the flags there's 'Down with autocracy', what bread is going to calm that down?" Back then though, after receiving the Tsar's order the necessary measures were implemented at once: at an immediately summoned meeting of the chiefs of police and commanders of military units it was proposed that "decisive action" be taken, i.e. to shoot into the crowds after "a warning signal given three times", the bridges over the Neva were placed under guard and additional troops were summoned to the capital. In the early hours of 26th February the *Okhrana* carried out mass arrests in the city; at the same time in the apartment of the Chairman of the Council of Ministers, Prince Nikolai Golitsyn, the Tsar's ministers were meeting. Flustered by what was happening and searching for a way out of the situation that had arisen, they even took a decision to ask the chairman and members of the State Duma to "use their prestige to calm the crowds". But it was all too late already.

On Sunday 26th February the streets of Petrograd were again filled with tens of thousands of

*People in front of the shop of the Society for Fighting High Prices waiting for groceries to arrive. Petrograd. 1916*

*A sugar-ration card from the period of the First World War. Petrograd. 1916*

pcoplc; meetings and demonstrations were going on everywhere. In a number of districts there were clashes with the police and troops who shot into the crowd (in particular, fire was opened on demonstrations on Znamenskaya Square and the corner of Nevsky Prospekt and Sadovaya Street) and hundreds were killed or injured. The mass struggle on the strccts that had gone on for four days in a row, the almost continuous anti-government meetings, the rapidly growing number of cases of "fraternization" with the soldiers finally shattered the main, and probably last, bulwark of tsarist autocracy — the army. On the cvcning of 26th February one of the companies of the Life Guards Pavlovsky Regiment mutinied, in the early hours of the 27th the Volhynsky Regiment revolted, then the Litovsky, Moskovsky, Preobrazhensky and other regiments. These soldiers refused to obey orders from their officers and opened fire on police and Cossacks who were dispersing and shooting at the people. This meant the beginning of the end: the army began to go over onto the side of the revolution.

As early as the morning of 26th February, the Chairman of the State Duma, Mikhail Rodzianko, urgently sent the Tsar an extremely eloquent telegram: "Situation grave. Anarchy in capital. Government paralysed. Transport ... has reached complete breakdown. Public discontent growing. Disorderly shooting occurring on the streets. Military units are firing on each other. Vital to call on a figure trusted by the country to form a new government. No time to lose. Any delay is as good as death. I pray God that in this hour the blame will not fall on Him who wears the crown." However surprising it may be, though, Nicholas II reacted to this more than alarming news with considerable calm. "That fatty Rodzianko," he told Count Fredericks, "has again written all sorts of nonsense to me, and I am not even going to reply." On that day as usual he attended Liturgy, later walked for quite some time along the highway leading to Bobruisk, received a senator, and in the evening played dominoes with his retainers. In a letter to the Empress dated 26th February he wrote: "I hope that Khabalov will be able to stop these street disorders soon. Protopopov should give him clear and definite instructions. Just so long as old Golitsyn doesn't lose his head!" He also reported that he had (as Alix had advised him the day before) visited the icon of the Virgin and touched his nose to Vyrubova's brooch which was pinned to the image. That same day the Emperor signed the decree (dated 25th February) on a suspension of the activities of the State Duma.

In the meantime on 27th February the revolutionary actions in Petrograd developed into an armed uprising embracing the whole city. Some 100,000 soldiers from the Petrograd garrison and sailors from the Baltic Fleet joined the civilians to take practically complete control of the capital. They gained possession of the bridges, mainline railway stations, the most important government and ministerial offices, the telegraph station and the main post-office, the Peter and Paul Fortress and the arsenal, where tens of thousands of rifles and ammunition were stored. Cars and lorries carrying armed workers and soldiers appeared everywhere. Police stations were smashed up, the District Court building set on fire. Political prisoners were released from the prisons that had been taken, while the arrests of tsarist ministers began.

General Khabalov, still trying to organize opposition to the insurrectionists had established himself with a small detachment of troops in the Admiralty building, but he was now forced to lay down his arms. "At about 12 noon on 28th February," the news was passed by telegram to Stavka by General Beliayev, the Minister of War, "the remains of the still loyal units, numbering 4 companies, 1 Cossack *sotnia*, 2 batteries and a machine-gun company... were led out of the Admiralty so as not to cause the destruction of the building. I did not consider it appropriate to transfer these troops to another position in the light of their lack of complete reliability. The units have been returned to barracks..." The streets and squares of the city filled with exultant crowds of people wearing red ribbons and bows, and waving red flags. Almost simultaneously with the military authorities, the tsarist Council of Ministers too was forced to surrender and tender its resignation. In a telegram to Stavka Prince Golitsyn asked the Emperor to meet the demands of the State Duma and form a new "responsible ministry". In Petrograd tsarist authority had already ceased to exist.

Instead, in the afternoon of that same 27th February, in the Tauride Palace divided into two parts, two new organs of power were formed and began to operate. One of them was the Petrograd Council or Soviet of Workers' and Soldiers' Deputies born on the crest of the revolutionary wave. The leader of the Menshevik party, Nikolai Chkheidze, was elected chairman of its executive committee, with, as his deputy, the leader of the Labour Group faction in the Fourth State Duma, Alexander Kerensky. The very next morning, 28th February, saw the appearance of the first issue of *Izvestiya*, the newspaper of the Petrograd Soviet which quickly spread the news of the victorious revolution throughout the country. The other new body which in effect received power from the hands of tsarism in those tense days was the Provisional Committee of the State Duma. After loyally resolving to obey the Emperor's decree on the dissolution of the Duma, at its meeting on the morning of 27th February that body's Council of Elders nevertheless proposed that the members of the Duma did not depart but immediately convene in "private session". In the break between these two meetings Rodzianko sent Nicholas II another anxious telegram in which he reported the complete paralysis of authority and the extremely dangerous development of events and called on the Tsar to acknowledge all that, urgently reconvene the Duma and appoint a new cabinet of ministers that enjoyed the trust of the people. "The government is completely powerless to put down the disorder. The troops of the garrison cannot be relied on. The reserve battalions of the guards regiments are gripped by mutiny. They are killing their officers...," the telegram said. "Sire, do not delay. If the movement spills over to the army, the Germans will be celebrating the downfall of Russia, and with it inevitably the dynasty as well... The hour that will decide your fate and that of our homeland has struck. Tomorrow may already be too late." Yet this, one might say desperate, missive too was received by the Emperor with equal indifference and even left unanswered.

In the afternoon of 27th February, then, the members of the State Duma met in "private session". An expressive word-picture of this session, the confusion of figures in the Duma and their fear of the revolution was painted by Vasily Shulgin in his memoirs: "So as to stress that this was a private meeting of members of the Duma and not a session of the State Duma as such, it was decided to assemble not in the large White Hall, but in the semicircular one ... There was barely room for us: the entire Duma was present. Behind the table sat Rodzianko and the elders. Round them the others sat and stood, crowded together, tightly packed... Alarmed, agitated, somehow mentally clinging to each other... Even people who had been enemies for many years suddenly felt that, for all of them, there was something that was equally dangerous, threatening and repugnant... That something was the street... the mob in the street... Its approaching breath could already be felt... From the streets came the thing that very few thought of then, but that very many, probably, sensed unconsciously, since they were pale, their hearts seized... Along the street, surrounded by the many-thousand strong crowd, Death was on the march..." After a stormy discussion of what was to be done, more or less undifferent solutions to the question of power (from the establishment of a military dictatorship to declaring the Duma a constituent assembly) general support was won by a proposal to form a Provisional Committee of twelve men headed by Rodzianko "for the maintenance of order in Petrograd and dealings with various bodies and individuals". "Fear of the street" as Shulgin acknowledged drove not only him, a convinced monarchist and nationalist, to join this Duma committee, but also the leaders of the middle-class, landowners' parties, the Constitutional Democrats Pavel Miliukov and Nikolai Nekrasov, the Octobrists V.N. Lvov and S.I. Shidlovsky, the Progressives I.N. Yefremov, V.A. Rzhevsky and others, and even (and this was particularly important for the subsequent course of events and the formation of a Provisional Government for Russia), the Social-Democrat Chkheidze and the Labourist Kerensky. Yet, having formed a Provisional Committee, this "private gathering" of Duma members broke up, without making any definite decision on the main question — what form was the new state power in the country to take. It was decided to await the Emperor's reply to the telegram sent to Stavka. Late in the evening of 27th February Nicholas II's reply did arrive, addressed to the last tsarist prime-minister Prince Golitsyn.

Alas, Nicholas had still not grasped the real meaning of events. Stubbornly not wishing to acknowledge that what was happening in the capital was not some "disorders" in isolated "recuperating companies", but a very real revolution, the Tsar as before gave no thought to the search for a rational compromise, but continued to follow the advice of his consort and to carry out "his will". Obstinately refusing to accept the suggestions put forward in numerous telegrams from Rodzianko, Generals Khabalov and Beliayev and the advice of General Alexeyev, and even his own brother Grand Duke Mikhail Alexandrovich, to make immediate concessions to the insurgent people and agree to the formation of a parliamentary government, the Emperor also categorically rejected the last loyal petition of the utterly frightened Council of Ministers regarding its resignation and the formation of a cabinet answerable to the Duma, telling Golitsyn by telegram: "Regarding changes in personnel [in the government — *The authors*] in the present circumstances I consider them unacceptible." In the same telegram he informed him that he had appointed an "Overall Head for Petrograd". This man, whom, as Nicholas wrote in his diary on 28th February "I am sending to Petrograd with troops to establish order", was Nikolai Ivanov, the Adjutant-General of the Royal Suite, who had "distinguished" himself by his harshness as long ago as the suppression of the first Russian revolution.

Already on 28th February the new commander-in-chief of the Petrograd military district "with emergency powers" set off at the head of a battalion of knights of St George in the direction of St Petersburg, reaching Tsarskoye Selo. On the orders of the Tsar General Ivanov was to have at his disposal four infantry regiments, four cavalry regiments and two machine-gun detachments, drawn half from the Northern Front, half from the Western. Additionally General Mikhail Alexeyev, the chief of the headquarters staff at

*Alexander Kerensky, Chairman of the Council of Ministers of the Provisional Government. Petrograd. 21st August 1917*

Stavka, ordered a further three regiments to be sent to Petrograd from the South-West Front. Later, in the twenties, Alexeyev authoritatively stated in his memoirs: "The operative, military element went into the background; the war was forgotten, before our eyes was only the internal political aspect... It was the lot of the troops moved to Petrograd under Ivanov's command to keep all the army in order."

We can see then that Nicholas II, his generals and others with him at Stavka were actively preparing to suppress the revolution. But the hope of "establishing order" in the insurgent capital with the help of troops was dashed. General Ivanov himself reached Tsarskoye Selo with his detachment but he did not have sufficient forces at his disposal to proceed. The conduct of a punitive expedition against Petrograd and the elimination of the "outrage" was hindered by revolutionary disturbances (including those

among railway workers) and mass defections of military units to the side of the revolution. The same circumstances also thwarted Nicholas's own attempt to travel with his retinue to Tsarskoye Selo: the two trains (marked with the letters "A" for the Tsar and "B" for his retinue) that set off on the Tsar's order were forced to return to the headquarters of the Northern Front. "In the night we turned back from Malaya Vishera, since Liuban and Tosno turned out to be occupied by insurrectionaries," Nicholas wrote of this in his diary on 1st March. "We went to Valdai, Dno and Pskov, where we stopped for the night. Gatchina and Luga also proved to be occupied. Shame and disgrace! Didn't manage to reach Tsarskoye."

New troubles awaited the Tsar in Pskov. By this time it had become absolutely clear both to the senior staff at Stavka under General Alexeyev and the commander-in-chief of the Northern Front Adjutant-General Nikolai Ruzsky, both of whom were in constant telegraphic contact with Petrograd and with Rodzianko in particular, that the only way out of a critical situation was for the Emperor to make all possible concessions. The telegram from General Alexeyev handed to Nicholas at 10.20 p.m. on 1st March stated: "Information being received gives grounds for hoping that members of the Duma, led by Rodzianko, may still be able to prevent a general collapse and that work with them might go well." The same telegram contained the text of a draft manifesto composed at Stavka which it was suggested that the Tsar issue. It proclaimed the formation of a cabinet answerable to the representatives of the people and to be headed by Rodzianko. When General Alexeyev received a return telegram in which the Tsar conveyed his royal consent to "publish the manifesto presented, as being issued in Pskov" it seemed for a moment at Stavka and in the headquarters of the Northern Front that the worst was already behind them.

But the two-hour conversation which took place on a direct line later that night between Rodzianko and Ruzsky quickly dashed barely kindled hopes. Contrary to expectations, the Tsar's agreement to the creation of a "responsible ministry" — something that only recently had been so fervently desired — failed to delight the Chairman of the State Duma when he was informed of it. This belated concession was already insufficient to stop the raging tide of revolt. "One of the most dreadful of revolutions has been in the offing, and it will not be that easy to avert it," Rodzianko said, "... what you are proposing is already inadequate, even the question of the dynasty is being put point-blank. I doubt if it will be possible to cope with this." Later he told the general: "I'm hanging by a thread myself... Anarchy has reached such a pitch that tonight I was forced to appoint a Provisional Government. The time has been missed, there is no turning back." Ruzsky immediately informed Alexeyev at Stavka of his nocturnal conversation with Rodzianko. Recognizing that "there is no choice and the Emperor's abdication should take place", Alexeyev sent urgent telegrams straight away to the commanders-in-chief of all the fronts, in which it was suggested that they express their opinion without delay by telegram to the Tsar at Pskov.

*Pavel Miliukov, member of the State Duma, one of the organizers of the Constitutional Democratic Party (Cadets) and Minister of Foreign Affairs in the Provisional Government, speaking in the State Duma. Petrograd. 1915*

Meanwhile, despite all the attempts of the Duma's Provisional Committee to establish control over the course of events, its chairman Rodzianko himself acknowledged that he was "far from successful": real authority had come to rest in the hands of the Petrograd Soviet. The true balance of power between the Duma committee at first, and then also the Provisional Government, and the forces of revolutionary workers and soldiers is probably best pictured from a letter written early in March by the new Minister of War, Alexander Guchkov, to General Alexeyev at Stavka. "I ask you to believe that the real state of affairs is as follows: 1) The Provisional Government exercises no real power and its orders are carried out only to the extent that this is permitted by the Soviet of Workers' and Soldiers' Deputies, who exercise the most important elements of real power, since the troops, the railroads, the post-office and the telegraph are in their hands. To put it directly, the Provisional Government exists only as long as it is permitted to by the Soviet of Workers' and Soldiers' Deputies. In particular, in the military department it presently appears possible to give only such orders as do not radically run contrary to the decisions of the above-mentioned Soviet." Under such circumstances it became clear once and for all to the leaders of the liberal-bourgeois and bourgeois-land owning parties who on 2nd March formed a Provisional Government with the agreement of the Socialist Revolutionary leadership of the Petrograd Soviet that it would be utterly impossible to leave Nicholas on the throne even as a constitutional monarch. "That Nicholas II was not going to reign any more was something beyond dispute for the widest circles of Russian society," the Constitutional Democrat leader Miliukov wrote in his memoirs. Nevertheless the majority of leading figures in the Duma strove to retain the royal dynasty in Russia with the throne passing to the Tsar's son and heir Alexis. And this striving prompted them to take action.

Late in the night of 1st March Guchkov drove to the Duma in the Tauride Palace. "And here that matter in particular was decided," Shulgin described events in detail in his memoirs. "We were not at full strength at that time. Rodzianko was there, and Miliukov and I — I cannot remember the rest... But I do remember that neither Kerensky nor Chkheidze were present. We were amongst ourselves. And so Guchkov spoke absolutely freely." What did Guchkov have to tell this confidential nocturnal gathering? He told them that they must decide on something, something big that "could get us out of a terrible situation with the least losses", that "in this chaos, in everything that is done, we must think above all of saving the monarchy", that "without the monarchy Russia cannot survive". It was impossible, though, for Nicholas to continue ruling — his orders simply would not be carried out. Consequently there was only one way out — the abdication of the present sovereign. Otherwise "all this revolutionary rabble will begin to look for a way out themselves... And settle matters with the monarchy themselves..." Rodzianko spoke next and explained that he had intended to travel on the morning of 1st March to hold discussions to that end with the Tsar, but he had changed his mind in the light of the demands of the Petrograd Soviet that he be accompanied by Chkheidze and a battalion of revolutionary soldiers. Then Guchkov proposed another plan:

*Yuri Miliutin* (seated), *Vice-Chairman of the St Petersburg City Duma, and Alexander Guchkov, member of the State Duma. St Petersburg. 1913*

"We must act secretly and quickly, asking nobody and taking no one's advice... We must present them with a *fait accompli*. We must give Russia a new sovereign." After general consent it was decided that Guchkov would go together with Shulgin who finally specified matters: "The Committee of the State Duma recognizes the only way out in the present situation is the abdication of the Emperor, entrusts the two of us with conveying this to His Majesty and, in the event that he agrees, with bringing the act of abdication to Petrograd. The abdication should be made in favour of the heir Tsesarevich Alexis Nikolayevich. We should travel the two of us alone, in complete secrecy." Early in the morning of 2nd March, unbeknown to the Petrograd Soviet, the Duma's envoys — Alexander Guchkov, a representative of the liberal bourgeois circles and the monarchist Vasily Shulgin — left for Pskov.

Meanwhile General Ruzsky had informed Nicholas II of his night time talk with the Chairman of the State Duma. Besides the transcript of this conversation, the Emperor was soon acquainted with the contents of telegrams from the commanders-in-chief of the fronts received in response to Alexeyev's inquiry mentioned earlier. All the generals — including Brusilov (Southern Front), Evert (Western Front) and even Grand Duke Nikolai Nikolayevich (Caucasus Front) — despite their different choice of words, all equally loyal, unanimously recommended the Tsar — for the sake of saving the dynasty and Russia — to abdicate from the throne in favour of Tsesarevich Alexis with Grand Duke Mikhail Alexandrovich as regent.

Curious enough to set it apart was the telegram which reached General Ruzsky at the headquarters of the Northern Front with some delay from General Sakharov, the commander-in-chief of the Romanian Front. The main body of his message was ardent in its expressions of loyalty: "Adjutant-General Alexeyev has confided to me the criminal and outrageous reply the Chairman of the State Duma gave you in response to the most gracious decision of Our Sovereign Emperor to grant the country a responsible ministry and has invited the commanders-in-chief to report to His Majesty through you their position in regard to the situation that has arisen. My warm love for His Majesty will not permit my heart to reconcile itself to the possibility of realizing the vile suggestion conveyed to you by the Chairman of the State Duma. I am certain that it was not the Russian people, who have never laid hands upon their Tsar, who thought up this evil, but the roguish handful of people going by the name of the State Duma who treacherously used a convenient moment to carry out their criminal ends. I am certain that the armies at the front would stand steadfast for their sovereign leader, were they not called to the defence of the Motherland from an outside enemy and were they not in the hands of those same state criminals who have seized the sources of the army's life. Such are the motions of my heart and soul." The remaining text of the despatch is such a turnabout that we can only read astonished at how the artful General managed "with tears in his eyes" to start on a happy note and finish on a sad one: "Passing on to the logic of reason and considering the hopelessness of the situation that has arisen, I, a steadfastly loyal subject of His Majesty, with tears in my eyes, am forced to say that, probably, the least painful way out for the country and for the retention of our capacity to fight the external enemy is a decision to meet the conditions already stated, so that procrastination might not prepare the ground for further and still viler pretentions."

So we see, not a single front, not a single army declared a desire to defend their sovereign emperor. Nicholas found himself not only without troops, but even without generals, and Alexeyev presented the Tsar with the already prepared draft of his abdication. This is what Nicholas himself wrote about all this in his diary entry for the first part of 2nd March: "This morning Ruzsky came and read through his extremely long telephone conversation with Rodzianko. From his words the situation in Petrograd is such that now a government drawn from the Duma would be powerless to do anything since it is being fought against by the soc[ial-dem]ocratic party in the guise of a workers' committee. My abdication is required. Ruzsky reported this conversation to Stavka and Alexeyev passed it on to all the commanders-in-chief. By 1/2 past 2 answers had come from all of them. The gist is that, for the sake of saving the Motherland and the maintenance of peace among the armies at the front, this step must be decided upon. I agreed. A draft of the manifesto has been sent from Stavka..."

Thus deprived of any real support, whether political, military or from his family (Alexandra Feodorovna and their children were at Tsarskoye Selo, you will recall) — not counting his small handful of noble retainers and adjutants — Nicholas II was obliged to agree to abdicate in favour of his son with his younger brother Mikhail as regent. Nevertheless it would seem that at this point the Tsar had still not given up hope of a chance to postpone or even alter the decision that he had taken. In this light it would probably be of some interest to learn what Alexandra Feodorovna was thinking as it is recorded in her letters to the Tsar written on 2nd March. In our opinion, these probably reflect the feelings that then gripped both the royal couple, since it is well known that their views seldom diverged.

"Everything is abominable and events are developing with colossal speed," the Empress wrote in the first of her letters that day. "But I firmly believe — and nothing will shake my belief — that everything will be all right. Especially since I received your telegram this morning — the first ray of sunshine in this mire." But for the present the situation was worse than poor. "Not knowing where you were, I acted in the end through Stavka, as Rodzianko pretended not to know why you were held up. It's clear that they do not want you to see me before you sign some paper or other, a constitution or some other horror of that kind. And you're alone, without the army behind you, caught like a mouse in a trap, what can you do? It is utterly base and mean, unparalleled in history — to detain one's sovereign." Alexandra Feodorovna then gives the Tsar what would seem like thoroughly judicious advice, without, incidentally, knowing what he had learnt from the telegrams of the commanders-in-chief: "Perhaps you will show yourself to the troops at Pskov and other places and gather them around you?" But the main thing the Empress went on to urge her husband was to remember, "If they force you to concessions then you are not in the least obliged to fulfill them, because they were obtained by unworthy methods." Here too she gave expression to what was obviously her innermost hope: "Two tendencies — the Duma and the revolutionaries — two snakes, which I hope will bite off each other's heads — that would save the situation." And in a postscript to the main body of the letter she gave the Tsar one more telling piece of advice: "Wear His [Rasputin's — *The authors*] cross, even if it's awkward for others, for my peace of mind."

In another letter to Nicholas also dated 2nd March, Alexandra Feodorovna again expounded the ideas she had expressed previously: "Nothing can divide us, although that is precisely what they want and that is why they are unwilling to allow you to see me, until you sign their papers about a responsible ministry or a constitution. It's a nightmare that, without the army behind you, you might be obliged to do it. But such a promise will have no force, once power is back in your hands. They have meanly caught you, like a mouse in a trap — something unheard of in history."

It would seem that the Empress either had an inadequate knowledge or a very personal interpretation of history. She considered it far more important to observe unswervingly the age-old tradition of all autocrats — to regard any obligation on them as nothing more than a piece of paper, which at a convenient moment could be torn up and thrown away, as had indeed been done in the past. For example, in the eighteenth century Empress Anna had behaved just this way after her accession to the throne with the "conditions" of the Supreme Secret Council which she had had to accept to get there, so too, much more recently, had Nicholas himself with the manifesto of 17th October 1905.

This attitude explains why, when soon after 3 p.m. General Ruzsky informed the Emperor of a despatch just received from Petrograd about Guchkov and Shulgin leaving for Pskov, Nicholas immediately gave orders not to send the telegrams giving his consent to abdication already prepared for transmission to Rodzianko and Alexeyev. The news of the imminent arrival of envoys from the Duma, particularly Shulgin who was known for his monarchist convictions, revived the hope in the Tsar that all was not yet lost. Late in the evening of 2nd March a train pulled into the main station at Pskov with a single carriage containing Guchkov and Shulgin, who were eagerly awaited. "At about 10 in the evening Colonel Mordvinov, the Emperor's aide-de-camp, Colonel the Duke of Leuchtenberg and I," General D.N. Dubensky wrote in his memoirs *How the Coup Took Place in Russia,* "went out onto the platform where the deputies' train was to arrive. In a few minutes it drew in. From the brightly lit saloon-car two soldiers with red armbands and rifles leapt out and stood either side of the carriage steps... After this first Guchkov, then Shulgin descended from the carriage, both wearing winter overcoats. Guchkov turned to us to ask how to get to General Ruzsky, but he was told, by Colonel Mordvinov, I think, that he was to proceed directly to His Majesty's carriage." On the way to the royal train which was standing in the sidings, Mordvinov enquired "What *is* going on in Petrograd?"

Shulgin's reply was far from heartening: "What's happening in Petrograd is unimaginable... We are entirely in their hands and we shall probably be arrested when we return." Shulgin, who was noted for his exceptional talent as a writer and publicist, has left us in his memoir sketches *Days* a detailed, eloquent and, most important, truthful account of the way in which Nicholas II's abdication took place that night of 2nd March in the saloon-car of the Russian Emperor's train.

"Our overcoats were taken off us. We went into the carriage. It was a large saloon-car. Green silk on the walls... A few tables... An old, tall, thin general yellowish grey with aiglets... That was Baron Fredericks...

"'The Emperor will come through in a moment... His Majesty is in the other carriage...' Things became even more dismal and difficult... The Tsar appeared at the door... He was wearing a grey Circassian coat... I had not expected to see him like that... His face? Calm... We bowed. The Emperor greeted us and shook hands. The gesture was friendly rather than otherwise...

"'What about Nikolai Vladimirovich?' Somebody said that General Ruzsky had asked him to say he would be a little late.

"'Then we shall begin without him.' The Tsar gestured for us to sit... The Tsar took a seat one side of a small rectangular table placed up against the green silk wall. Guchkov sat on another side of the table. I was alongside Guchkov, diagonally across from the Emperor. Baron Fredericks was opposite the Tsar...

"Guchkov spoke. He was deeply agitated. He was obviously speaking well-thought-out words, but had trouble dealing with his emotion. He spoke unevenly ... and flatly.

"The Emperor sat leaning slightly on the silk wall and looked straight in front of him. His face was completely calm and inscrutable. I did not take my eyes off him. He had changed greatly from before... Lost weight... but that was not it... No, it was that around his blue eyes the skin was brown and all criss-crossed with the little brown lines of wrinkles. And in that instant I felt that brown skin with its wrinkles was a mask, not the real face of the Emperor, and his real one was perhaps rarely seen by anybody, perhaps the others had never seen it, not even once...

"Guchkov spoke about what was happening in Petrograd. He became a little more in control of himself... He had a habit of slightly covering his forehead with his hand when he was speaking as if to concentrate, and he did it now. He did not look at the Emperor, but spoke as if addressing some inner figure, sitting inside himself. As if he were speaking to his conscience. He spoke the truth, exaggerating nothing and keeping nothing back. He spoke of what we had all seen in Petrograd. There was nothing else he could say...

"The Emperor looked straight in front of him, calm, absolutely inscrutable. The only thing it seemed to me one might have read in his face was: 'This long speech is superfluous...' At this point General Ruzsky came in and took a seat between Baron Fredericks and me... That same moment, I think, I noticed that another general was sitting in the corner of the room, black-haired

with white shoulder straps... That was General Danilov. Guchkov again became agitated. He came to the point that perhaps the only way out of the situation was to abdicate... General Ruzsky whispered to me: "'That matter's been decided...'

"Guchkov finished. The Emperor replied. After A.I.'s [Guchkov's] agitated words his voice sounded calm, simple and precise. Only the accent was slightly strange — like a guardsman:

"'I have taken the decision to abdicate... Up until three today I thought I could abdicate in favour of my son Alexis... But at this time I have changed my decision in favour of my brother Mikhail... I hope you will understand a father's feelings...' The last sentence was spoken more quietly..."

The Tsar's decision to renounce the throne not only for himself but also on behalf of the Tsesarevich was wholly unexpected for all present, and moreover was not in accordance with the law on succession. But at that moment these were mere "details". It was far more important to effect the voluntary abdication as quickly as possible, to set the revolutionary wave in disarray and at the same time attempt to preserve the royal dynasty in Russia. For all the participants of the meeting this was the main thing, which meant there was no need to discuss legal niceties, although the Tsar rejected the draft abdication manifesto presented by the envoys of the Duma and, declaring that he would draw up his own text for the document, went off into his carriage.

When Nicholas returned to the saloon some time later, General Danilov stated in his memoirs, he "brought with him the text of the manifesto typed on several blank telegram forms. As far as I recall, it was the draft drawn up at Stavka, only slightly amended in accordance with the Emperor's last decision." This was indeed the text of the unsent telegram to General Alexeyev at Stavka. In a voice muffled by emotion Guchkov read the text out loud, then, at the request of the Duma envoys and with Nicholas's agreement Shulgin inserted a few clarifying words. Finally, bearing in mind that "the deputies return journey is fraught with risk", Guchkov suggested that to be sure more than one copy of the manifesto should be signed. Nicholas agreed to this request too and besides that wrote then and there the text of two decrees to the Ruling Senate: one at Ruzsky's suggestion appointing Grand Duke Nikolai Nikolayevich supreme commander-in-chief, the other asked for by Guchkov and

Shulgin appointing Prince Georgi Lvov chairman of the Council of Ministers.

Although Nicholas signed all three documents almost simultaneously at about midnight on 2nd March, they were all dated 3 p.m., which understandably was intended to attest to the independent and voluntary nature of the Tsar's decision to abdicate even before the arrival of Guchkov and Shulgin from Petrograd. We see then that in the course of a single day Nicholas II signed three different documents: at about 2 a.m on 2nd March the manifesto on "the granting of a responsible ministry", at 3 p.m. his abdication in favour of his son Alexis with his brother Grand Duke Mikhail Alexandrovich as regent, and between 11 p.m. and midnight of the same day the abdication in favour of his brother Mikhail.

"After talking for a few minutes more, the Emperor said farewell to everyone, shook our hands affably and left for his own carriage. That was the last time I saw the former Emperor," General Danilov recollected. "We all began to leave the carriage... Bringing up the rear, I glanced back to take a last look at the now empty saloon that had been mute witness to such a significant event. A small decorative clock hanging on the wall of the carriage showed a quarter to twelve. There were crumpled scraps of paper scattered over the red carpeted floor... The chairs had been moved back to stand in a disorderly manner against the walls... In the middle of the carriage an empty space gaped glaringly, as if a coffin containing a body had just been removed from it!.."

Two copies of the manifesto on the abdication of Nicholas II were produced: the first — typed on telegram forms — remained with General Ruzsky, the second retyped on a large separate sheet was given to the envoys of the State Duma who had to sign for it: *Royal manifesto of 2nd March 1917 received, Alexander Guchkov, Shulgin.*

The final version of the manifesto read as follows:

Stavka

To the Chief of Staff

In the days of the great struggle against an external enemy who has been striving for almost three years to enslave our homeland, the Lord has been pleased to impose on Russia a new terrible trial. The popular domestic disturbances that have begun threaten to have a calamitous effect on the further conduct of the stubborn war. The fate of Russia, the honour of our heroic army, the well-being of the people, all the future of our dear homeland demand that the war be prosecuted to its victorious end, cost that what it may. The savage enemy is straining his last strength, and the hour is already close when our valourous army together with our glorious allies will be able to break the enemy once and for all. In these decisive days in the life of Russia, we have considered it a duty of conscience to ease our people's establishment of close unity and the consolidation of all the nation's forces to achieve victory in the shortest time and, in agreement with the State Duma, we have acknowledged that it will be of benefit to abdicate from the throne of the Russian State and to lay aside the supreme power. Not wishing to be parted from our beloved son, we transfer our inheritance to our brother Grand Duke Mikhail Alexandrovich and bless him on his accession to the throne of the Russian State. We enjoin our brother to manage the affairs of state in full and unbreakable unity with the representatives of the people in the legislative institutions, on such principles as shall be established by them, taking an unbreakable oath to that effect. In the name of our dearly beloved country we call on all loyal sons of the Motherland to fulfill their sacred duty to her through obedience to the Tsar in this grave time of trials for all the nation, and to help him together with the representatives of the people to lead the Russian State onto the road of victory, prosperity and glory. May the Lord our God grant Russia His aid.

*Pskov*                                            *Nicholas*
2nd March 15 hours 5 minutes 1917
Minister of the Imperial Court
Adjutant-General Count Fredericks

The text of the manifesto (and also the contents of the two decrees to the Senate) was immediately telegraphed to Stavka and to the Chairman of the Provisional Government in Petrograd, and then — on 5th March — published in the *Bulletin of the Provisional Government.* On reading the document one is immediately struck by some glaring inconsistencies. For some reason the text opens with the word "Stavka" and the entire document so important for the whole of Russia as a whole and intended for all its population was also, for reasons completely incomprehensible for its contemporary readers, addressed personally to one definite individual — the "Chief of Staff". The explanation is fairly simple, though. It has already been mentioned that in the afternoon of 2nd March General

Alexeyev sent the Emperor a draft act of abdication; this draft, however, did not meet with Nicholas's approval and a different version of the manifesto was drawn up there and then on the royal train. Prepared for sending to Stavka as a telegram to the Chief of Staff of the Supreme Commander-in-Chief, Mikhail Alexeyev, the document, as we have seen, then remained unsent. Later this selfsame text — retyped, but retaining the telegram form including the addressee — was signed by Nicholas II, countersigned by Count Fredericks, Minister of the Imperial Court, and, finally, entrusted to Guchkov and Shulgin who set off back to Petrograd about three in the morning. Roughly an hour earlier the two lettered trains had left Pskov to journey via Dvinsk to Mogilev, bringing the former Russian Emperor and his retinue back to Stavka. The concluding part of Nicholas's diary entry for 2nd March is eloquently laconic: "... In the evening Guchkov and Shulgin arrived from Petrograd, I had discussions with them and gave them the signed and reworked manifesto. At 1 a.m. left Pskov with a heavy feeling from the experience.

"Treachery and cowardice and deceit all around!"

By that time revolutionary events had reached such a pitch that not merely the question of Nicholas II's personal abdication was on the order of the day, but also that of the total elimination of the monarchy in Russia. Even in the course of 2nd March the "Petersburg moods", to use Miliukov's phrase, continued their progress leftward. The Cadet leader came to feel this particularly strongly as a result of one incident. In the afternoon he had addressed a crowd that had gathered in the Column Hall of the Tauride Palace and spoken in support of the idea of Nicholas abdicating in favour of the heir Alexis with the Tsar's brother Mikhail as regent, but that same evening a group of agitated officers sought him out when he was with Rodzianko and declared that they were unable to return to their units unless Miliukov repudiated his words. The new Minister of the Interior was forced to declare that he had expressed only his own personal opinion — although in reality what he had said reflected the position of the majority of the Duma. Given the powerful expressions of antimonarchist sentiment among the masses, the leading figures in the State Duma and the newly-formed Provisional Government realized that it would be useless and even harmful to publish

*The seal of the Provisional Government, Petrograd, 1917*

the former Tsar's manifesto on his abdication. It was precisely for this reason that in the series of regular direct conversations with General Ruzsky, the commander of the Northern Front, Rodzianko stressed above all the extreme importance of not making public the manifesto on the abdication and transfer of power to Grand Duke Mikhail Alexandrovich. "A mutiny has flared up unexpectedly for all of us among the soldiers, the like of which I have never seen," the Chairman of the State Duma said. "You could only hear in the crowd: Land and freedom, Down with the dynasty, Down with the Romanovs, Down with the officers." Rodzianko went on to explain that proclaiming Mikhail Alexandrovich emperor would only "pour oil on the fire... We will lose and let slip all power and there will be no one to calm the popular unrest."

Concurrently with these discussions Miliukov barely managed to telephone Shulgin at an intermediate station and warn him, that to make the manifesto known was not opportune. When on their return to Petrograd the Duma envoys nevertheless attempted to announce the transfer of power to His Imperial Majesty Mikhail II at meetings in the halls of the station and in the railway workshops, the indignant workers and employees all but arrested them.

From the morning of that same day leading members of the Duma's Provisional Committee headed by Rodzianko and ministers of the newly formed Provisional Government (Prince Lvov,

195

Miliukov, Guchkov, Tereshchenko, Kerensky and others) began to gather in the apartment of retired General Prince Putiatin on Millionnaya Street, where Grand Duke Mikhail Alexandrovich had been staying since the last days of February. The meeting took place in an atmosphere of apprehension that news which had already begun to spread of the talks with Nicholas in Pskov and of the preservation of the Romanov dynasty would provoke a new explosion of indignation from the revolutionary masses. It had become clear to the majority of those assembled that tsarist autocracy had utterly discredited itself and its fate was predetermined. Miliukov and Guchkov alone spoke out against the abolition of the monarchy (the former in particular spoke of the necessity of urgently leaving for Moscow so as to gather military forces for the defence of the new emperor). Grand Duke Mikhail Alexandrovich, weighing up all the pros and cons, decided to renounce (conditionally, it is true — pending the decision of a future Constituent Assembly) the supreme power.

"The Grand Duke came out," Shulgin wrote of the event in his memoirs. "It was about twelve noon... We understood that the moment had come. He walked as far as the middle of the room. We crowded around him. He said:

"'Under these circumstances I cannot accept the throne, because...' He never finished, because... because... and burst into tears. The Grand Duke went to his room. We began to talk of how to word the abdication."

The complete text of this document — a renunciation with a first draft in which Nekrasov, Kerensky and Shulgin participated and with a final formulation by the noted politicians and lawyers Vladimir Nabokov and A.E. Nolde — reads:

A heavy burden has been laid on me by my brother's will in transferring to me the Imperial throne of All Russia at a time of an unprecedented war and of unrest among the people. Inspired by the thought common to the whole nation, that the well-being of our homeland comes above all, I have taken the hard decision to accept supreme power only in the event that it shall be the will of our great people, who in nationwide voting must elect their representatives to a Constituent Assembly, establish a new form of government and new fundamental laws for the Russian State. Therefore, calling on God's blessing, I ask all citizens of the Russian State to obey the provisional government which has formed and been invested with complete power on the initiative of the State Duma, until a Constituent Assembly, to be convened in the shortest possible time on the basis of general, direct, equal, secret ballot, express the will of the people in its decision on a form of government.

Signed *Mikhail*

3rd March 1917, Petrograd

Soon after the train carrying the former Tsar arrived in Mogilev late in the evening of 3rd March, General Alexeyev reported the latest news to him, which he had learned from Rodzianko. "It turns out Misha has abdicated," Nicholas wrote in his diary before going to sleep. His manifesto ends with tailpiece calling for the election of a Constituent Assembly in six months. God knows what got into him to sign such trash!"

Meanwhile, in the early hours of 4th March in the Tauride Palace in Petrograd two historic documents were finally being prepared for simultaneous official publication: the *Act on the abdication of Emperor Nicholas II from the throne of the Russian state in favour of Grand Duke Mikhail Alexandrovich* and the *Act on the renunciation by Grand Duke Mikhail Alexandrovich of the adoption of supreme power and on the acknowledgement of the complete power of the Provisional Government that has formed on the initiative of the State Duma*. More than three hundred years of autocratic rule by Romanov monarchs in Russia had come to an end. This fact was, incidentally, far from being realized by all involved. When Grand Duke Pavel Alexandrovich, the younger brother of Alexander III and commander of the First Guards Corps, was summoned by the Empress to the palace on 3rd March, he had as he recalled "a fresh copy of *Izvestiya* in my hands containing the manifesto on the abdication. I read it out to Alexandra Feodorovna. She had known nothing about the abdication. When I finished reading, she exclaimed:

"'I don't believe it; it's all rubbish. Newspaper invention. I believe in God and the army. They still haven't deserted us.'

"I was obliged to explain to the disgraced Tsarina that not just God, but all the army too had joined the revolutionaries."

Nevertheless, even knowing of Nicholas's abdication, Alexandra Feodorovna wrote to him on 3rd March 1917: "Pavel [Alexandrovich] was just here — told me everything. I fully understand your action, o, my hero! I know you could not sign something opposed to what you swore at your coronation. We know each other perfectly, we have no need of words and, I swear by my life, we shall see you on your throne again, carried back by your people and troops to the glory of your reign." Truly, hope dies last...

*Grand Duke Nicholas Alexandrovich. 1870s*

*The Heir Apparent Nicholas Alexandrovich and his attendants visiting Greece. 1890*

*Alix of Hesse. Darmstadt. 1888*

*Grand Duke Tsesarevich Nicholas Alexandrovich
with his bride Alix of Hesse. Coburg. 1894*

Лобунь. 1894.

# Grand Duchess Elizabeth (Yelizaveta) Feodorovna

Grand Duchess Elizabeth (Yelizaveta) Feodorovna (1864—1918), the daughter of Grand Duke Ludwig IV of Hesse-Darmstadt, was the older sister of the last Russian Empress, Alexandra Feodorovna. As the wife of Grand Duke Sergei Alexandrovich from 1884, she undoubtedly played a special role in the relationship and eventual marriage between Alix of Hesse and the heir to the Russian throne.

A deeply religious woman, "highly respected and extremely unfortunate" as Witte characterized her, Elizabeth Feodorovna devoted herself with great enthusiasm to charitable deeds, founding and financing a whole series of institutions and committees dealing with such matters.

From 1891, when Sergei Alexandrovich moved to Moscow as governor-general, she was mainly active in the old capital. During the Russo-Japanese War the Grand Duchess had several hospital trains fitted out at her own expense. She visited the hospitals daily and provided material support for the widows and orphans of fallen soldiers.

After her husband's murder in 1905 by the anarchist Ivan Kaliayev — for whom with her inherent magnanimity she pleaded unsuccessfully for mercy from the Tsar — Elizabeth Feodorovna divided her fortune into three unequal parts, for the State, her husband's heirs and charitable needs, and founded a convent in Moscow, known as the Convent of SS Martha and Mary after the church constructed there in 1911. Working under its auspices eventually were an exemplary hospital with the best doctors in the city, a free out-patients department, pharmacy, a shelter for young girls, a library and more besides. At the beginning of the World War some of the sisters, who had grown to number 97 by 1914, went to serve in field hospitals.

Elizabeth Feodorovna was arrested in April 1918. Her last place of confinement was the ill-starred school at Alapayevsk, sixty versts from Yekaterinburg. Together with other members of the Romanov family she was executed in the night between 17th and 18th July 1918. An eyewitness reported that she left this life with Jesus' words on her lips: "Father, forgive them, for they know not what they do."

*Grand Duchess Elizabeth Feodorovna. St Petersburg. 1887.*
*Photograph by Bergamasco*

*Nicholas II with his wife Alexandra Feodorovna. St Petersburg. 1894.*
*Photograph by Pasetti*

*Alexandra Feodorovna and her sister Grand Duchess Elizabeth Feodorovna.*
*Tsarskoye Selo. Mid-1890s. Photograph by K.E. von Gan*

*Grand Duke Sergei Alexandrovich with his wife Grand Duchess Elizabeth Feodorovna.*
*St Petersburg. 1884*

*Nicholas II and Alexandra Feodorovna. Tsarskoye Selo. 1894.*
*Photograph by K.E. von Gan*

*Emperor Nicholas II. St Petersburg. 1894.*
*Photograph by Zdobnov*

*Empress Alexandra Feodorovna. St Petersburg. 1894.*
*Photograph by Zdobnov*

*Cavalry regiment on Palace Square in front of the Winter Palace.*
*St Petersburg. Late 19th century*

*Great courtyard of the Imperial Winter Palace. St Petersburg. Early 20th century*

*St George's Room in the Imperial Winter Palace. St Petersburg. Ca. 1903*

The Emperor's marriage with Princess Alix of Hesse had not been prompted by reasons of state. They had from the first been drawn together by feelings of mutual affection, and their love for each other had grown stronger with every passing year. Ideally happy though they were in their married life, the Emperor's choice was nevertheless an unfortunate one. Despite her many good qualities — her warm heart, her devotion to husband and children, her well-meant but ill-advised endeavours to inspire him with the firmness and decision which his character lacked — the Empress Alexandra was not a fitting helpmate for a Sovereign in his difficult position. Of a shy and retiring disposition, though a born autocrat, she failed to win the affection of her subjects. She misjudged the situation from the first, encouraging him, when the political waters were already dangerously high, to steer a course fraught with danger to the ship of State. The tragic element is already discernible in the first act of the drama. A good woman, bent on serving her husband's interests, she is to prove the chosen instrument of his ruin. Diffident and irresolute, the Emperor was bound to fall under the influence of a will stronger than his. It was her blind faith in an unbridled autocracy that was to be his undoing. Had he had as his consort a woman with broader views and better insight, who would have grasped the fact that such a regime was an anachronism in the twentieth century, the history of his reign would have been different...

George Buchanan,
*My Mission to Russia*

*Nicholas II and Alexandra Feodorovna with their daughter Olga.*
*St Petersburg. 1896. Photograph by Levitsky*

## 14-го Ноября 1897 года.

Въ память дорогаго для Россіи дня рожденія Императрицы МАРІИ ѲЕОДОРОВНЫ и бракосочетанія Ихъ Величествъ Императора НИКОЛАЯ АЛЕКСАНДРОВИЧА и Императрицы АЛЕКСАНДРЫ ѲЕОДОРОВНЫ.

Настоящее изображеніе счастливой Царственной Семьи, осѣняемой Покровомъ Небесной Владычицы, да послужитъ благодатнымъ утѣшеніемъ искони Царелюбивому Русскому народу, окрыляя его свѣтлыя упованія при видѣ того, какая нѣжная любовь и неистощимая доброта окружаютъ Царя подъ Его семейнымъ кровомъ.

Царица Мать, со старшей Внучкой на рукахъ, сердобольная, всей душой отдавшаяся дѣламъ милосердія, благотворенія, образованія дѣвицъ всѣхъ слоевъ общества, помощи больнымъ и раненымъ, спасенія погибающихъ на водахъ и проч. Рядомъ съ Нею, съ радостно-нѣжною заботой поддерживая младшую Дочь Свою.—Царица-Супруга, спутница Царя въ жизни и сподвижница во ввѣренномъ Ему Богомъ дѣлѣ. Лелѣя Своихъ Дѣтей, отраду Царственнаго Супруга, Она посвящаетъ всѣ Свои заботы попеченію о домахъ трудолюбія и обезпеченію бѣднякамъ насущнаго хлѣба. Русскій народъ, чуткій ко всему доброму, возлагаетъ горячія надежды на молодую Царицу, перенося на Нее дорогія воспоминанія о незабвенной Императрицѣ Маріи Александровнѣ, Супругѣ Императора Александра II, происходившей изъ того-же Гессенъ-Дармштадтскаго Велико-Герцогскаго Дома, которая такъ любила Россію, что незадолго до Своей кончины, почувствовавъ въ Дармштадтѣ опасный недугъ, потребовала скорѣйшаго отъѣзда въ Россію, говоря: «Послѣ Бога всего болѣе люблю Россію». Наконецъ, двѣ юныя Царевны, Ольга и Татіана, какъ два Ангела Хранителя, скрѣпляютъ этотъ союзъ мира и любви, услаждая труды и заботы Вѣнценоснаго Родителя, подъемлемые Имъ на благо всей многомилліонной Русской Семьи.

БЕЗПЛАТНО.                    Русскому народу на добрую память отъ Издателя «Каѳедры Исаакіевскаго Собора».

*On one of the avenues in the park at Peterhof:* (left to right)
*Alexandra Feodorovna, King Christian IX of Denmark, his daughter the Dowager*
*Empress Maria Feodorovna, Nicholas II and Grand Duchess*
*Olga Alexandrovna. Peterhof. 1896*

*Members of the Imperial family relaxing in the park:* (left to right)
*Grand Duke Alexander Mikhailovich with his wife Grand Duchess*
*Xenia Alexandrovna and Nicholas II with Alexandra Feodorovna;* (in the centre)
*Grand Duchess Olga Alexandrovna. Gatchina. 1897*

← *Reproduction of the lithograph* The Family of Nicholas II. *14th November 1897*

*Nicholas II and Carol I of Romania on manouevres. Krasnoye Selo. 1898*

*Nicholas II* (fourth from left) *and Grand Duke Mikhail Alexandrovich*
(first) *with the King of Siam* (second). *Tsarskoye Selo. 1897.*
*Photograph by K.E. von Gan*

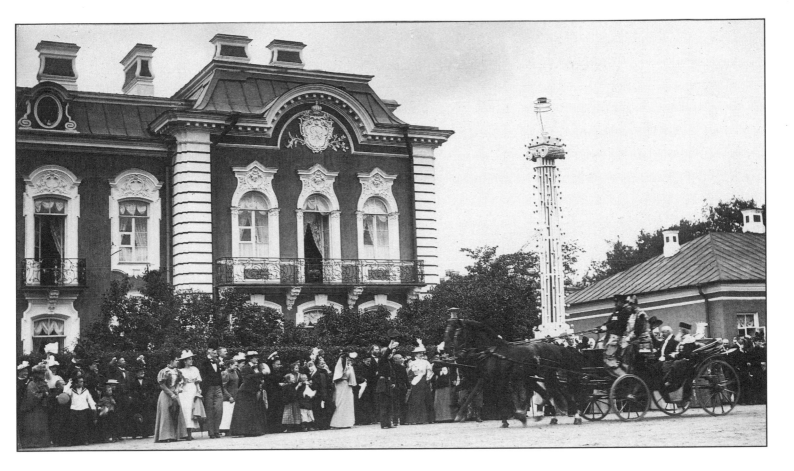

*The arrival of the President of France in Peterhof. 1897*

*Members of the Imperial family leaving on a motor-launch from the slipway of the Baltic Ship-Building and Mechanical Works after the launching of a ship. St Petersburg. 1902*

*Emperor Nicholas II reviewing the crew of the battleship* Prince Suvorov
*formed up on the quay of the Baltic Ship-Building and Mechanical Works.*
*St Petersburg. 1902*

*Nicholas II and Maria Feodorovna greeting the sailors.*
*St Petersburg. 1902*

*Launch of the battleship* Pobeda *from the slipway of the Baltic Ship-Building and Mechanical Works. St Petersburg. 1th May 1900*

*Nicholas II and Alexandra Feodorovna leaving the Evangelical-Lutheran
Church of St Peter after the requiem for the German Empress.
St Petersburg. 6th August 1901*

*Nicholas II and King Victor Emmanuel of Italy* (centre) *with a group
of generals on the parade-ground. Tsarskoye Selo. 1902* →

*Nicholas II and Émile Loubet, President of France, in a carriage.* →
*Peterhof. 1902*

*The court church at the Great Palace. Peterhof. 1900s*

*The Great Palace in Peterhof from the Lower park. Peterhof. 1900s*

*Grand Duchess Tatyana riding a pony. Tsarskoye Selo. 1902.*
*Photograph by K.E. von Gan*

←   *Grand Duchesses Tatyana* (left) *and Maria riding goats.*
*Tsarskoye Selo. 1902. Photograph by K.E. von Gan*

←   *Nicholas II's daughters: Grand Duchesses Anastasia and Maria*
(in the arms of governesses), seated *Grand Duchess Tatyana*
(first from right) *and Olga* (second). *1902*

234       *Nicholas II, grand dukes and generals reviewing the Life-Guards Preobrazhensky Regiment. Tsarskoye Selo. 1902*

*Nicholas II* (centre); seated in the second row below (from left) *Grand Duchess Olga Alexandrovna* (fourth), *Grand Duchess Elizaveta Mavrikiyevna* (fifth), *Alexandra Feodorovna* (sixth), *Dowager Empress Maria Feodorovna* (eighth), *Grand Duchess Xenia Alexandrovna* (ninth) *with the officers and wives of His Majesty's Life-Guards Cuirassier Regiment; standing behind Olga Alexandrovna is Grand Duke Pavel Alexandrovich. Krasnoye Selo. 1902*

237

*Iconostasis of the court Cathedral of the Vernicle at the Imperial Winter Palace. St Petersburg. Ca. 1903*

← *Interior of the Rotunda Room in the Winter Palace with portraits of emperors. St Petersburg. 1903*

← *The Golden Drawing-Room in the Imperial Winter Palace. St Petersburg. Ca. 1903*

# Anna Alexandrovna Vyrubova

Anna Alexandrovna Vyrubova, *née* Taneyeva, was the daughter of a courtier who administered the royal chancellery. In 1903 she became a maid-of-honour in the Empress's court and quite soon grew close to Alexandra Feodorovna. The development of their relationship was in no small part due to Vyrubova's unsuccessful marriage. After her divorce in 1907 she involved herself more intimately with the royal family. "My friendship with the Empress grew stronger," she wrote. "Together we sewed, drew and sang at Iretskaya's, the professor of the Conservatoire." A woman of no great intelligence, she won affection by her naive, boundless devotion to her royal friend and was her confidante for many years.

Vyrubova met Rasputin, like Alexandra Feodorovna, through Militsa Nikolayevna and soon became an ardent admirer, having herself experienced both the strength of the *starets*'s influence and his gift of second-sight (curiously, the very first time they met, just before Vyrubova's wedding, he predicted that her marriage would fail). For her part Anna Alexandrovna was one of the few people to whom Rasputin was truly well-disposed.

It is not surprising, therefore, that in the 1910s her little house in Tsarskoye Selo became in its way the "portal of power", as Protopopov, the Minister of the Interior, wrote, observing that "this place indubitably played a great role in the story of the last phase of the monarchy. People at court, who had access to the family, divided themselves up into 'Us' and 'Them'. 'Us' meant those who conformed to the demands and were accepted in both halves: the Tsar's and the Tsarina's — and knew Vyrubova and Rasputin... The little house had a great many visitors; some were summoned when the Tsarina, Tsar or princesses were present. Rasputin too often spent time there. People came with requests of a personal or official nature, for recommendation or protection; what they said there was meant to be passed on."

*Participants in the fancy-dress ball in the costumes of young*
*Russian boyarinas; on the left, the maid-of-honour Anna Vyrubova.*
*St Petersburg. 1903*

*Society fancy-dress ball in the Hermitage Theatre of the Winter Palace. St Petersburg. 1903*

St Petersburg's 200th anniversary was an event of great importance in the life of the capital. Preparation for it began well in advance. Jubilee almanacs and historical publications appeared. Exhibitions were held in different parts of the city: in the Yekaterinhof Palace — the first palace museum in St Petersburg, which housed a collection of items that belonged to Peter the Great or were typical of his era; in the Summer Gardens; in Peter's Log Cabin, in the Technological Institute, where an extensive display related the rise in science in Peter's time and followed it up to the beginning of the twentieth century.

The main festivities took place in the historic centre of the city: on St Isaac's and Peter I's (Decembrist) Squares, the Admiralty, Palace and Petrovsky Embankments, in the Peter and Paul Fortress and the Summer Gardens. Around the Bronze Horseman monument the coats-of-arms of the ruling House of Romanov were on display, a royal tent and places for guests of honour were set up. The whole city was a colourful display of flowers and flags, with which "the residents of the capital were permitted to decorate the houses on the day of 16th May..."

*Nicholas II in the uniform of the Life-Guards Semionovsky Regiment,*
*Alexandra Feodorovna and accompanying officers from that regiment*
*passing through Palace Square. St Petersburg. 1903*

*Nicholas II with his entourage accompanying the carriage*
*of Empresses Alexandra Feodorovna and Maria Feodorovna.*
*St Petersburg. 2nd May 1903*

Seraphim of Sarov (1759—1833), whose secular name was Prokhor Isidorovich Moshnin, was the first figure to be canonized during Nicholas II's reign. His life was little different from that of others recognized as saints by the Orthodox Church. The boy lost his father at an early age and his mother brought him up on her own giving her child his first lessons in piety. After spending two years at the Kiev Monastery of the Caves, he arrived as a nineteen-year-old youth at the monastery in Sarov, which according to legend he had been told by the *starets* Dosifei would be a place where he would achieve great spiritual feats. There he became a monk, taking the name Seraphim ("Ardent") and after some time became a priest as well — a hieromonk. More than once he left the monastery to communicate with God alone and in silence, and came to be a *starets*, helping people with his advice and prayers. He was also the founder of the Diveyevo Convent near Sarov, where he preached and exhorted the nuns towards particular reverence of the Virgin.

His canonization took place against the objections of Pobedonostsev, the Chief Procurator of the Synod, and despite the fact that when his remains were exhumed neither the local bishop, nor the Metropolitan of St Petersburg confirmed their incorruption. Nevertheless the necessary rites were performed and were extensively reported in the press, after which Sarov, as R. Wortman observed, became a Russian twin of Lourdes and the national centre for adoration of the miracle-worker.

The festivities were attended by the Emperor and Alexandra Feodorovna, whose insistence had brought about Seraphim's canonization, the Dowager Empress Maria Feodorovna and other members of the royal family. Watched by many thousands of the faithful the coffin was carried three times around the convent cathedral, with the tsar supporting it without being relieved for the whole length of the ceremonial procession. The Empress for her part, despite her poor state of health, stood through the whole four-hour canonization service.

The political significance of this action was not lost on contemporaries. "The whole land of Russia, one can say, has now gathered around the relics of this sainted priest," *Moskovskiye Vedomosti* (*The Moscow Gazette*) wrote. "It is a representative gathering so impressive that any possible universal popular election pales before it."

*Nicholas II and members of the Imperial family transferring the relics of St Seraphim of Sarov. Sarov Monastery. Tambov Province. 1903*

*Nicholas II leaving the church during the Sarov festivities. Sarov Monastery. Tambov Province. 1903*

*Grand Duchesses Olga Nikolayevna and Tatyana Nikolayevna in a carriage of the royal train. Skernevitsy. 11th September 1903*

248

The seven-carriage Imperial broad-gauge train, consecrated in March 1896, was constructed in the workshops of the Alexandrovsky Mechanical Works.

The train was built under the supervision of the Special Commission for the Construction of Imperial Trains headed by the engineer V.S. Sumarokov. The carriages were painted in a mid-blue colour against which the gilded bronze handles stood out, while the Tsar's own carriages were decorated with golden eagles. Every door had its own short flight of steps which could easily be adjusted to platforms of different heights. The train was fitted with two automatic brake systems — Westinghouse (compressed air) and Hardy (air discharge). The entire train was lit by electricity supplied by a self-contained mobile power station located in the seventh, end carriage.

There was evidently quite some curiosity among ordinary people about the train's facilities and its appearance inside and out, so that the *Vsemirnaya Illiustratsiya* (*Universal Illustrated*) printed a detailed description: "The saloon-car consists of two compartments: a drawing-room lined in olive-coloured silk, with furniture of the same colour, a mirror and three small wooden tables of Karelian birch and with an exquisite mosaic of different woods on the tops — a flower pattern. The door from the drawing-room to the dining-room is also decorated with marquetry. In the dining-room there is also a mirror, while both places have attractive electric lamps. A door leads from the dining-room to a buffet section, then by an enclosed link one can pass through to the kitchen; the kitchen next to the dining-room is spacious with a real stove, and has several sections, including one, by the way, for tubs of ice. The luggage van incorporates several service compartments and a simple space, like a hall, for luggage. Here too pieces of apparatus are installed: the *Graphtia*, which records the speed of the train, and the telephone. At the end of the carriage there is a compartment for servants. The Tsar's own carriage contains two studies and also bedrooms, and between them a nursery that can be divided into two by a partition. A corridor runs from one end to the other and is lined with grey silk wallpaper.

"Of the two end rooms in the carriages one is for a lady-in-waiting, the other for a valet; beyond the first room is the Empress's in which the furniture and walls are in sandy-coloured silk with small bouquets of flowers; there is purple velvet drapery at the windows and the same on the table; the nursery is lined in reddish silk wallpaper. The Emperor's room, faced in American walnut, has furniture upholstered in dark green shagreen leather. On the desk is an attractive gilded writing set in Renaissance style. The carriage for the retinue, also with a corridor and lined with silk, has two compartments for ladies and three for men with comfortable divans (not counting the servants' compartments). The service and administration car contains several compartments with divans, desks and filing cabinets."

*Nicholas II's sleeping-car on the royal train. 1896* →

*Saloon-car on the royal train. 1896* →

*Dining-car on the royal train. 1896* →

*Nicholas II's study on the royal train. 1896* →

*Nicholas II and his generals leaving the Church of the Holy Trinity*
*after the anniversary service for the founding of the Life-Guards Izmailovsky Regiment.*
*Krasnoye Selo. May 1904*

*Nicholas II receiving a report from the commander of H.M. Empress*
*Maria Feodorovna's Life- and House-Guards Regiment, Prince Felix Yusupov,*
*Count Sumarokov-Elston. Peterhof. 1904*

*Nicholas II congratulating the cadets of the Infantry Cadet School
on their promotion to the rank of officer. Krasnoye Selo. 9th August 1904*

*Nicholas II with a group of members of the Council of War.
St Petersburg. Early 1900s*

*The royal party with retinue setting off to the palace church for the baptism
of the Heir Alexis Nikolayevich. Peterhof. 11th August 1904*

*The Romanov family:* (right to left) *Grand Duchess Olga, Nicholas II,
Alexandra Feodorovna holding Tsesarevich Alexis and Grand Duchess Tatyana,
seated below* *Grand Duchess Anastasia. St Petersburg. 1904.
Photograph by Boasson and Egger*

*Nicholas II and his son Alexis. Inscribed:* Nicky with his son. *St Petersburg. 1905*

*Alexandra Feodorovna with her son Alexis. 1904*

"It would have been difficult to find four sisters so dissimilar in character and at the same time so closely bound together in friendship...," their French tutor Pierre Gilliard recalled. "From their initials they made up the collective name *Otma*. They sometimes signed themselves that way, when making presents or sending letters that one of them had written on behalf of all four...

"Circumstances taught all four early to be content with their own company and natural gaiety. There are few young girls who would have accepted without murmur such a way of life, devoid of any outside entertainment. Its only consolation was the delights of a close family life that are so scorned nowadays...

"They never attended a single ball; they only had occasion to take part in two or three soirés given by their aunt, Grand Duchess Olga Alexandrovna. From the moment the war broke out they had only one thought — to relieve the concerns and fears of their parents. They surrounded them with their love, which expressed itself in highly touching and tender signs of affection."

*The daughters of Nicholas II.(left to right) Grand Duchesses Maria, Olga, Tatyana and Anastasia. St Petersburg. 1905. Photograph by Boasson and Egger*

*The Great Palace at Tsarskoye Selo. Tsarskoye Selo. 1913*

*View of the bedchamber in the Great Palace at Tsarskoye Selo.*
*Tsarskoye Selo. 1905*

←   *Part of the drawing-room in the Great Palace at Tsarskoye Selo.*
*Tsarskoye Selo. 1905*

←   *Part of the study in the Great Palace at Tsarskoye Selo.*
*Tsarskoye Selo. 1905*

*Nicholas II receiving a welcome with bread and salt on his arrival to address troops departing for the front. Kobeliaki Station. 1904*

*Nicholas II reviewing troops about to leave for the front during the Russo-Japanese War. Kremenchug. 1904*

*Nicholas II and Alexandra Feodorovna with retinue and priests on the way to a service in the church of Grand Duchess Anastasia Nikolayevna's 148th Infantry Caspian Regiment before its departure for the front in Manchuria. Peterhof. 1905* →

*Nicholas II leaving the church of Grand Duchess Anastasia Nikolayevna's 148th Infantry Caspian Regiment after the service preceding the regiment's departure for the front in Manchuria. Left, in the background: Empress Alexandra Feodorovna. Peterhof. 1905* →

Reflecting on Count Witte's achievements, Buchanan wrote later: "Though I, personally, mistrusted Witte on account of his pronounced pro-German views, I fully recognize his merits as an able and far-seeing statesman who rendered his country invaluable services. He introduced the gold currency, he negotiated the Treaty of Portsmouth that reestablished peace with Japan, and he induced the Emperor to publish the October manifesto of 1905 that called the Duma into existence. ... Now, the Emperor and Witte were mutually antipathetic, and the latter's dislike of his Sovereign so biased his judgement that, in his eyes, His Majesty could do nothing right..." This was evidently the reason why on learning of the Count's death Nicholas gave orders for the private study at his former chief minister's home to be sealed, fearing the publication of his memoirs, which he perfectly well knew existed. At the same time secret agents carried out a search of the Witte villa in France, hoping to find the papers there, but without success. The prudent courtier kept the typewritten manuscript of his memoirs in his wife's safe-deposit box at the bank and it was only this that saved them and they were published later in Berlin.

*Count Sergei Witte. St Petersburg. 1905*

*Nicholas II reading the manifesto on the opening of the First State Duma in St George's Room of the Winter Palace. St Petersburg. 27th 1906. Photograph by K.E. von Gan*

Оставил Госуда.
ремъ Императеи
Александра Федоровна
у Себ.
15 Октября 1907.

*The Romanov family:* (right to left) *Grand Duchesses Olga and Tatyana, Nicholas II,*
*Alexandra Feodorovna, Grand Duchess Maria, Tsesarevich Alexis, Grand Duchess*
*Anastasia. 1907. Photograph by Boasson and Egger*

← *Tsesarevich Grand Duke Alexis riding a donkey. Tsarskoye Selo. 1906. Photograph*
*by K.E. von Gan*

← *Tsesarevich Grand Duke Alexis clearing a path in the park*
*at Tsarskoye Selo. 1907*

← *Censor's signature on the back of an authentic print showing Tsesarevich Alexis*
*in the park. 1907*

*Alexandra Feodorovna and her son Alexis. St Petersburg. 1907*

← *Nicholas II with his children on the Gulf of Finland. Peterhof. 1908*

← *Nicholas II and his children on the coast of the Gulf of Finland: Tsesarevich Alexis (left),
Grand Duchess Anastasia (right). Peterhof. 1908*

← *Tsesarevich Alexis on the deck of a yacht. 1906. Photograph by K.E. von Gan*

Deprived of many usual childhood amusements, Tsesarevich Alexis was very attached to his pets. He had a dark brown lapdog named Joy, a pony and Van'ka the donkey, who those who knew him said was an absolutely inimitable and highly intelligent creature. He had come into the palace stables from Cinizelli's Circus, because he was already old and not up to performing. Van'ka could do many tricks which charmed children and adults alike.

*Tsesarevich Alexis riding a pony. Tsarskoye Selo. 1909. Photograph by K.E. von Gan*

*Tsesarevich Alexis in a car. Tsarskoye Selo. 1909. Photograph by K.E. von Gan*

The Tsesarevich's education did not begin until he was over eight years old. His tutor was Pierre Gilliard who taught him Russian and French, arithmetic, history, geography and scripture. There was no particular system: Alexis was often ill and lessons were disrupted. We learn from his tutor's own memoirs that the teaching day began with lessons about nine in the morning and at about eleven they were interrupted for a walk or often a carriage, sleigh or car ride after which they resumed until lunch (at one o'clock). That was followed by a regulation two hours in the fresh air, and then back to lessons, roughly from four until seven which was the time when the Tsesarevich took dinner.

As a seriously ill child and thus the focus of attention for the whole family, Alexis had as far as Gilliard could see "never been subjected to any sort of discipline". He sought refuge in inactivity from the boring work and concentration which was urged upon him and tried to resist the very process of education. He was possibly somewhat backward for his age, but he was far from stupid. As he came to know his pupil better, Gilliard even noted quite a few attractive qualities in the Tsesarevich. "He completely revelled in life as an active boy full of *joie de vivre*," Gilliard wrote. "His tastes were very modest. He did not in the least boast of being the heir to the throne; he cared less about that than anything. His greatest pleasure was to play with the sailor Derevenko's two sons, who were both a little younger than him.

"He had a very lively mind and judgement and could be very thoughtful. He could strike you now and then with questions too mature for his age, which were evidence of a delicate and sensitive soul. I could easily understand," the tutor continued, "how those who did not have to instill discipline in him, as I did, might with no further thought succumb to his charm. Inside the capricious little creature he seemed at first, I discovered a child with a heart that was loving by nature and sensitive to suffering, since he himself had already suffered much."

*Tsesarevich Alexis in sailor's uniform. St Petersburg. 1910—11*

*The imperial yacht* Standart. *Copenhagen. 1893—96*

*Nicholas II's study aboard the imperial yacht* Standart. *Copenhagen. 1893—96*  →

*Children's bedroom aboard the imperial yacht* Standart. *Copenhagen. 1893—96*  →

*Ceremonial service before the unveiling of the monument to the Bicentennial*
*of the Battle of Poltava attended by Nicholas II and Grand Duke Nikolai Nikolayevich.*
*Poltava. 1909*

*Monument to Alexander III by Pavel Trubetskoi on Znamenskaya Square.*
*St Petersburg. 1909*

ИМПЕРАТОРУ АЛЕКСАНДРУ III

ДЕРЖАВНОМУ ОСНОВАТЕЛЮ

ВЕЛИКАГО СИБИРСКАГО ПУТИ

*Nicholas II, members of the Imperial family and their retinue at the consecration of the church commemorating*
*the sailors who perished at Tsushima (Church of Our Saviour on the Waters, Novoadmiralteisky Canal).*
*St Petersburg. 1911. Photograph by K.K. Bulla*

*Nicholas II, Grand Duchesses Olga Nikolayevna and Tatyana Nikolayevna with the pupils*
*of the Imperial Philanthropic Society for the Collection of Donations*
*for the Education of Poor Children in Handicrafts. 1911*

*← Church of Our Saviour on the Waters. St Petersburg. 1911*

*Nicholas II inspecting a parade of the Life-Guards Izmailovsky Regiment.*
*Tsarskoye Selo. 1909*

*Nicholas II and Tsesarevich Alexis by the royal tent during a parade of the Life-Guards Chasseurs Regiment.*
*Peterhof. 17th August 1912*

← *Nicholas II reviewing the Poteshny (Toy) Regiment on the Field of Mars. St Petersburg. 1912*

← *Nicholas II. 1910s*

*Nicholas II, Grand Duchesses Olga ahd Tatyana with a group of officers of H.I.M. Own Escort
at the entrance to the Great Catherine Palace. Tsarskoye Selo. 1911*

*Members of the Imperial family on the main porch of the Catherine Palace on the day of the Tsarskoye Selo Bicentennial: (from right) Grand Duchess Tatyana (second), Grand Duchess Victoria Feodorovna, wife of Cyril Vladimirovich (third), Grand Duchess Maria (fifth), Grand Duke Alexis, Alexandra Feodorovna, Grand Duchess Olga (ninth) and Grand Duchess Anastasia (tenth). Tsarskoye Selo. 1911*

*Alexandra Feodorovna taking a ride with her daughters. Livadia. 20th April 1912*

*Nicholas II* (third from right) *and Grand Duchess Tatyana* (second) *after a game of tennis. Tsarskoye Selo. 1912—13*

*Tsesarevich Alexis on a jetty. Finland. 1912* →

*Nicholas II's children, Grand Duchesses Tatyana, Maria, Olga, Anastasia and Tsesarevich Alexis, taking part in the campaign against consumption. Livadia. 20th April 1912* →

*Nicholas II and members of the Imperial family with officers of the Life-Guards Grenadiers. 1912*

*Nicholas II and Grand Duke Nikolai Nikolayevich with their retinue reviewing the platoons
of the Life-Guards Chasseurs Regiment. Peterhof. 17th August 1912*

*Celebrations of the Tercentenary of the House of Romanov: the arch of Gostiny Dvor decorated
for the festivities. St Petersburg. 1913. Photograph by K.K. Bulla*

*A group of participants in the celebration for the Tercentenary of the House of Romanov
by the Emperor Nicholas II's Narodny Dom (People's Palace)* →
*which is decorated with royal emblems. St Petersburg. 1913*

*Main gates and railing of the State Bank (21, Sadovaya Street) decorated for the celebration
of the Tercentenary of the House of Romanov. St Petersburg. 1913* →

*Nicholas II and members of the Imperial family at the unveiling of the model of the monument commemorating the Tercentenary of the House of Romanov. Nizhni Novgorod. 1913*

*The arrival of members of the Imperial family in Rostov for the celebrations of the Tercentenary of the House of Romanov: Nicholas II (on the left), Tsesarevich Alexis (being held by an "uncle"), Grand Duchesses Maria, Tatyana, Anastasia and Olga. Rostov. 1913*

*Nicholas II being welcomed with bread and salt by the townspeople.*
*Kostroma. 1913*

*Alexandra Feodorovna with Tsesarevich Alexis in a carriage on Red Square*
*during the celebrations of the Tercentenary of the House of Romanov. Moscow. 1913*

*Members of the Imperial family driving across Palace Square during the celebrations of the Tercentenary of the House of Romanov. St Petersburg. 1913*

## Grand Duchess Olga Nikolayevna

H er abilities made Grand Duchess Olga Nikolayevna (1856–1918), the eldest of the Emperor's daughters, stand out from her sisters. In the words of her tutor Pierre Gilliard, she "possessed a very lively mind. She had great discretion and frankness at the same time. She was very independent of character and could be amusingly quick-witted in her ripostes... She grasped everything with surprising speed and had the ability to put an original construction on what she had absorbed... She read a good deal outside of lessons."

However the circumstances of Olga's life — not enough attention to her education from her mother who was completely taken up with the Tsesarevich's illness — did little to further the development of her remarkable capacities, which faded rather than flourished with the years.

In 1914 fate presented the young princess with a chance of escape from her family's terrible lot. A summertime trip to Romania on the royal yacht *Standard* was connected with a possible match between Olga Nikolayevna and Prince Charles of Romania, which under the prevailing political conditions was looked on favourably by both sets of parents. The settlement of this question was, however, put off indefinitely, at the insistence of Olga Nikolayevna herself as it seemed to Gilliard. Before leaving for Romania she had guessed at the true reason behind the visit and had told him that she did not want to leave Russia. When he responded that she would be able to return whenever she wanted, she is supposed to have said: "Despite everything I will be a stranger in my own country, but I am Russian and want to stay Russian!"

*Grand Duchess Olga Nikolayevna in the full-dress uniform of Her Own Hussar Yelizavetgradsky Regiment among the ladies of the regiment. Peterhof. 5th August 1913*

*Grand Duchesses Olga, Tatyana and Maria with V.N. Orlov,*
*the commander of the Imperial Headquarters Staff, at a parade.*
*Krasnoye Selo. 3rd August 1913*

*The commander of the 3rd Hussar Yelizavetgradsky Regiment reporting*
← *to the regiment's patron Grand Duchess Olga Nikolayevna. On the right:*
*Nicholas II and Grand Duchess Tatyana Nikolayevna.*
*Peterhof. 1913*

*Tsesarevich Grand Duke Alexis, Grand Duchesses Olga, Tatyana, Maria*
← *and Anastasia by the Catherine Palace. Tsarskoye Selo. 1913*

*Nicholas II with the personnel of a motorized training company. St Petersburg. 1913*

"A nother figure who had great influence over the Emperor during my ministry was Grand Duke Nikolai Nikolayevich. This influence was bound up with the particular mystic diseases which the Emperor caught from his most august spouse, and which Grand Duke Nikolai Nikolayevich had suffered from for a long time. He was one of the chief, if not *the* chief initiator of that abnormal mood of Orthodox paganism and searching for miracles, into which they obviously strayed in the highest circles (the story of the Frenchman Philippe, Seraphim of Sarov, Rasputin-Novykh; all fruits of one and the same tree). One could not say he was insane, nor that he was abnormal as that word is usually understood, but neither could one say he was right in the mind; he was touched, like all people of that kind, who practice and believe in table-turning and similar forms of charlatanism. On top of that the Grand Duke was by nature a fairly narrow-minded man and not highly cultured.

*From Sergei Witte's memoirs*

*Nicholas II about to lay a brick for the new building of the Life-Guards Cavalry Regiment. St Petersburg. 26th June 1914*

*Nicholas II and Grand Duke Nikolai Nikolayevich on manoeuvres. Krasnoye Selo. 1913*

*Nicholas II, Grand Duchesses Olga Nikolayevna and Tatyana Nikolayevna with officers of the 148th Caspian Infantry Regiment by the Catherine Palace. Tsarskoye Selo. 1914*

*Nicholas II and Kaiser Wilhelm II in a carriage. Germany. Early 1913*

←   *King Friedrich August of Saxony and Nicholas II inspecting the guard of honour
at the railway station. Tsarskoye Selo. 7th June 1914*

←   *Crown Prince Ferdinand of Romania and Nicholas II inspecting the guard of honour
on the platform of the railway station. Tsarskoye Selo. 22nd March 1914*

*Nicholas II and Alexandra Feodorovna on the balcony of the Winter Palace before the proclamation of the manifesto on the declaration of war against Germany. St Petersburg. 1914*

*A demonstration at the corner of Nevsky Prospekt and Sadovaya Street
following Serbia's rejection of the Austro-Hungarian ultimatum.
St Petersburg. 28th July 1914. Photograph by K.K. Bulla*

← *A recruiting centre. Petrograd. 1914*

← *Mobilized soldiers and their relatives in front
of the recruiting centre. Petrograd. 1914*

*Ward prepared for the reception of the wounded in the hospital of the Imperial
Winter Palace. Petrograd. 1914*

*The Grand Duchess Maria Nikolayevna Hospital Column of the Imperial Russian Motor Society →
on the Field of Mars before departure for the front. Petrograd. 1915*

*Nurses by patients' beds in the hospital of the Imperial Winter Palace. Petrograd. 1914   →*

*Nicholas II inspecting the unit of H.I.M. Escort being sent to the front. Mogilev. May 1916*

← *Nicholas II with his family on the platform of the railway station on their arrival at Stavka. Mogilev. May 1916*

← *Officers at Stavka welcoming Nicholas II's daughters. Mogilev. 1916*

During the war the Emperor more than once took his son to Stavka, which was located at Mogilev from 8th August 1915. They occupied two rooms in the governor's house, one of which served as a bedroom, the other as a study. According to Gilliard who accompanied him, Tsesarevich Alexis slept on a camp-bed alongside his father. Every day at about half past nine Nicholas went to headquarters where he stayed, as a rule, until one, while the heir was busy in the Tsar's study at this time with his tutor. "Lunch was served in the main hall of the governor's house," Gilliard wrote. "Daily up to thirty invited people gathered for it. These would include General Alexeyev, his main assistants, the heads of all the allied military missions, the royal retinue and a few officers who were passing through Mogilev. After lunch the Emperor dealt with urgent matters, following which, at about three, we went for a drive in the car. After driving a certain distance from the town, we stopped, got out and walked for about an hour in the surrounding area... On our return from the drive, the Emperor again set to work, while Alexis Nikolayevich prepared his lessons for the next day in his father's study." Another component of this life was the Emperor's trips with the Tsesarevich to the front.

*Nicholas II, a Catholic priest and attendants in the area of military operations. 1915*

← *Alexandra Feodorovna and Tsesarevich Alexis making the round of troops before the parade of reserve guards battalions on the Field of Mars. Petrograd. 19th April 1916*

The difficult military situation prompted the Emperor to summon an extraordinary session of the Council of Ministers at Stavka. The day appointed was 14th June, and even on 13th those invited gathered there. "That day Stavka presented an unaccustomed sight," wrote Major-General Dmitry Dubensky, in a way a royal biographer for the war years. "In the pine forest by the carriages and along the paths you could see groups of ministers, engaged in lively discussion amongst themselves. The white frock-coats of their uniform stood out distinctly against the green background of grass and forest. A whole row of ministerial carriages was drawn up on one of the side-tracks." The session took place on the day appointed after prayers said kneeling and a royal lunch attended by some fifty people. For three hours, roughly from 2 to 5, the ministers, gathered in a large open-sided tent close to the imperial train, discussed the problems of the military emergency. Nicholas II himself took the chair. The result was that he became confirmed in his intention to fight to a victorious conclusion, uniting all the efforts of the Russian land. With this goal in mind, he recognized the necessity of convoking the most authoritative legislative institutions — the recommencement of sessions of the State Council and State Duma. He also entrusted the Council of Ministers to draft laws made necessary by the demands of wartime.

*Nicholas II at the fronts in the First World War:* seated *Nicholas II and Grand Duke Nikolai Nikolayevich (junior);* standing *General Yu.N. Danilov* (left) *and N.N. Yanishkevich, Chief of Staff. Western front. 1916*

*The Council of Ministers:* first row (left to right) *P.A. Kharitonov, State Controller; Grand Duke Nikolai Nikolayevich (junior); Nicholas II; I.L. Goremykin, Chairman of the Council of Ministers; V.B. Fredericks, Minister of the Imperial Court and Domains, Adjutant-General;* second row *Prince N.B. Shcherbatov, Minister of the Interior; S.V. Rykhlov, Minister of Communications; S.D. Sazonov, Foreign Minister; A.V. Krivoshein, Minister of Agriculture; P.L. Bark, Minister of Finance; N.N. Yanishkevich, Chief of the Headquarters Staff, Infantry General; A.A. Polivanov, Minister of War, Infantry General; and Prince V.N. Shakhovskoi, Minister of Trade and Industry. Stavka—Baranovichi Station. 14 June 1915*

By the time Rasputin appeared in St Petersburg, met the royal family and developed into an influential figure at court, he already had behind him a long and in large measure remarkable life. Born into a moderately well-to-do peasant family in the village of Pokrovskoye in the Tiumen district of Tobolsk Province, he fairly soon became notorious in his home area as a man with an ungovernable temper, extremely effusive, sly and self-assured. Rasputin was seen stealing on several occasions and once he was savagely beaten by a man from the same village (he was struck a very heavy blow on the head with a stake, causing him to bleed from the mouth and nose, and to lose consciousness), after which, according to eyewitnesses, he turned strange and even slightly stupid.

But his real transformation came as a result of a pilgrimage to the Monastery of Verkhoturye in Perm Province, which he undertook to escape a legal action brought by the local populace, not wishing to share the fate of those of his friends whose disorderly and immoral conduct had already earned them deportation to Eastern Siberia. This journey, which lasted some three months, brought about a real change in his behaviour, prompting those who had known him earlier to suggest that he was patently suffering from some psychological disorder. He completely changed his way of life: he stopped drinking and smoking, gave up eating meat and began to read texts in Church Slavonic, the liturgical language of the Orthodox Church; he cut himself off from people, prayed a lot and talked with wanderers representing various sects and dogmas, including those whom the official Church called "*khlysty*" — a sect which believed that one should sin more in order that one's salvation would be the greater. Over a period of several years he spent time at dozens of monasteries in Siberia and European Russia, and even on Mount Athos, returning each time to his native village, where a completely closed circle of his admirers formed, with new female companions.

The numbers of those who looked on him with mystical adoration and blind faith, despite the scandalous tales which followed him, grew apace, embracing people from the most varied circles and greatly increasing his reputation. "Father Grigory", as they came to call him, could in the minds of his many female followers be compared with Tikhon Zadonsky, who was the same sort of "ordinary mortal, when he walked on the earth, but then came into glory".

In an incredible manner fate impelled Rasputin into the highest court circles, making the simple Tiumen peasant the all-powerful favourite of the supreme authorities, whose whim decided the rise and fall of many statesmen. Rasputin had a tremendous effect on the Empress who saw him not only as the healer of her only son but also as a genuine oracle whose word she believed absolutely. This gave him an immense influence on all aspects of state policy under the last of the Romanovs and this influence was unflagging, despite Rasputin being compromised by numerous facts it was impossible to ignore. The St Petersburg period of his life, according to the reports of the agents who kept him under constant surveillance, was marked by ever-growing unrestrained debauchery, drinking-bouts and orgies, embroiling even highly placed figures. For the immediate royal family, however, his "holiness" and "piety", enhanced by renewed wanderings about Russia and more than one pilgrimage to Jerusalem, were not a matter for question.

On various grounds — some seeking advice or support, others out of pure curiosity — many high society ladies visited Rasputin. The Provisional

Government's Extraordinary Investigative Commission established for certain, though, that members of the Tsar's and grand dukes' families were never at his home. Nevertheless, this relationship had already dealt a shattering blow to royal prestige. All attempts to separate the *starets* from the Emperor's family came to naught, and it was only the violent death of this man, so disastrous for the ruling dynasty, that put an end to a whole period of Russian history connected with his name.

*Grigory Rasputin among his female admirers:* standing third from left *Anna Vyrubova. St Petersburg. Early 1910s*

Recalling this time Grand Duke Alexander Mikhailovich (Sandro), father-in-law of the instant celebrity Felix Yusupov, wrote that when he arrived in Petrograd he "was absolutely struck by the prevailing dense atmosphere of common rumour and vile gossip, now combined with gloating over the murder of Rasputin and a yearning to glorify Felix and Dmitry Pavlovich". Concerned for the fate of his daughter Irina, who had married Yusupov two years previously and was indirectly involved in the scandalous business, he did not share the general delight and was probably truly shaken by the savagery of the act that his relatives had committed. It is clear from his own admissions that it was fatherly duty which caused him to join the campaign set in motion by members of the royal family to defend the "national heroes" who had saved the state. As a result Yusupov's punishment was limited to banishment on the Kursk estate of Rakitnoye, where he was soon joined by his family.

After the revolution Prince Yusupov and other members of the family lived abroad. The allure of scandalous fame remained with them all their lives and was of quite some benefit to them. One of their sources of income was damages which they claimed from companies that made films about Rasputin without their permission. In 1934 a London court awarded Irina Yusupova the equivalent of $125,000 for moral damage caused her. Besides this, the Yusupovs ran a fashion salon called *Irfe* from the first letters of their two names. "The salon was a success," Alexander Vertinsky recalled. "Rich American women, gluttons for titles and sensation, paid crazy sums for their designs — not so much because they were so good, as for the right to meet the man who had killed Rasputin." Many Russian stage performers, artists and writers visited the Yusupov house, including Kuprin, Bunin, Aldanov and Taffi.

*The "Saviours of Russia": Felix Yusupov and his wife Irina in a hospital for wounded soldiers (42 Liteiny Prospekt):* seated in the second row (from right) *Irina Yusupova* (fifth), *Felix Yusupov* (sixth), *Dowager Empress Maria Feodorovna and Grand Duchess Xenia Alexandrovna. Petrograd. 1915*

*Grand Duke Dmitry Pavlovich. 1910s*

*The Provisional Executive Committee of the State Duma:* scated (left to right)
*Prince V.N. Lvov, Rulevsky, S.I. Shidlovsky and M.V. Rodzianko;* standing *V.V. Shulgin,*
*I.I. Dmitriakov, B.A. Engelhardt, A.F. Kerensky and M.A. Karaulov.*
*Petrograd. March 1917*

← *The Gendarmerie Building in Tverskaya Street, burnt out during*
*the February revolution. Petrograd. March 1917*

← *Participants in the events of February—March 1917. Liteiny Prospekt,*
*Petrograd. 1917*

*Packing up paintings in the rooms of the Catherine Palace
at Tsarskoye Selo after the departure of Nicholas II and his family.
Tsarskoye Selo. October 1917*

*Nicholas II in the uniform of the Life-Guards Cavalry Regiment with his son Alexis.*
*St Petersburg. 1913*

*Nicholas II. 1910—14*

*Nicholas II and Alexandra Feodorovna with their children:* (left to right) *Maria, Tatyana, Olga, Anastasia and Alexis. St Petersburg. 1913*

*The Grand Duchesses:* (left to right) *Maria, Tatyana, Anastasia and Olga. St Petersburg. 1914*

*Nicholas II after his abdication. Tsarskoye Selo. 1917*

# EPILOGUE

---

*Nicholas II: "I sense with a firm and
absolute certainty that the fate of Russia,
my own fate and the fate of my family
are in the hand of God, Who set me in the place where I
am. Whatever may happen,
I bow to His will, in the awareness that
I never had another thought than to serve the
country which He entrusted to me.*

FROM ALEXANDER IZVOLSKY'S
*Memoirs*

AS YOU TURN THE PAGE TO THE LAST PHOTOgraph in this book, you get a strange sensation, as if scenes from some astonishing play had flashed before your eyes — it opens with the Russian Emperor Nicholas II on a white horse surrounded by his splendid retinue making a grand entry into the Moscow Kremlin for the magnificent coronation ceremony, and in the end the same man, having just abdicated from the throne, is left, abandoned by everyone, in bitter solitude...

And this last photograph of Nicholas sitting on a tree-stump in the park at Tsarskoye Selo would seem a fitting conclusion to what is in effect a visual chronicle reflecting the family story and life of the last Russian tsar. A historical drama which lasted over three centuries, in which the main roles were played by the rulers of the Romanov dynasty on one side and their subjects — the many peoples of an immense empire — on the other, has here come to its end. Already at this point the former Russian autocrat — now plain Citizen Nikolai Romanov — would have been able from his seat on the stump to see preparations being made in the palace at Tsarskoye Selo to evacuate the possessions of the royal family — the "props" being carried off the stage of history.

What thoughts might have been going through the mind of this main character still left at the front of the stage? Usually people who find themselves at present in a bad position and are fearful of the future tend to remember the past, all the more so, if it was such a splendid one as the last Russian monarch had. Again and again Nicholas must have recalled episodes from his untroubled childhood among his august family, from his youth in the role of tsesarevich, his fascinating journeys to countries near and far, his unforgettable coronation, the parades and military reviews that were so dear to his heart, the countless palace receptions and society balls, his travels through his own country, meetings with gatherings of nobles and officers, and much else that left a lasting impression and is recorded in this book.

On the other hand, Nicholas probably had no great wish to recall things left almost totally unrecorded in the official chronicle and therefore, naturally, not reflected in the present volume — other events of the past twenty-two years in which he had reigned over the country. This is how the famous historian Sergei Melgunov, who can in no way be regarded as a Bolshevik sympathizer or a supporter of Soviet power (suffice it to recall his widely known book *Red Terror* published in the 1920s), wrote about these matters in 1917: "The reign of Nicholas II really was one of the bloodiest in history. Khodynka, two debilitating wars, two revolutions, and, in between them, civil disturbances and pogroms: disturbances put down by the savagest of punitive expeditions with 'Take no prisoners!' and 'Don't spare the bullets!' as their mottoes, and pogroms inspired by proclamations written in Tsarskoye Selo and printed at the department of police... They say that General Gaunitz of Tambov had him in ecstasy with his descriptions of the executions and shootings he carried out. On a report from Rediger, the Minister of War, about bringing one of the 'faint-hearted' pacifiers before the courts, the Tsar wrote, out of pure light-heartedness it would seem, 'That's the style!'. There are plenty more such shameless aphorisms... 'All these revolutionaries should be drowned in the Gulf,' Nicholas said in 1906, contemplating the muddy waves of the Gulf of Finland after the execution of sailors of the Baltic Fleet."

One of Nicholas's own contemporaries, the celebrated lawyer and publicist, Anatoly Koni, agreed with these words in his own observations: "Suffice it, finally, to recall his [Nicholas's] indifference to General Gribsky's conduct when he drowned five thousand peaceful Chinese inhabitants in Blagoveshchensk on the Amur in 1900 and the bodies disrupted river traffic for a whole day... or the unconcerned connivance at Jewish pogroms under Plehve; or his savage attitude to the members of the Dukhobor sect exiled to Siberia, where, as vegetarians in the north, they were doomed to die of hunger, as Leo Tolstoy said in his passionate letter to him... I must mention too his approval of the vile bestialities committed by that blackguard I.M. Obolensky, the governor of Kharkov, when he put down agrarian disturbances in 1892. And can we forget the Japanese War, an adventurous exercise in defence of mercenary gains, and the sending of Nebogatov's squadron with its 'old buckets' to an obvious fate despite the Admiral's pleas? And that after the initiative of the Hague Peace Conference. Can we forget his complete failure to express sorrow over Tsushima and Mukden, and, finally, his cowardly flight to Tsarskoye Selo which accompanied the shooting of unarmed workers on 9th January 1905? This same heartlessness explains his unwillingness to put himself in the position of others and his dividing the world up into 'I' or 'we' and 'them'."

All this, and much else that has already been mentioned besides, meant that an ever bloodier shadow fell over Nicholas's reign and led inevitably to its tragic denouement. As a fairly intelligent and sensitive man he could not have failed to be aware of this. The French ambassador Maurice Paléologue recalled:

"Stolypin once suggested an important measure in domestic policy to His Majesty. After hearing him out pensively, Nicholas the Second made a sceptical unconcerned gesture, as if to say 'that or something else — does it really matter...'"

"Do you know on what day my birthday falls?" the Tsar asked Stolypin.

"How could I forget it?" came the reply. "It is May 6."

"What Saint's Day is it?"

"Forgive me, Sire, I am afraid I've forgotten."

"The Patriarch Job," Nicholas continued.

"Then God be praised!" Stolypin tactfully observed. "Your Majesty's reign will end gloriously, for Job, after piously enduring the most cruel test of his faith, found blessings, and rewards showered upon his head!"

"No, no, Peter Arkadievich, believe me! I have a presentiment — more than a presentiment, a secret conviction — that I am destined for terrible trials..."

Of course at that time, and even later, after his abdication, Nicholas could not have known that fate had in store for him and those close to him no more than a year and a half of life and a terrible death; that after the Petrograd Soviet's decision on 20th March 1017 to "deprive Nicholas Romanov and his wife of their freedom" the family would spend some five more months under house-arrest in the Alexander Palace at Tsarskoye Selo; that the persistent attempts of the Provisional Government throughout that period to arrange the legal transfer of Nicholas and his family to one of the countries in Europe would come to nothing; that the former emperor and his close relatives would prove unwelcome in a whole number of European states where the thrones were occupied by his own cousins or Alexandra's sister — George V in Britain, Christian X in Denmark, Constantine I in Greece, Queen Eugenia in Spain, Kaiser Wilhelm in Germany; that seeing the growth of revolutionary passions in Petrograd the Provisional Government, and in particular Kerensky, would decide on the advice of Archimandrite Hermogen of Tobolsk (a friend of Rasputin) to send Nicholas and his family to the distant Siberian town of Tobolsk, where the Soviet had no great influence and all power lay in the hands of the provincial commissar of the Provisional Government; that there, in the specially repaired former governor's house, which stood in its own gardens and had eighteen rooms, electricity and running water, guarded by a special detachment of 350 soldiers and a small number of officers — the majority of them war heroes and knights of St George, he and his family would spend the autumn and winter of 1917—18 in relative peace; and that from there Nicholas, his wife and children, would set off with the detachment of the special commissioner of the All-Russian Central Executive Committee of the Soviets, Vasily Yakovlev, on their last journey; and that, finally, on this journey the unforeseen would occur: in spite of the orders of the Central Executive Committee to bring the Romanovs to Moscow for a public trial, the leaders of the Ural Regional Soviet of Workers', Peasants' and Red Army Deputies, in view of a genuine threat from the White Guard forces, would dismiss Yakovlev and disarm his detachment, taking all responsibility upon themselves.

Yes, there was much that Nicholas still did not know sitting on that stump in 1917... But, strange as it may seem, even now in the 1990s we are far from knowing all there is to know about that final period in the life of the last tsar. Who, in fact, was it who arranged for the members of the Romanov family to be sent away from the great cities of central Russia? Who really gave the order for the sentence of death to be carried out on the former Emperor and his immediate family, and when? And whose intervention prevented it being enforced on those members of the royal family who were then in the south of the country — near Yalta and in Kislovodsk?

In particular, under whose orders was the Sebastopol sailor Zadorozhny acting when he saved the life of Nicholas's mother, Maria Feodorovna, and his two sisters? It was no coincidence that in an interview with the *Izvestiya* correspondent in Italy published in the spring of 1990, Grand Duke Nikolai Romanov quoted something Zadorozhny said and which his father had remembered all of his life: "My duty to Soviet power is to preserve all of you safe and free from harm." Who was Vasily Yakovlev (K.Ya. Miachin) in reality? A Socialist Revolutionary who had participated in an armed revolt of sailors during the first Russian revolution and was condemned to death in his absence by a tsarist court, yet at the same time a man who, on the authoritative evidence of Nikolai Sokolov, an investigator in the service of the White Guard leader Admiral Kolchak who published a book about the murder of the royal family abroad in 1925, quickly established a good relationship, even one of trust, with Nicholas? What were the true motives of this envoy of Yakov Sverdlov, the president of the Central Executive Committee, who was invested with special authority and persistently tried to carry out the orders of the central Soviet power and deliver the former tsar and his family to Moscow? Finally, what was the true meaning, exact date (16th or 17th July 1918) and time of sending of the famous coded telegram which began with the figures *393435422935364926273...*, dispatched from Yekaterinburg (the name of the town was also the key to the code) via Petrograd to Moscow, to Gorbunov, the secretary of the Council of People's Commissars, in the Kremlin and meant for Lenin and Sverdlov?

All these unanswered questions... Despite the fact that almost seventy-five years have gone by since that bloody reckoning in the night between 16th and 17th July 1918 in a semi-basement room of the house of the mining-engineer Ipatyev in Yekaterinburg, there are still more than enough unsolved puzzles linked to the dreadful end of the Romanov family. To this day, sad to say, neither professional historians, nor writers, nor journalists have succeeded in shedding complete light on all the causes and circumstances, on the true guilty parties behind the shooting of the imperial couple and the horrible murder of their totally innocent children and of the last loyal people who remained with the family.

But, despite the fact that there are several versions of events — from the astonishing theory that Nicholas alone died and the family by some miracle was saved to the categorical insistence on the death of the whole imperial family. Whether the decision to execute the Romanovs was taken by the foremost members of the Bolsheviks and of the Soviet government in Moscow or the leaders of the Ural Soviet, one thing would, however, seem to be beyond doubt: that the deaths of the royal family can only be re-garded as something horrible and beyond rational justification, but that also there was in some way a certain inevitability to them. First and foremost because while alive the Emperor or members of his family indisputably presented a danger to the new Bolshevik power, if only as figureheads for the White opposition.

What occurred was a tragedy, and it too was a profoundly personal tragedy of a man who fervently believed in his God-given destiny and yet was unable to fulfil his duty to his family and his people. "A man of moderate abilities" in the eyes of General Danilov, he proved incapable of bringing to an immense bureaucratic monarchy the democracy and change needed for social and economic advance.

Inseparably bound up as it was with the personality of Nicholas II, Russian autocracy was unable to transform itself into a functioning constitutional monarchy as had happened in a number of Western European countries, nor to resolve successfully any one of the numerous problems in the domestic and foreign policy of the country. Because of this, autocracy proved doomed as a historical phenomenon, or to put it more accurately — it condemned itself to death.

Like the French Bourbons, the Russian ruler could remember everything well, but never learnt a thing. And while the first Russian revolution only "tickled" the Emperor, as he himself said to one of his cousins, the second toppled Nicholas from the throne, and the third led to his tragic end.

The news of the events of October 1917 had an oppressive effect on the former tsar and those around him when it reached them in Tobolsk. "It is sickening to read the newspaper accounts of what happened two weeks ago in Petrograd and Moscow," Nicholas wrote in his diary on Friday, 17th November. Vasily Pankratov, the commissar of the Provisional Government in charge of guarding Nicholas Romanov and his family while they were in Tobolsk, wrote that the explanation which he gave his charge in reply to a question about the plundering of the wine-cellars of the Winter Palace in Petrograd "was completely incomprehensible to the former tsar. After keeping silent for several minutes, he said:

'But why destroy the palace? Why not stop the crowd?.. Why allow the theft and destruction of treasures?..'

"The former tsar pronounced these last words with a tremor in his voice. His face turned pale and his eyes sparkled with indignation. At this point Tatishchev and one of the daughters joined us. Our conversation on the subject was interrupted. Later I very much regretted this. I very much wanted to know myself how in fact the former tsar did regard the events that had taken place. Was he aware that the 'impetuous' crowd had been formed and raised not the day before, not in the last year, but over the preceding centuries of a bureaucratic regime which sooner or later was bound to summon up a crowd to 'impetuous' action? Nicholas II had apparently had a poor understanding of this impetuosity in March 1917 and was even worse at imagining it in October. To do that he would have had to have known not just the military history he taught to his son, but the history of the people, the history of the crowd. Apparently the revolts of Stenka Razin and Pugachev, the revolts of the military settlements had been forgotten by the former ruler. Apparently he never asked himself why neither in England, nor in France, nor in Austria, nor anywhere else, had the people and the forces risen in such a way during the war. Why could it only happen in Russia, where the power of the tsar and the bureaucracy seemed so strong, so unbreakable, yet it collapsed to its very foundations in two or three days. Was this not ever the fate of despotism?.."

That Russian revolt poured over into revolution in the dramatic months of 1917, swept away the old autocratic Russia, and naturally could not but sweep with it its symbol and apex — the Romanov dynasty. As the outstanding Russian philosopher Nikolai Berdiayev said in this regard: "The people in the past sensed the injustice of a social order based on the oppression and exploitation of the workers, but they bore their lot of suffering meekly and submissively. But the hour came when they no longer wished to tolerate it..."

To look back now in an attempt to find who was right and who was guilty is a very difficult, and probably pointless, task. At his coronation Nicholas II was not only given the orb and sceptre, but also burdened with a cross which he then had to bear to the end of his days. This burden was an immeasurably heavy one and proved to be beyond the last Russian tsar. And three-quarters of a century later we should not try to cast judgement on the course he took. We should try to understand and to forgive — as he himself did.

"Father asks you to tell all those who remain loyal to Him, and those with whom they might have influence, not to take revenge for Him, because He has forgiven everyone and prays for everyone, and to remember that the evil that is now in the world will be stronger yet, but that it is not evil which overcomes evil, but only love."

It would seem that the spiritual testament of the last Russian emperor, which his daughter Grand Duchess Olga conveyed from Tobolsk in the spring of 1918, was addressed not only to his compatriots and contemporaries, but also to their descendants. To those who need to find the sense and courage to look for a way towards a general reconciliation and concord, and, remembering the past, to step forward in peace and hope to the future in the twenty-first century.

# Chief Sources and Related Literature

*Arkhiv Russkoy Revoliutsii*, published by I.V. Gessen in 20 vols., Berlin, 1921—37

S.P. BELETSKY, *Grigory Rasputin*, Petrograd, 1923

A.V. BOGDANOVICH, *Tri poslednikh samoderzhtsa*, Moscow—Leningrad, 1924

G. BUCHANAN, *My Mission to Russia and Other Diplomatic Memories*, Boston, 1923

*The Central State Archives of the October Revolution*, funds 130, 161

*Commemorative booklet for the year 1899* (in Russian), St Petersburg, s.a.

*Complete collection of the speeches of Emperor Nicholas II: 1894—1906*, St Petersburg, 1906

*Correspondence of Wilhelm II and Nicholas II: 1894—1914*, Moscow—Petrograd, 1923

YU.N. DANILOV, "Moi vospominaniya ob imperatore Nikolaye II i velikom Knyaze Mikhaile Aleksandroviche" *in Arkhiv russkoy revoliutsii*, Vol. 19, Berlin, 1928

*The Diary of Nicholas II. 1890—1906*, Berlin, 1923

"The Diary of Nicholas II. 16 December 1916 — 30 June 1917" *in Ot pervogo litsa*, Moscow, 1990

*The Diary of Member of the State Duma Vladimir Mitrofanovich Purishkevich*, Riga, 1924

*Dom Romanovykh. Biografichesky spravochnik*, 2 vols, Leningrad, 1989

N.YA. EIDELMAN, *Revolutsiya sverkhu*, Moscow, 1990

*Encyclopaedic Dictionary (in Russian)*, published by F.A. Brockhais and A.I. Efron, Books 1—82, St Petersburg, 1890—1904

"The family correspondence of the Romanovs: the letters between Nicholas Romanov and Alexandra Feodorovna (4 December 1916 — 7 March 1917)" *in Krasny arkhiv*, Vol. 4, Moscow—Petrograd, 1923

"The February Revolution of 1917 (Documents from the Stavka of the supreme commander-in-chief and from the staff of the commander-in-chief of the armies of the Northern Front)" *in Krasny arkhiv*, Vols. 21—23, 1927

M. FERRAULT, *Nikolai II*, Moscow, 1991

P. GILLIARD, *Thirteen Years at the Russian Court*, London, 1921

*His Imperial Majesty the Sovereign Emperor Nicholas Alexandrovich with the fighting army. The routes of the first to fifth royal journeys in September—October and November—December 1914, January—June 1915 and July 1915—February 1916*, compiled by Major-General D. Dubensky, Petrograd, 1915—16

A.A. IGNATYEV, *50 let v stroyu. Vospominaniya*, Moscow

*Istorichesky opyt trekh rossiyskikh revoliutsiy. Vtoraya burzhuazno-demokraticheskaya revoliutsiya v Rossii*, Moscow, 1986

G.Z. JOFFE, *Veliky Oktyabr i epilog tsarizma*, Moscow, 1987

*The Voyage of the Heir and Tsesarevich (in 1890—1896)*, written and published by Prince E.E. Ukhtomsky, illustrated by N.N. Karazin, Vols. 1—11, St Petersburg—Leipzig

M.K. KASVINOV, *Dvadtsat' tri stupen'ki vniz*, Moscow, 1987

A.F. KERENSKY, "Otyezd Nikolaya II v Tobolsk" in *Izdaleka*, Paris, 1921

*Khodynka. Krovavye zhertvy koronatsii*, Geneva, 1900

V.O. KLIUCHEVSKY, *Istoricheskiye portrety. Deyateli istoricheskoy mysli*, Moscow, 1990

A.F. KONI, *Collected Works* (in Russian), 8 vols., Moscow, 1966

V.S. KRIVENKO, *Puteshestviye naslednika tsesarevicha na Vostok*, St Petersburg, 1891

V.S. KRIVENKO, "Ot Gatchiny do Bombeya: Ocherki puteshestviya naslednika tsesarevicha" in *Pravitelstvenny vestnik*, 1891, Nos 41, 48, 56, 78, 100

*Krizis samoderzhaviya v Rossii: 1895—1917*, Leningrad, 1984

*Krusheniye tsarizma. Vospominaniya uchastnikov revolutsionnogo dvizheniya v Petrograde (1907 — fevral 1917)*, Leningrad, 1986

*Legal Acts of the Transitional Period 1904—1906*, St Petersburg, 1907

M.K. LEMKE, *250 dney v tsarskoy Stavke*, Petrograd, 1920

S. LIUBOSH, *Posledniye Romanovy*, Leningrad—Moscow, 1924

A. LUKOMSKY, "Iz vospominaniy" in *Arkhiv russkoy revolutsii*, Vol. 2, Berlin, 1922

S.P. MELGUNOV, *Posledny samoderzhets. Cherty dlya kharakteristiki Nikolaya II*, Petrograd—Moscow, 1917

P.N. MILIUKOV, *Vospominaniya (1859—1917)*, 2 vols., Moscow, 1990

S. MSTYSLAVSKY, *Pyat dney*, Moscow, 1922

*Nikolay II i velikiye knyazya: Rodstvennye pis'ma k poslednemu tsariu*, Leningrad—Moscow, 1925

*Otrecheniye Nikolaya II: Vospominaniya ochevidtsev, dokumenty*, Leningrad, 1927

*Padenie tsarskogo rezhima: Stenograficheskiye otchety doprosov i pokazaniy, dannykh v 1917 godu v Chrezvychainoy sledstvennoy komissii Vremennogo pravitelstva,* Leningrad, 1924

M. PALÉOLOGUE, *Le roman tragique de l'empereur Alexandre II,* Paris, 1923

M. PALÉOLOGUE, *An Ambassador's Memoirs,* New York, 1923

V.S. PANKRATOV, *S tsarem v Tobolske: Vospominaniya. Ubiystvo tsarskoy semyi i eyo svity. Ofitsialnye dokumenty,* Leningrad, 1990

A.YE. PRESNIAKOV, *Rossiyskiye samoderzhtsy,* Moscow, 1990

*Revoliutsia i grazhdanskaya voina v opisaniyakh belogvardeitsev,* 6 vols., Moscow—Leningrad, 1926—27

*Revoliutsiya i RKP(B) v materialakh i dokumentakh,* Vol. 7, *Epokha imperialisticheskoy voiny (iyul 1914 — fevral 1917),* Moscow, 1924

M.V. RODZIANKO, *Krusheniye imperii,* Leningrad, 1929

B.V. SAVINKOV, *Vospominaniya terrorista,* Leningrad, 1990

L.YE. SHEPELEV, *Otmenennye istoriyey. Chiny, zvaniya i tituly v Rossiyskoy imperii,* Leningrad, 1977

V. SHULGIN, *Dni,* Leningrad, 1926

A. SIMANOVICH, *Vospominaniya byvshego sekretarya Grigoriya Rasputina,* Riga, 1924

S.M. SOLOVYEV, *Chteniya i rasskazy po istorii Rossii,* Moscow, 1990

N. SOKOLOV, *Ubiystvo tsarskoy semyi,* Berlin, 1925

V.A. SUKHOMLINOV, "Diaries" in *Dela i dni,* 1920, No 1

V.A. SUKHOMLINOV, *Vospominaniya,* Berlin, 1924

"Sviatoy chert" (Hieromonk Iliodor's writings about Rasputin) in *Golos minuvshego,* 1917, No 3

V.A. TELYAKOVSKY, *Vospominaniya 1898—1917,* St Petersburg, 1924

V.N. VOYEYKOV, *S tsarem i bez tsarya: Vospominaniya poslednego dvortsovogo komendanta gosudarya imperatora Nikolaya II,* Helsinki, 1936

A.A. VYRUBOVA (TANEYEVA), *Memories of the Russian Court,* New York, 1923

S. YU. WITTE, *Memoirs,* Vols. 1—3, Moscow, 1960

S. YAKOVLEV, *Posledniye dni Nikolaya II. Ofitsialnye documenty. Rasskazy ochevidtsev,* Petrograd, 1917

N.P. YEROSHKIN, *Istoriya gosudarstvennykh uchrezhdeniy dorevolutsionnoy Rossii,* Moscow, 1983

N.P. YEROSHKIN, *Samoderzhaviye nakanune krakha,* Moscow, 1975

P.A. ZAYONCHKOVSKY, *Pravitelstvenny apparat samoderzhavnoy Rossii v XIX veke,* Moscow, 1978

*1 Marta 1881 goda: Kazn' imperatora Aleksandra II,* Leningrad, 1991

DK 258 .I765 1992
Iroshnikov, M. P.
The sunset of the Romanov
  Dynasty

DK 258 .I765 1992
Iroshnikov, M. P.
The sunset of the Romanov
  Dynasty